Prologue

I t was late one night when a young boy arrived at the massage parlour in Tottenham, London, where I worked. He was with two friends. They were all drunk but he looked quiet. Short with light brown hair and a stocky body, he was in his early twenties and English.

I was sitting in reception as usual. The customers would come in, look over the girls who weren't already occupied with a client and then choose which one they wanted to go with.

I looked at the boy with only a slight flicker of interest. They were all the same to me, these men who came in looking for a piece of meat to fuck. But the night had been a quiet one for me and if I didn't get a customer soon, I would suffer for it. My pimp, Ardy, was waiting for me, as he always did, first to get hold of all the money I might have made during the evening, and second to make sure I didn't run. If I escaped from him, his income would vanish with me and he'd made it perfectly clear that if that happened, he'd hunt me down and kill me. As it was, even a quiet night could mean punishment for me, for failing to line Ardy's pockets adequately.

The boy was staring at me. His eyes held the dazed look of a drunk man but he was young so perhaps he would be satisfied with a massage or even a blow job. When we caught each other's gaze, he smiled at me.

'Can you go with me?' he asked.

'Sure. Why not?' I replied.

'You're not English,' he said. 'Where are you from?'

'Turkey,' I lied. It was the story I told everyone. It was easier somehow. How could I begin to tell anyone the truth about what had happened to me?

As we walked into the small massage room, he tried to touch my bottom.

'Don't do that,' I told him firmly.

'Of course. You don't like that.'

'No.'

I closed the door. 'It's forty-five pounds for half an hour.'

He dug into his pockets and handed me some crumpled notes. I took them. 'I've got to give reception their money, then I'll be back.' I went out and returned a few minutes later to find the boy sitting on the chair by the massage table. 'So ... do you want a massage?' I asked him.

'No. I just want to fuck you.'

I looked at him. I could see he was drunk and I'd learned to be careful of men like that – they could surprise you, behave badly – but I couldn't help being a little shocked. He seemed so young. 'Wouldn't you like a nice, soft massage?' I said slowly. It was better for me if we started that way.

'No. Just take your clothes off now.'

I would do what he wanted, but calmly and seriously, to keep things gentle. 'Okay. But aren't you going to as well?'

'No. Take yours off first.'

I unbuttoned my dress. As I let it fall to the floor, revealing my underwear, I felt scared. He was too cold and too commanding for my liking. Why wouldn't he undress? Did he have something in his pockets? He nodded with satisfaction as I stood in front of him, semi-naked.

'I want a blow job now,' he said.

I took a condom from the box beside the bed.

'No. No condom.'

'It's the rules.'

'But I'll pay you a hundred pounds.'

'I don't care. Condom or nothing.'

'Oh, come on. I'm clean.'

'No. If you're not happy then change the girl.'

The boy was silent as I knelt down in front of him. It was difficult to put the condom on him because he wasn't ready so I tried to prepare him with my hand.

'Did you drink a lot today?' I asked.

'Not much. What's the problem?'

'Well, I can't get you hard.'

'But you're a fucking prostitute. That's your job.'

I didn't like the edge in his voice. I felt instinctively that I needed to defuse him, so I tried to sound reasonable. 'I know but if you've drunk a lot or taken drugs, I can't do it.'

He pushed me away. 'I know how to do it,' he slurred. He rolled the condom down over his semi-hard penis. Then he stood up and, in a quick movement, pushed me round so that I had my back to him. With sudden force, he pushed me down so that I was leaning over the massage table, my back exposed to him. With one hand, he forced my head down so that my cheek was pressed against the cheap cotton cover on the table. He grabbed a fistful of my hair and, with the other hand, he held my hip. He began to press against me and I could feel that he had regained his potency – he was hard now. He pushed and pushed and eventually found his way inside me.

I did not bother to struggle – I knew that it would do no good. He was strong and determined. I didn't have a chance against him.

He began to move back and forward, his body slapping against my buttocks as he went.

'Tell me you want a fuck,' he said suddenly. 'Tell me you're a bitch, a whore.'

I was silent. Wasn't it enough that I had to endure this?

'Say it.'

'No.'

'Yes.'

He pulled my hair as he started hitting my buttocks. 'Say it or I won't finish. Come on. Tell me. You're a fucking slag, a bitch, a whore.'

I wouldn't say it to him, couldn't say it to him.

'No,' I whispered as he pushed harder and harder inside me.

'Say it,' he said as I felt a pain in my stomach.

'No.'

'You're a whore.'

He gripped my head tighter as he rammed into me.

'Say it.'

Anger hardened inside me.

'Say it.'

'No.'

'Just say it,' he screamed.

He was hurting me so much. My body kept slamming into the side of the table. I just wanted him to stop – for the shouts to be silent. My anger died.

'I'm a whore,' I said.

'Again,' he shouted.

'I'm a bitch.' My voice was utterly expressionless.

With a moan he stopped moving on top of me and I reached back to take the condom, push him away and pick up my dress. The boy didn't look at me as he walked towards the shower. Later, after he'd got out and put his clothes on, he turned to give me £5.

'I'm sorry,' he said, his eyes not meeting mine.

'Just go,' I said. 'I don't want your money.'

The boy said nothing as he left. I sat down quickly, feeling my legs lose their strength.

'I cannot stand it,' I whispered, my head in my hands. 'I cannot bear this life much longer. I would rather be dead than suffer this.' I could see blood in my mind, feel aggression in my heart and, for the first time, feared I wouldn't be able to control whatever was trying to rip out from inside me. I wasn't sure what I might do if I saw the boy again. I sat in silence and stared at the wall, trying to push down the animal which was clawing to get out from inside me.

I knew I had to win the struggle for control. My desire for survival was still strong. It had to be. I had to get home to my children. They were all that had kept me going through all the terrible hardships and abuses I had suffered. I had told them that Mummy would come home and I knew I had to survive if I was ever going to keep my promise.

Mummy,
Come Home

Chapter One

I believe your birth is like your life and you are born with good or bad luck which follows you forever. I weighed just over two pounds when I was born three months prematurely and no one thought I would live. But I fought, held on to my life and survived just as I have done ever since.

I came into the world in Ukraine at about 6pm on 16 January 1976, after my mother Alexandra slipped on an icy street as she ran for the bus. Her waters broke and I had been born by the time my father Panteley arrived at the hospital. The doctors warned my parents I would not survive but my father had me moved to another hospital where I spent three months until I was well enough to go home. They called me Oxana.

We lived in a town called Simferopol in Ukraine, which was then part of the Soviet Union, and my parents were rich compared with many in the Communist country. My father was a lorry driver and my mother worked in a nursery. They'd met at college and my mother was just seventeen when she married and my brother Vitalik was born. Six years later I arrived and together we lived in a huge apartment block of more than six hundred flats. We were lucky because we had two bedrooms and a large balcony and could afford to eat meat every day. My mother, who was small, beautiful and smelled of a perfume called Red Moscow, was an excellent cook, and Sunday was the best because we would have chicken livers or lamb with white sauce and onions followed by biscuits or cakes. That was my favourite day of the week, when we were all laughing together and my parents weren't working.

But things started to change when my father gave up his driving job to run his own car repair business. Suddenly my world wasn't quite as happy. I don't know what came first – my father's jealousy or my mother's nights out – but after that the beatings started. I would lie in bed listening and praying to God to protect me. Papa was like a bull who couldn't control himself, while Mamma couldn't stop her tongue. I listened to the awful noise of their rows, wishing that they would stop and terrified that it was my fault they were no longer happy.

The noise from our flat must have been horrendous, but no one ever got involved in the arguments between my parents because anything between a husband and wife was considered private. Besides, there were plenty of other families like mine in our apartment block and if you got married then it was no one else's business what your husband did to you. Women were the ones who provoked men after all – if they answered back they were hit, if they wore a short skirt they were a slapper who deserved what they got. One day a policeman came and sat with my father in the kitchen. By the time he had left, Papa had signed a document saying he wouldn't touch my mother but what good is a piece of paper against a powerful fist? Nothing could heal the rift between my parents.

'He's a bastard,' my mother would tell me as we lay in the bedroom we shared. Vitalik had the other while my father slept in the living room. 'I'm going to leave him. You can come with me, Oxana, and we'll be happy together.'

I wanted us all to be happy but I wished that we could stay together too. I loved my papa, even though he was so angry all the time with my mother. I was also frightened of my mother because she had drunken rages of her own and could turn against me in an instant. Sometimes she would scream at me after one of Papa's beatings that I hadn't protected her, and she would hit me. Once she beat me with a bunch of roses; I was covered in scratches and had to stay off school for a week.

Maybe it was because of all this that my brother Vitalik changed. We'd always been friends when we were young but he lost interest in me as he became a teenager and soon the arguments between my parents often included him. He started smoking, stopped going to school and hung around with a bad crowd which worried my father. Then when I was nine, my parents' wedding rings and a gold necklace disappeared. Papa was furious; he was convinced that Vitalik had stolen them and it was the first time I realised that it wasn't just my mother he could hit.

'Why are you doing this?' my father screamed. 'I'm working hard to make a better future for you and your sister and you do this to me.'

Then one day, the police arrived at our home. A car had been stolen and there had been an accident. After that Vitalik disappeared. He was just fifteen.

* * *

After my brother had left, I felt almost invisible. I was a good girl who never caused my parents any trouble but I was also a very sensitive child. Every day I would write in my diary how many bad things my mother or teachers had said to me and it made me sad that nobody liked me because I was the clever girl at school. Things got worse when Vitalik went away.

'There's the thief's sister,' my classmates would snigger as I walked by.

People would turn their backs as I walked into the playground and teachers would mark my homework down for no reason. At that time, Ukraine was a Soviet country where many things weren't accepted. Religion was one. Lenin was our god and people who believed otherwise could get into trouble. I remember one day when a girl came into school wearing a cross. We didn't see her for a whole year after that. There were some churches of course and I was baptised into the Greek faith but my family never practised their religion openly. We celebrated Christian festivals but there was no Bible at home or trips to church.

In Ukraine, difference wasn't trusted. Children were taught to hate homosexuality, black skin and anything foreign. Everybody had to be the same. There was just one big supermarket where everyone shopped and it didn't sell any luxury goods or foreign foods – things like tampons and disposable nappies were unheard of. Instead we ate simple meat and vegetables, women used pads of gauze every month to stop their blood and children drank milk. When Coca-Cola arrived in Ukraine there were a lot of people who believed it would make them sick and I didn't have my first sip until I was thirteen – the same day I tried chewing gum.

My country was hard in other ways too – it wasn't wealthy and everyone had to work. Just a dollar a day could mean the difference between eating and starving, and I always knew that some people had a lot less than my family.

What I loved more than anything else was Bollywood films. The singing, the dancing, the colour, the costumes – everything about them was beautiful and I was convinced that India must be heaven on earth. My favourite one was called *Disco Dancer* and starred Mithun Chakrabarti. He was so tall and handsome that I saw it twenty-three times and couldn't stop crying when it finally stopped being shown. I loved the way that Bollywood films always had a happy ending full of love. They made me believe that one day my prince would find me and we would live together happily ever after. I just had to wait patiently for that day to come.

Then something happened that turned all the colour in my dreams to grey.

Chapter Two

It was the summer of 1990, I was fourteen and on a secret day out at the beach with two friends, Natasha and Alina. I knew I'd be in trouble if Papa found out, but I had had a wonderful time sunbathing and chatting with my girlfriends. Now we were going to buy some food before walking to the station ready for the hour's train journey home.

As we stood in the queue for pastries, a handsome boy waited behind. He looked about eighteen and was wearing shorts, no shirt and good sunglasses.

'Excuse me, could you tell us what time it is, please?' Natasha asked as she turned towards him.

He looked at his watch. 'Nearly six o'clock,' he replied.

I was worried. It was much later than I'd thought. 'We have to go,' I said urgently. 'We'll miss the train and we'll never be home in time. I have to get back before Mama comes home from work.'

'Don't worry, Oxana,' said Natasha breezily. 'There's plenty of time.'

She didn't seem at all worried as she started chatting and laughing with the older boy. I didn't like it – she seemed so open and free with him, and it wasn't how I'd been taught to behave.

'Why don't you come and meet my friends?' he asked, when we'd bought our pastries.

'Sure,' replied Natasha, and she began walking off with our new friend.

'But we've got to get home,' I cut in, looking at Alina.

'Not yet,' she said as she turned to follow Natasha and the boy. 'We can always catch the next train. Don't be a scaredy cat, Oxana.'

I stood for a moment. What should I do? I could go on my own to the station or for once try to fit in with my friends. I didn't want to be left alone. I turned to follow as the boy led us behind the shops to the edge of a small wood.

'My friends are in there,' he said, gesturing at the trees.

Twigs cracked under our feet as we walked into the sudden darkness. I saw a group of about seven boys a little way ahead. They looked between sixteen and eighteen, and were sitting on blankets with food and bottles of homemade wine surrounding them, smoking. We went over and sat down with them. Natasha accepted a bottle immediately but I felt more and more nervous. We were going to be so late.

Then I heard two boys muttering behind me.

'What are we going to do?' one asked in a low voice.

I strained to hear and made out a few other words.

'… and you can take her,' the other said as he looked at me.

Fear filled me. Something was wrong.

'Come on, let's leave,' I whispered to Alina. I turned to the boy next to me and said with a smile, 'We need to go to the toilet.'

'Over there.' He gestured at some bushes. Alina and I got up and started to walk casually away.

'We need to get away from here,' I told her in a low voice.

'What do you mean?' she replied.

'Trust me. There's something wrong. I'll count to five, then we'll run.'

'Okay,' Alina said and my heart beat as I waited to count down.

'Five, four, three, two, ONE,' I shouted and started running through the shadowy wood. I couldn't hear Alina behind me, she must have gone in a different direction, but I couldn't stop. I just had to run. That was all that mattered.

Suddenly I felt hands on my back and was pushed to the ground before being pulled roughly around. Looking down at me was a boy of about seventeen with blond curly hair, blue eyes and big lips.

'Listen,' he snapped. 'I can make you a deal. Either all these guys are going to fuck you or you accept just me.'

'No way,' I screamed. 'Never.'

'All right then,' the boy said as he started getting up. 'I'll just call the others.'

I could sense he was nervous, unsure of what he was doing. 'No, please don't,' I begged. 'Don't call them. I'll go with you.'

'Good,' he said as he pulled me to my feet. 'Now follow me.'

I was very afraid as the boy took my arm and we started walking through the woods. What was he going to do? Why wouldn't he let me go?

'Please don't hurt me,' I sobbed. 'My parents are expecting me home.'

'If you're good I won't give you to anyone else but if you're not then I have a lot of friends.'

My heart beat fast. I hardly understood what happened between men and women but I knew that I didn't want this boy to touch me and there was no way to get away from him. Even as my eyes scanned the floor for something to use as a weapon – a plank, a stone – he held tightly on to me.

'Please don't hurt me today,' I pleaded as we reached a deserted house and he pushed me into an old shed at the back. 'Can't you just leave me tonight?'

The longer he didn't touch me the better. I'd been told again and again that I had to be a virgin to be a good wife and I knew that meant not letting boys touch me. I couldn't let this boy do anything to me or the word 'whore' would follow me forever.

'Don't worry,' he replied. 'I'm not going to hurt you. You just need to drink some wine and then it won't be so painful.'

He lay a blanket on the ground and offered me a bottle before lifting his eyes to me once again. The silence was thick between us as we stared at each other. I saw in his eyes that he was determined to do it.

'Please don't hurt me,' I whispered as the boy pushed me back onto the hard ground.

I was so scared I couldn't move. I'd hit boys at school if they'd ever tried to touch me but this was so different. My body froze. Maybe he would let me go when he realised how afraid I was.

'I won't tell anyone about this,' I sobbed. 'Please let me go. I won't tell the police or my parents.'

But the boy did not listen and started pulling at my clothes as I folded my arms around my body.

'No,' I pleaded as he ripped the thin straps of my pink top. 'I'm a virgin.'

'Oh, come on,' he snapped in a low voice. 'You must have had a boyfriend.'

Tears ran down my face as the boy pulled at my shorts and I stiffened my legs to hold them tightly together. He pushed himself onto me and I could hardly breathe. He was too heavy and strong to resist as he forced my legs open. I tried screaming but a hand clamped down on my mouth.

A hot jab of pain flooded in between my legs. I didn't want him to do this to me and neither did my body. It hurt so much. The boy pushed again and again until he went inside me. I screamed.

'Shut up,' he shouted. 'Relax and you'll be fine.'

But pain filled me as millimetre by millimetre the boy robbed me of myself. I could feel his sweat dripping on me, his tongue licking me and smell the stink of his armpits. Sickness rose up in my throat.

I don't know how long it was before he stopped moving and rolled away onto his back.

'You see, it was nothing,' he said. 'I'm tired now. Tomorrow I'll take you to the train station and you can go home.'

He dozed off straight away while I lay awake trembling, too terrified to move, until I finally fell asleep, grateful for the oblivion.

Early the next morning we woke up. I saw dried blood on my thighs as I pulled on my shorts. It hurt to move as I shifted from one leg to the other. I felt freezing, so cold I was almost shaking, and I wondered what he was going to do now. Home felt so far away.

He led me out of the shed and we started walking along a deserted road with trees on either side until we reached an empty beach.

'Clean yourself up,' the boy said as he gestured at the sea. 'And then I'll take you to the station.'

I looked at a toilet block on the edge of the beach – the kind of low building with no roof, low walls and holes in the ground that were found by the seaside.

'Can I go?' I asked.

'Yes, but don't lock the door.'

The boy waited outside as I walked into the latrine and looked at the back wall. I could climb it and run. If I could just get away, perhaps I could forget this had ever happened. No one need ever know.

I stayed still for a moment as I listened for the boy. I couldn't hear him moving, just the sound of the sea as it rolled onto the beach. Holding my breath, I pulled myself up onto the wall. As my head appeared over the top, I looked down to see two men waiting on the other side.

'She's trying to escape,' one called and I heard a grunt of frustration as the boy rushed into the cubicle.

'You've made a real mistake,' he shouted as he grabbed me. 'And now you're going to pay for it.'

Panic filled me as the boy pulled me outside to where the two men were waiting. One was in his early thirties with blond hair and a well-built body while the other was tall, thinner and older.

'Hello there, little girl. Nice to meet you. Now, let's go,' the tall man said as he dug his fingers into my arm and started dragging me towards a tent pitched nearby.

I looked back to see the blond man handing over some money to the boy as I was pushed inside the tent. The light inside glowed yellow and the air was hot, hard to breathe.

'So what shall we do now?' the blond man smiled as he crawled in behind us.

Without a word, he grabbed my hair and pushed his lips onto mine. I felt teeth bite into me as the man held my shoulders and pulled open his shorts. He pushed my head towards his nakedness as he knelt. My mind went black. What was he trying to do? I gritted my teeth, forcing myself not to cry or scream, as the man forced himself towards me. Suddenly fingers wrenched open the sides of my mouth and I tasted blood as my skin split.

'Hold her nose,' a voice said and fingers pinched my nostrils shut.

Whatever happened I must keep my mouth closed, mustn't let this man into me. But as the world went from red to black and my body gasped for air, the blond man thrust himself into me. I bit him.

'Fucking bitch,' he shouted.

A fist smashed into my mouth and a knee flew towards my face. Pain flooded into my head. I could taste blood and feel the salt sting of tears melting into my cuts.

'Here, wait,' the tall man said as he grabbed me by the neck and pulled out a roll of masking tape. He pushed a strip over my mouth. Blood and tears rushed into my throat as my arms were pulled behind my head and I was forced back onto the ground.

The blond man pulled up my T-shirt and suddenly his weight was crushing me. He wanted what the boy had taken yesterday. It had hurt so much. I had to stop him. Once again I went rigid as he forced himself into me.

'You're only hurting yourself,' he said.

It was worse, much worse, than the night before as the grown man pushed into me with a violence the boy did not yet know he had. I wanted to die. Just fall into the sea, out of the sky, and die. Tears fell wet down my face as the man moved on top of me. I had never known pain like it so deep inside, at the centre of me.

'Sshh,' he said as his hips pushed into mine again and again, his voice suddenly soft, the kind of voice you use to speak to a little girl. 'Don't cry. You'll be fine.'

But still he heaved on top of me until suddenly a thick, musky smell filled the air. I felt warmth spread on my stomach as he rolled off me.

Silently I sat up and pulled the tape off my mouth as the men lit cigarettes. It felt like there was an animal inside me which wanted to scream but I couldn't let it out.

'It was all right, wasn't it, even though you were tight?' the blond man smiled as he smoked.

'Can I have one?' I asked, gesturing at the cigarette.

'You smoke?'

'Yes,' I lied as he put a cigarette into my bleeding mouth and held a match to it. I felt dizzy as chemicals rushed into my brain and, without thinking, I pushed the burning cigarette onto the back of my hand. I wanted to see if I was alive but couldn't feel a thing as the burning tip scorched my skin. Only the small white scar it left on my hand reminds me still that the day was real. But I didn't know that back then. It all felt like a dream. When would I wake up at home?

I felt a slap on my face.

'Are you crazy?' the tall man shouted.

I looked at him silently.

'She needs to clean herself,' the blond man snapped as he took my arm and pulled me out of the tent.

I stood up and stumbled towards the sea where I started splashing myself. The water felt cold and my nose and mouth stung as the salty water bit into my cuts. Inside I felt nothing.

'Are you all right?' a voice asked.

I turned to see a police car parked on the beach and an officer standing near the tent. Another sat in the car.

Suddenly a flash lit up inside me. I was safe. They could help me.

But then fear filled me again. No one must ever know what had happened. My father could never find out. I would be shamed forever if he did. I started shaking as the sea rushed over my feet and I pulled down my wet T-shirt. I had no underwear. What kind of girl would they think I was?

'I'm fine,' I told the policeman.

He looked at me.

'She's my cousin,' the blond man said.

'Is that true?' the officer asked.

'Yes,' I replied.

The policeman stared at me for a moment. 'Well, get your things anyway because I want you to come with me.'

I dragged a hand over my mouth to wipe away the blood as I stood up to follow the man. Silently, I got into the front seat of the car as the other officer put the two men into the back. They didn't say anything and neither did I. I wouldn't tell, I decided as the car drove away. I'd lie if I had to. If Papa found out I wasn't a virgin anymore then he'd either kill me or I'd be labelled a whore – either way my life would be over.

I was scared when I got to the police station. I knew what the police were like – they could do whatever they wanted – and so, even though a kind man asked me again and again what had happened, I didn't tell him.

'So where are your friends?' he asked.

'I don't know.'

'And your clothes?'

'I lost them.'

'What were you doing with the men we found you with?'

'Just talking.'

There was silence while the policeman considered my answer. Then he said, 'Did these men do something to you?'

'No.'

'Are you sure, Oxana?'

'Yes.'

Soon a woman doctor arrived to take me to another room. I cried again as she asked me to sit in a chair with stirrups before looking at every part of me, the parts no one had ever seen until that day. The woman was silent as she examined me before turning away to write notes. Later she left the room, came back with a white gown and I was taken back to the room where the investigator sat.

'Why have you lied to me?' he asked softly. 'You've been raped, haven't you? The doctor says you've been treated very roughly. You must have been in a great deal of pain. Why keep silent?'

I stared down at the table. Would my body always tell my story to those who looked closely enough? I felt sick. Would my husband know in the years to come?

'I'm scared,' I sobbed. 'My father mustn't know what's happened to me.'

'But why?'

'Because he'll kill me. Please, please don't tell my parents. I'll do whatever you want but please don't tell them.'

'I won't,' he said.

So I told him everything. He kept his promise and did not call my parents. Instead, we called my second cousin,

Yula, who came to pick me up and take me home. She lived not far from us with her husband and two children and I saw her often. I trusted her to help me. The investigator told her that I'd been found at the beach alone and needed clothes.

Yula came bringing clothes for me and, after speaking to the investigator, took me home in her car. We had only been driving for about fifteen minutes when she stopped the car and climbed into the back seat beside me.

'What were you doing at the beach alone, Oxana?' she asked gently.

I started sobbing. 'You must never tell Mamma and Papa,' I whispered.

Yula began crying as well. She knew my father was very strict. 'But I have to,' she said. 'You're fourteen. A girl. They need to know.'

'Well, then I'll kill myself,' I cried. 'I know how to die and I'll do it.'

'We have to say something, Oxana,' she insisted. 'You've been gone nearly two days.'

'You'll think of something,' I said in a rush. 'Please, Yula, you have to help me.'

We didn't talk anymore as she drove me back to her house and waited for my mother to arrive.

An hour later, my mother came rushing in. 'Where have you been?' she screamed as she started slapping me. 'Your father has had heart pain all day and night. We haven't been to work because of you. You are a bad girl! Such trouble. We had no idea what had happened.'

'Alexandra,' cried Yula, 'you don't understand! Poor Oxana has been through a terrible ordeal. Yes, she was naughty – she went on a secret trip to the beach with her friends – but she and the others were set upon by thieves.

They were badly beaten and had all their things stolen before being dumped in the middle of nowhere. She's lucky to be alive.'

My mother's anger vanished. 'Oh, my poor baby!' she said, with tears in her eyes. She put her arms round me and hugged me. I couldn't remember when she had last done that.

Back at home, I climbed into my pyjamas and went straight to bed. The next day I told the story Yula had invented to Papa and he stopped asking questions when I began crying. He didn't do as I'd expected and beat me. Instead my parents sent me to see relatives in the country for a week and we never mentioned what had happened again.

I still find that day at the beach almost the worst of everything that was to come. I was a child until I started running through the dark forest away from those boys. But in that moment I was forced into the painful world of adults. In the months that followed, I started seeing the devil in my dreams. I was sure that one day he would kill me.

Chapter Three

'Hello,' said the young man as I approached his table to take his order. He was sitting on the terrace outside the café, reading a paper and smoking a cigarette. 'Can I have an orange juice, please?'

It was the fourth time he'd been back to the café and I knew he was here to see me.

'Hello again,' the man said as I returned to the table with his drink. He was older than me, with green eyes, light brown hair and the same square jaw as my favourite actor, Arnold Schwarzenegger.

I knew he wanted to talk but although I liked his looks, I didn't feel up to speaking to him. Strange men made me very nervous and I kept my distance. I went back inside and started drying glasses. There were only a couple of hours to go before I finished work and went back to the room I shared with Mamma. She'd probably be out so I'd have it to myself.

After that day at the beach a year ago, I had changed completely. I never talked about it or saw the other girls when I got back because I didn't want their parents to ask questions. But still I couldn't stop thinking about what had happened and soon I stopped speaking. I avoided my parents and stayed silent for many weeks. A couple of months later I met Alina who told me Natasha had not been found after that day. I didn't know if it was true or not but believed her when she said she'd spent a month in hospital after being raped by thirteen men. I felt so guilty. She was younger than me and I should have protected her.

Apart from Alina, only Yula knew what had happened. When the case came to court, I wasn't called because I was so young and Yula went on my behalf – once again my parents knew nothing about it. The fifteen-year-old boy who raped me first was jailed for three years. The blond man got twelve years and the tall one three. But I didn't really care. All I could think about was the sin I had committed as I stared at myself in the mirror. I hated what I saw. I was marked, dead inside and couldn't feel anything anymore. School, my family, my friends – nothing mattered because I was empty. I just carried on living as I had before, going to school and coming home, but feeling nothing.

Six months later, my parents finally split up. We left Papa in the apartment, and Mamma and I moved to a dirty room furnished with a single bed, table and chair. I'd hoped we would become closer but, free of my father, Mamma went out most nights. The most I usually saw was a shadow getting into bed beside me, smelling of alcohol and cigarettes.

A few months after that, I stopped going to school. Our new home was on the other side of Simferopol and anyway I wasn't interested anymore. My dreams of doing well in my exams and getting a good job meant nothing after that day at the beach. Mamma had tried to persuade me to go back but I wouldn't change my mind and after a few weeks at home she'd told me I had to start paying my way.

'If you're not going to study then you need to make some money,' she said. 'You can't keep eating my food and not paying anything. Now you'll realise how hard life is.'

That is how I'd ended up working in the café where I stood now as the man got up and stared through the window. I put my head down and carried on drying the glass.

Whenever my mysterious friend returned to the café, I was always quiet and never responded to his attempts to break the ice. Nevertheless, a few weeks later, I left work one evening to find him standing outside holding a big bunch of flowers.

'Hi,' he said, offering them to me. 'My name is Sergey. Would you like to go for a walk?'

I couldn't help smiling – the flowers were beautiful and my stomach fluttered nervously to be so close to this handsome man.

'Come on,' he said, seeing that I was wavering. 'What's your name?'

'Oxana,' I said hesitantly.

'Well, Oxana – I'd be very honoured if you'd walk a little way with me. Do you live far from here?'

Without thinking, I answered him and we began to stroll off together. Soon we were talking away and then we sat down in the park to chatter on together. Sergey was twenty-two, funny, and so good-looking he made me tremble. When we said goodbye, I was full of excitement, but I was also afraid. I'd been dead inside so long that I felt safer that way – did I really want to come back to life again and risk more pain? And surely Sergey would soon notice that I was worth nothing, that there was a sin inside me and then it would all be over. But he didn't. Day after day, he came back and waited for me so that we could walk together, holding hands in the park as night fell. I felt warm inside when he smiled and I blossomed under his attention. Then, one night, he kissed me under a tree in the park – a soft delicious kiss that was everything I dreamed it would be.

'Now you're my girl, Oxana,' said Sergey softly.

'Yes,' I replied, happier than I'd ever thought I could be again.

'Is this what you want, Oxana?' Sergey asked, his green eyes anxious.

I nodded. We were in the bedroom of a flat that belonged to a friend of his. It was early afternoon but the curtains were drawn against the daylight. I was wearing only my bra and pants.

'Good,' he said. 'It's what I want too, but you have to be sure.' He came over and sat beside me on the bed and stroked my arm.

'I am.' I was. I had decided that I wanted to give myself to Sergey and belong to him completely. I had found the man I wanted to marry and whose children I wanted to bear. Why wait? Besides, there was always the horrible possibility that if I did not, he might leave me for someone who would, even though he told me how much he loved me. My great fear was that he would realise that I was not a virgin when he first made love to me, and that he would turn away from me in disgust.

He lay me down on the bed. 'You're so beautiful,' he whispered and then he kissed me. A few moments later, I felt him pushing against me and then he moved inside me. It was not at all like the experience I had had with those men on the beach – this was gentle and sweet and did not hurt me, though I made a small whimper as he entered me.

'Don't worry,' he soothed. 'It's only painful the first time, I promise.'

It was over very quickly and then he lay beside me dozing.

'Do you still love me?' I asked. He hadn't noticed that I was not a virgin but I feared that he might lose interest now that he had had me.

'Of course I do. Don't worry. Didn't I say that you're my girl?' And he fell asleep.

'I love you too,' I whispered, gazing at his face. I knew that I never wanted to leave his side. Three months later, we moved in together, into a rented room in an apartment block.

I didn't tell my mother where I was going – she would not have cared anyway.

Sergey and I were very happy in our little room together, although I was the only one bringing in a wage from my job at the café. Sergey was looking for work but he hadn't yet found anything. In the meantime he spent time with his friends and going about the city while I was at work, and in the evening we were together.

Then, in late 1991, I found out that I was pregnant.

'Well, we'd better make the best of it, I suppose,' Sergey said uncertainly when I told him the news. 'Weren't you being careful?'

I just looked at him. I was only fifteen and didn't really know anything about the facts of life. There was no sex on television, no half-dressed women in adverts and no sex education at school. I'd heard older girls talking of course but didn't understand and had trusted Sergey to know what we had to do. He was so much older than me.

'Do you think ...' I hardly knew how to say the words. It wasn't what I had dreamed of at all. '... do you think we should get married?'

He knew as well as I did that unless I was married I would be branded a slut and our child would have a miserable life, bullied at school and looked down on forever. Only a ring on my finger could prevent it.

'Yes, I suppose we'd better,' said Sergey with a smile, although he didn't look as happy as I'd hoped he might at the prospect. 'And I really will have to find a job – otherwise how am I going to support my wife and child?' He smiled and kissed me, and I tried to be positive. He must be pleased, mustn't he? Wasn't this what we had been planning all along?

While we arranged our wedding, which took time, my stomach began to swell and it was obvious I could no longer work at the café. I had to go somewhere safe where I could escape the looks and the whispers until I was married.

'You're not coming back here!' shouted my mother. 'I'm not taking you in because you've been a little tart! Get rid of it, that's my advice. Children are only a thankless burden.'

There was only one person I could turn to – my father. I had not seen him for over a year and I was frightened of what he would say when I turned up on his doorstep, but I needn't have worried.

'Oxana!' he cried, smiling and wrapping me in a huge hug. 'Where have you been? Come in, come in. It's wonderful to see you.'

Relieved, I went inside our old apartment. It was so nice to be back. It felt like home again. I explained to Papa what had happened: that I had met Sergey and was going to get married, but that I couldn't live with Mama any longer. He looked down at my growing stomach.

'I assume that this is the reason you need to get married,' he said.

'Well … I …' I couldn't meet his eye.

'Let's not worry about that now,' he said kindly. 'You are welcome to live here as long as you need to. And your fiancé can come too, if he likes. There's room here and I'm tired of living on my own. Some company would make a nice change.'

'Oh, thank you, Papa!' I cried, throwing my arms round his neck. At last, things were beginning to go well for us.

Silently the happiness grew inside me with my baby.

I was married just after my sixteenth birthday, wearing a white flower in my hair and a blue blouse and skirt. Sergey and I exchanged vows and cheap metal rings, and then we were man and wife. I knew some people believed it was bad luck to get married without a dress and gold but I told myself they were wrong.

Sergey and my father seemed to get on well and we all lived together happily enough, waiting for the arrival of the child. Sergey got a job in a metalwork factory and I was so happy that we could save up for our own house. But times were hard after Ukraine became independent following the fall of the Soviet Union and he often came home without wages. He wasn't alone and anger filled the air as prices went up and electricity and food shortages got worse. I was still one of the lucky ones, though, who had butter, eggs and meat as often as my father could get them, and I began to grow fat with my pregnancy and plenty of good food.

I had no idea what was happening when my waters broke on 31 May 1992. Papa knew though, and he took me at once to the hospital. My labour was difficult and painful but it was also short, and my beautiful son Alexander – or Sasha for short – was born quickly. When they handed him into my arms, I was shaking.

'Don't look so worried,' a nurse said to me when she saw tears on my face. 'He's fine.'

But I wasn't crying because of fear. I was happy. I had been born again in the moment that my son came into the world. The day at the beach was far behind me now. I was a different person, a mother, and my life could begin again.

When we got home, I spent hours staring at Sasha as he slept. He looked so peaceful – his skin the colour of milk and his cheeks like peaches – and so perfect that I felt almost scared to touch him. What if I dropped him? But Papa showed me what to do when I needed help.

'Here,' he said when I first tried to give the baby a bath and he kept slipping in my arms. 'Watch and learn.'

There were so many new things and sometimes I wondered if I'd ever be able to learn them all. But gradually I discovered how to massage Sasha's belly when he cried or stroke his head to help him sleep. I loved being a mother in so many ways and it gave me a warm feeling to live for someone else. The past seemed so far away now. I had another life to live for, another person who would carry my blood when I was gone.

It was not easy though, and Sasha was a difficult baby. He hardly slept at night but only cried and cried until the noise filled my head and felt like the only sound in the world. I began to feel more and more exhausted, and locked into a world where there was only the baby and me, as I fed him, changed him and tried to stop him crying. Sergey had seemed pleased with his new son but he couldn't care for him the way I did – he could not offer his breast – and sometimes got angry during the night when the baby's cries woke him.

Soon he began to spend more and more time with his friends. Now I was alone all day when he and Papa were at work, and without my husband in the evening too. As the weeks turned into months, I grew terribly lonely.

'Why can't you come home to see us?' I'd ask, when he finally got home. 'Your son needs you – I need you.'

'Because I want to relax away from a crying baby,' he'd reply. 'It's your job to look after him not mine.' There was a hardness in his eyes that I hadn't seen before and it scared me.

Soon I couldn't sleep or eat and my weight had started dropping. Within six months I'd lost five stone – my cheeks were sunken, I had black circles under my eyes and felt tired all the time. I was almost scared to go to sleep in case I didn't wake up when the baby needed me. It was like being sucked into a whirlpool and there was nothing I could do to stop it.

It was no good turning to my mother – she had no interest in me or her grandchild, and spent her time drinking greedily with her friends. Papa was the only person who did all he could to help – going out first thing to buy me milk and leaving work early to help me at the end of the day. I forgave him for all the events of the past and was grateful for his love and support now, when I truly needed it.

But however difficult it got, there were moments when Sasha made it all worthwhile – a smile or a laugh could lift my heart and I knew then that whatever happened I would love him forever.

Sasha was about three months old when my father suggested that we go to collect Sergey from work. It sounded like a good idea to me; I'd never seen him at his factory before and I was curious. When we got there, I left Papa and Sasha outside while I went to ask when Sergey would be leaving.

'There's no such person here,' replied the receptionist bluntly.

'Yes, there is. You must be mistaken,' I said with a smile.

But then I was shown into an office where a supervisor sat surrounded by files and he said the same thing. 'I'm sorry, Mrs Kalemi, but I can't find your husband's name anywhere,' he said after looking through his papers. 'He isn't listed as an employee.'

'But he must be here,' I replied. 'My husband has worked here six days a week for eight months.'

The man pulled another a pile of papers off a shelf. 'Ah, yes,' he said eventually. 'A Sergey Kalemi did apply to work here last October.'

'Yes, that's him.' I was relieved.

'But I'm afraid he never showed up.'

I stared at the man. I didn't understand what he was saying. 'You must be wrong. He's been working here for months.'

'I'm sorry but I'm not. Your husband applied for a job last October and got it but never turned up to start work.'

My heart thumped. How could Sergey not be working here? He'd been out twelve hours a day since before Sasha was born. Maybe he'd got a job at a different factory and hadn't told me. There must be an explanation.

I walked out to meet my father.

'So where is he?' Papa asked as I lifted Sasha into my arms. 'Not finished yet?'

'No.'

'What time will he be out?'

I held the baby tightly as I stared straight ahead. 'He won't,' I said slowly.

'What do you mean?'

'They say he's never worked there.'

There was a second of silence as colour flooded into Papa's face. 'What?' he said quietly.

Fear suddenly filled me as my father's face twisted with fury. I knew that look well.

'Papa, please be calm,' I pleaded. 'We just need to find Sergey and he'll explain.'

'I hope so,' my father said softly, and we turned for home.

When Sergey got back to the apartment, I took him into our bedroom while Papa waited outside. I told him everything that had happened.

He saw at once that there was no way to deny it, so he said defiantly, 'I didn't take the job because I couldn't get a reference.'

'But why not?' I cried.

'Because I've never worked anywhere.'

I looked at him as the breath left my body.

'What?'

'I didn't want you to know the truth so I lied. I'm sorry. I have a criminal record because I stole something when I was young and now I can't get a job.' He shrugged.

'But where did you get the money you've been giving me all these months?'

'I've got a deal with a family who rent my parents' house from me. It's been empty ever since they died and these people pay me each month in cash.'

I knew it was true that Sergey had a house but I'd never wanted to live there. It was in a different part of Simferopol and it was more like a village place with no running water or electricity, and I had much preferred it at Papa's. But now I stared at Sergey. 'Why are you saying these things? Why are you telling me fresh lies? If someone was paying rent then you'd have brought more money home each month.'

'Oxana, believe me,' Sergey pleaded. 'I gave you everything I had.'

I knew he was lying. What about all those nights he'd come home late and drunk? He'd spent whatever money he'd got on alcohol and his friends rather than his wife and baby.

There was no remorse in Sergey, only cold defiance. Was my whole life based on lies? Why didn't my husband want to work and support us? I hoped that now I had learned the truth, he would change and take responsibility for us. I had to be a good wife to him – give my husband another chance and show him that I still loved him. But soon it was clear that things were not going to be so simple.

'Well?' demanded Papa when I finally went to see him. 'What was his excuse? It had better be a good one.'

When I told him what Sergey had said, he was furious. 'How can a man live like that? How he can sponge off me and not look after his own wife and child? It's incredible!'

'Please don't hurt him!' I begged. I could see that Papa wanted to beat him up.

'I won't – for your sake,' he answered. 'But it's quite simple, Oxana. Sergey has to go.'

'No, no! Please don't separate us! Give him another chance.'

'No. I've had enough. I want him out, at once.'

I felt sick as I heard those words. What would we do? My place was with my husband whatever trouble we were in. My fear turned to anger and hysteria, and I started screaming until my father slapped me. Sadness wrestled with anger in his eyes but all I felt was fury. Once again he'd shown what he was really like.

'That's it,' I cried. 'I'm going now and you'll never see me again.'

'But you can't take Sasha. You can't just leave.'

'Yes I can. Sergey is my husband, the father of my child.'

This time I was the one who lost control and behaved like the sixteen-year-old I was. Papa said nothing as I packed our bags, walked into the living room and threw my keys at him.

'I hope you're happy,' I shouted as I slammed the door behind us.

Chapter Four

The snow cracked under the pram wheels as I pushed Sasha along the street. It was January 1995 and I was eight months pregnant with my second child. I was on my way to see Mamma in the early evening and my head was full of thoughts. So many things had happened since leaving Papa's eighteen months before and none of them were happy.

Sergey and I had gone to the only place we could think of when we left Papa's. He hadn't been lying when he'd said that he'd rented out his parents' house, so we couldn't stay there. Instead, we moved into an outbuilding in the garden called the summer kitchen, a one-room stone building with no glass in the windows, no running water and no stove. I tried to make it a home but it was impossible: it was always cold, draughty and miserable. On top of that, Sergey obviously felt that now I had found out about his lies, there was no need to pretend any longer. His love for me seemed to have died the day I confronted him with the truth about himself and now I finally saw him for what he was – a drunk who hated work and would rather see his wife and child go hungry than give up the little money he earned doing odd jobs and bought vodka with. There were many days without food and it was hard caring for Sasha – nappies didn't dry because the summer kitchen was so cold, his skin was raw and his stomach always empty.

Sergey and I rowed and fought all the time and one night, after a terrible fight when he flew at me with his fists, I knew I had to leave. I went back to Papa's apartment that night, taking Sasha with me. I cried with relief when Papa welcomed us into the warmth and light of my old home. At last we were safe. Somehow, I'd start again and put Sergey out of my life.

But my happiness was cruelly short-lived. Two months later my dear father died quite suddenly at the age of only forty-six, worn out from a life of unrelenting hard work. I sobbed at his funeral, overwhelmed with sadness and guilt. I couldn't help the awful feeling that I had killed him because of what I'd put him through. I had thrown all his kindness back in his face and it was my fault he was dead. My brother Vitalik soon returned to claim everything of Papa's for himself. I saw enough to know he was taking drugs – he brought flowers to the house and cooked them in the kitchen, the house was full of needles and the smell of burning – and, as I looked into his empty eyes, knew he would never give me a penny. Sasha and I were alone again.

Soon Sergey found us. He had heard about my father's death and returned, remorseful and crying, telling me that he loved me and the baby, and wanted us back. Things would be different, he promised. He'd stop drinking and find work, he'd make a proper home for us all. He loved me, he said, and was sorry for everything that had happened.

I believed him. I had to. In Ukraine, there was no help from the government for women like me so with no one to protect me, nowhere left to run and a child to care for, I had no choice. I had to trust that my husband was a reformed character. Besides, I couldn't help loving him in spite of it all. The power of what I had felt for him once was still strong.

But within weeks I'd realised that Sergey hadn't changed when I fell pregnant and he hated the baby from the moment it came to life inside me.

'Who were you fucking when you were living with your father?' he'd scream as we fought in that cold outbuilding while Sasha cried his heart out.

'No one! I don't want this baby either!' I yelled back, weeping. It was true. I already had Sasha and we were living in such terrible circumstances – how could I care for another child? I decided I had to have an abortion but when the doctor told me it would cost me $15 I knew I could never find such money and realised I would have to try to rid myself of my unborn child. I lifted heavy furniture, had long hot baths and even pushed my fists into my stomach as I tried to loosen its hold on my body. But nothing happened and so I went to see an old lady who told me to soak dill in hot water before drinking it and another who gave me some tablets which she said would stop the pregnancy. Nothing worked.

But as the months passed, I gradually began to realise that my child was meant to come into the world. God wanted me to have another baby and I had to learn to love it. Deep down, though, I was scared of what it would be like when it was born. I had committed a terrible sin when I'd tried to kill my own child and was sure it would be born sick and full of anger just like me. The guilt which I felt then had never left me and even now – days before the baby was due – I still felt it.

Walking through the cold winter day, I breathed in a lungful of freezing air as I turned into the street where Mamma lived. A few nights before, Sergey had kicked me in the base of my swollen stomach before locking me out in the snow during an argument. He'd let me back inside eventually but I'd had to sleep on a chair because he said I was too fat to share his bed. It felt as if all he had done was beat me since this baby came to life inside me. Tonight I needed some food – bread maybe or eggs – and I hoped Mamma would have something to spare. I'd just had my eighteenth birthday and maybe she would feel kind towards me. The baby needed something and so did Sasha.

I put my head down as the cold wind blew into my face. It wasn't far to go and then I would be inside. I just hoped Sasha would stay asleep and not anger Mamma with his crying.

When I arrived, I found my mother and her friends drunk as usual.

'What do you want now?' she bellowed, a cigarette hanging out of her mouth. 'Look at you! You look like a sow.'

'I just want something to eat …' I said. She grunted and I followed her into the warm kitchen where she put a loaf of bread and some cheese on the table in front of me. I ate it gratefully.

'Why can't that lazy oaf of a husband of yours provide for you? I knew he was rotten right from the start. How could you let him get you pregnant again? He can't even look after one child, let alone two.'

'He'll beat me if I refuse him,' I muttered.

She snorted. 'Just don't expect me to keep bailing you out, that's all. I've got problems of my own. I can't afford to feed you and your brats, so you might as well stop coming round.'

The food turned to ashes in my mouth. Was my own mother really refusing me help? She knew how we lived, and what it meant for the baby and for me. After a while, Mama rejoined her friends as they guzzled their vodka and, after I'd fed Sasha, I let myself out into the cold darkness, back to the icy summer kitchen.

I was almost happy when I found blood in the toilet the next day – the baby had died and I was going to have a miscarriage. Maybe it was for the best. What kind of life could I offer this child? I told myself to wait as the pain got worse throughout the night and following day but eventually it got so bad that I had to go to hospital.

'The baby is fine,' a doctor told me but I felt nothing.

Three days later my second son was born.

Chapter Five

Pavel, known as Pasha, was small, with thick black hair like a cap and huge blue eyes which were so dark they looked almost black. I thought of my father as I looked at him.

'He'll need lots of attention,' the doctor said as he handed him to me. 'He has slight jaundice but he should be fine.'

I said nothing as I felt the weight of my son in my arms for the first time. Pasha stirred in my arms and I stared down at him as his eyes fluttered open. Tears slid down my cheeks. Somehow I had to find my love for him, forget the sin I had committed in trying to stop him coming into the world and the fierce beatings Sergey had given me as he raged that another child was coming. My baby needed me.

'I will look after him carefully,' I said as I looked up at the doctor.

But even though I was filled with tenderness for my new son, life did not get any easier. Pasha was a sickly baby and I felt scared when I changed his nappy for the first time. His skin was thin like paper, his long legs scrawny and, instead of a fat peachy bottom, his was skinny and slight. He was an unsettled baby who spat out my nipple when it was offered even though he was screaming for food and he would cry for hours on end as Sergey shouted.

'Shut him up! I can't stand this noise. Why is this bastard child here? Why am I feeding him, giving him a home?'

Pasha was just as I'd feared he would be – I was sure that his weakness came from the way I had once tried to rid myself of him, and I was certain that his cries were filled with grief. How could he be anything other than sick and unhappy after what had happened? It only made me more desperate to care for him and bring him to health and happiness, like Sasha. My older son was nearly two and doing as well as he could in the circumstances. I tried to make sure that he always had enough to eat and milk to drink, and he was growing big. He toddled about the summer kitchen, chatting away and playing. He even managed to charm Sergey out of his rages, though I was grateful he slept through the worst of my husband's drunken furies.

I knew that Sasha was strong. My great fear for Pasha was that he wouldn't be able to survive the life we were living. Even while I fed him, dressed him and kept him warm, I suffered agonies of fear that he would die; when he screamed and cried I felt sure he was telling me of his unhappiness and that he could not bear it.

'Why don't you just put him into an orphanage?' Sergey would shout. 'He's going to die anyway so you might as well save yourself the trouble of looking after him.'

My relationship with Sergey deteriorated more every day. I despaired that he would ever be able to care for us. There was a glimmer of hope when he got a job as a labourer, earning the few dollars a day we needed for food and clothes; but he lost it after brawling with another worker. We were back to living on what Sergey stole and did not drink. But even a thieving husband and a few dollars for food was better than no husband at all.

One evening, Sergey was sitting at the table, trying to repair an old radio he had found. Sasha was playing at his feet with some of the bits and pieces that Sergey was discarding as he went. I sat as close as I could to the fire, holding Pasha in my arms. I felt more protective of him than ever because earlier that day we had been to see a doctor who'd told us Pasha had a hernia and muscular problems. I'd known my son was weak but was shocked when the doctor told me he should go to an orphanage where he could have an operation and be cared for.

'But I can't do that,' I said. 'He's my son. How could I sleep at night if I left him?'

'Well, it may be better for him if you did.'

I could see his disgust for me in his eyes. What the doctor really wanted to say was: 'Why have a baby if you can't look after him?'

I was full of shame, wanting to explain how things had got this way, but I stayed silent.

Now I looked up at Sergey as he played at fixing the radio. What would it achieve if he mended it? Would he sell it for a dollar and give the money to me so I could buy food? I doubted it. I pulled Pasha close, feeling anger rise up inside me.

'We have to find work,' I said. 'The baby is sick. We need money to buy proper milk. You heard what the doctor said. We have to help Pasha become strong.'

Sergey looked at me. 'I do my best. I find work when I can.'

'But we have to do more. We need just two or three dollars a day to buy food and if you can't find work then maybe I can.'

Sergey's eyes widened. 'Me?' he asked. 'Look after children while you work?'

'Yes. It's the only choice we have.'

'Well, you wouldn't need to work if we just put Pasha in the orphanage.'

Fury hardened in my stomach. Pasha, Pasha, Pasha … Sergey wanted to blame everything on him.

'Why can't you understand?' I snapped. 'We all need food and you don't provide it. What kind of father are you? Look at us. We're thin, sick.'

'But I'm always thinking about you, Oxana.'

Suddenly I forgot all the lessons beaten into me by Sergey in the past. I put Pasha down in his basket and stood up to face him. 'What?' I screamed. 'When do you think of anyone but yourself? You spend money on vodka when your own children can't eat. All you do is drink and steal. You'll never change. You're not a man, you can't even provide for us!'

Sergey's eyes blazed but I didn't care as a river of rage washed through me. I couldn't look after my children properly, Pasha was sick, we were always hungry and I was hated as a thief just like Sergey because I was his wife. His crime was my crime.

'You're a joke,' I laughed. 'All you can do is hit women because you can't stand up to men. You're pathetic.'

His hand cracked across my cheek. 'You fucking bitch,' he shouted.

'Oh go on, hit me,' I screamed back. 'You can't hit a man, can you? Come on. Do it. I'm your wife, aren't I? That's what I'm here for.'

Still the words didn't stop as they poured from my mouth.

'Come on!' I screamed as tears streaked my cheeks. 'Do it. Be a man. Show me what you can do.'

Sasha began to cry and hid under the table. I saw his frightened eyes looking out at us and part of me longed for it all to stop so that I could gather him up in my arms and comfort him. But it had all gone too far for that: Sergey and I were both riding high on a torrent of rage and frustration. Miserable in our lives, we could only blame each other for our wretchedness.

'You are a laughable excuse for a man,' I spat.

Suddenly Sergey lunged for me and grabbed my hair. 'I'm going to take your scalp off,' he shouted. 'See if I don't.'

'So try it,' I shrieked. 'You'll need to cut me. Do you want to cut me?' We stared at each other as my challenge hung in the air. I wasn't scared of him. I was sick of the bruises and split lips.

'Go on,' I spat. 'Do it.'

Sergey pulled off his belt – an army belt made of thick leather with a big buckle which he loved – as he pushed me into the corridor, folded it into a strap and lifted it into the air.

'No!' I screamed and tried grabbing it from him, kicking my legs into the air, aiming for his groin. Somehow I wrenched the belt into my hand and hit him with it before running out of the front door and into the yard where I grabbed a piece of wood.

'I'm going to kill you,' Sergey shouted as he ran after me and I saw a glint of silver in the darkness.

Fear bit my throat. There was a meat knife in his hand. His eyes were dead and lifeless. I had to run. But Sergey caught me by the hair and started dragging me towards the summer kitchen. What had I done? Had I pushed him too far this time? He pulled me into the corridor and I broke free for a second as I tried to get away. But suddenly I felt a searing pain in my back and saw the knife falling through the air beside me. It landed on the floor and dark drops of blood dripped one by one around it. Whose were they?

I drew my hand around to my back and pulled it away to see a crimson stain. I fell onto the floor, crying as my breath came in gulps. Sergey didn't move as he stood above me, confusion and fear written across his face. I stayed still as I lay on the ground.

'It's the last time,' I screamed as I looked up at him. 'I'm going to the police.'

But we both knew I wouldn't. I'd seen it so many times with my parents. I knew the police couldn't give me a place to live or money to buy food so what was the point in asking for help?

Sergey bent down and put his arms around me. 'I'm sorry, Oxana,' he whimpered. 'I didn't mean to, I'm sorry. It's just a cut, don't worry. I'll clean it.'

But I said nothing as the courage which had filled my veins drained away like the blood flowing out of the wound. As I looked into Sergey's eyes, all I could see was darkness. I was his now. He had defeated me. Finally I knew there were no limits to what he would do to me. The knife may have missed its mark tonight but next time it would not.

I wanted to scream as Pasha cried – a high, thin wail he'd been making all day.

'Sshh,' I said as I bent down to pick him up out of his cot.

Anxiety and annoyance twisted my stomach. Sergey would be home soon and he'd scream at me if Pasha wasn't quiet. His hatred of our son – and me – had only got worse in the weeks since the night he'd cut me. I hadn't gone to hospital after the fight and the cut had left a thin, white scar snaking across my back.

All I could do was live in the shadows, hoping not to anger Sergey again because I couldn't run. Day after day Sergey asked if I loved him and stayed close to me to make sure I didn't try to leave again. I wasn't going to. Once I'd had my father, now there was no one, so where could I run? Sergey had shown what he could do and I felt more powerless than ever. All I could do was trust that one day things would change.

As I picked up Pasha once again, I thought of what the doctor had said all those weeks ago. We were due to see him again soon and my son hadn't got any better however much I'd tried to coax milk into him. The more I thought about the orphanage, the more I wondered if it might be right to put him there. My neighbour Janna who gave me food sometimes when I had none, the doctor and Mamma all told me it would be right, that the baby could be cared for properly there. Everyone said the same thing and I knew deep down what I had to do. I would put Pasha into the orphanage for six months to give me enough time to find a job and someone to look after Sasha while I worked. Then Pasha would be well enough to come home.

Sergey was so pleased when I told him later that night. 'At last you've seen sense,' he said with a smile.

It might be the right decision but I was seized by sadness as I packed Pasha's few clothes into a bag the next day. Would he ever forgive me? I had never really learned how to love him properly and now I was sending him away.

'He'll have the operation he needs,' the orphanage director told me the next day as she took him. 'We'll feed him up and make him strong.'

'But when can I see him?' I asked.

'Whenever you want but most parents visit at weekends.'

'Then that's what I'll do.'

Pasha looked so old as he stared at me. He was such a serious baby who hardly ever smiled.

'Shall I take him?' the director said and moved towards me.

A pain leapt up in my chest as his weight was lifted from my arms.

'It's for the best,' I told myself as I started crying. 'You'll improve your life, make it better for the children and then he'll come home. You have no other choice. You have to do this to keep him safe and well.'

Sergey took my arm as the door closed.

'What's wrong?' he asked roughly. 'I'm glad he's gone. Now let's go.'

I didn't say a word as we walked outside and I held tightly onto Sasha's hand. I had given my baby away to strangers, failed him just as I had from the moment I knew I was having him, and I felt sick inside.

'May God forgive me,' I said silently to myself.

Chapter Six

Soon after Pasha left I got a job in a café through a new friend. Her name was Marina and she lived on the same street as us. She was seventeen, tall and slim with long black hair and beautiful eyes but most of all she was kind. Marina could see how hungry I was and fed me whenever I went to visit her at her parents' home. I was so happy to have a friend. A lot of people didn't want to know me because of Sergey but Marina didn't care. I'd felt so old and tired but with her I could almost feel like a real teenager again.

Soon we had started working in the café together, a place owned by a Muslim man called Aziz. At first Sergey hadn't been at all happy about it, but he changed his mind when he heard about the $3 I would be making every day. My shifts lasted twelve to fourteen hours, so now I could put food on the table. One day, I hoped, I would save enough tips to rent my own room and leave with Sasha.

Sergey looked after Sasha during the day but one night he decided to come and pick me up and, as he waited outside, saw me joking with Aziz. He quickly flew into a jealous rage.

'Why were you kissing that man? Are you fucking him?' he shouted as we walked home.

'You know I'm not and I didn't kiss him,' I replied.

'Yes, you did and now I know why you don't want to have sex with me anymore.'

'Oh, come on,' I said wearily. 'I'm just tired.'

Sergey slapped my cheek. 'Don't lie to me,' he said.

'Why are you doing this?' I started to cry. 'I promise you that I haven't done anything wrong. You know I'd never cheat on you.'

'No, I don't,' he shouted. 'And today is your last day at work. You can't go back.'

I didn't argue with him as we walked back to the summer kitchen and got into bed. But when I woke the next morning, I got up to dress for work as usual and put some money on the table before leaving. Sergey would realise he was better off if I worked when he saw it.

Marina was waiting for me outside as I closed the door and it was quiet as we started walking. But yells suddenly filled the air and I turned around to see Sergey running towards us.

'You fucking bitch,' he shouted. 'I told you that you couldn't go back to that place. What the fuck are you doing?'

Marina looked so confused. I'd never told her the truth about Sergey. I didn't talk to anyone about it and, although she'd been shocked when she saw how we lived in the summer kitchen, she had no idea how things really were.

'Let's go,' I said as I started running. We managed to stay ahead of him for a while but as we reached the road, Sergey caught me. Blows flew into my body as I fell to the ground.

'Why didn't you listen?' he screamed. 'I meant what I said, you know. Fucking bitch!'

A fist smashed into my stomach. 'Please help me,' I cried to Marina, but she was scared and didn't know how to stop Sergey as he ripped at my clothes. 'Why are you doing this?' I screamed at him. 'We need the money. I can't just leave my job.'

'Whore! You're doing all those Muslims and now you don't want me.'

'What are you saying?' Marina suddenly shouted. 'It's not true. Stop this. Leave her alone.'

Sergey said nothing but the punches stopped as suddenly as they'd begun and I looked up to see a car parked beside us. Two customers I knew from the café were getting out as Sergey walked quickly away. I lay on the ground and pulled my cardigan around me, trying to hide my underwear as I sobbed.

The customers were kind and helped me up. I managed to put my dress back on and hold the rips together until I could pin them at the café. My eye had started to blacken by the time Aziz arrived and Marina told him what had happened.

'Is he crazy?' Aziz asked when she'd finished.

I said nothing. All I could think about was going home later. I was so scared. What would Sergey do to me this time? I knew what he was capable of – a belt, a knife, he didn't care what he used to hurt me. But, however much I wanted to run, I couldn't leave Sasha.

Later that evening, I stood outside the door to the summer kitchen and held my breath. I'd been standing there for a few minutes trying to make my hand reach out and turn the handle. I knew I couldn't fight back if Sergey beat me. I'd tried in the past and look what had happened. I was weak and he was strong – I'd never win.

But the summer kitchen was in darkness when I finally opened the door. Maybe my neighbour Janna would know where Sergey and Sasha were. She made vodka and so Sergey often went to see her.

'Oxana,' she exclaimed when she opened the door.

'Do you know where Sergey is?' I asked. 'He's not at home and I want to find Sasha.'

'The baby is here with me. But don't you know what's happened?'

'What do you mean?'

'Sergey is in hospital.'

'What?'

'In hospital,' Janna exclaimed, her eyes widening in excitement.

'But why?'

'He got beaten up. Some men arrived earlier to see him and the next thing I knew Sergey was staggering out of the summer kitchen covered in blood. Barely walking. Half dead.'

I felt sick as I stared at Janna. Finally Sergey knew what it was like to be beaten but, although I knew I should be happy, all I felt was fear. What had he done now? Would those men come back for me?

It was too late to go to the hospital that night but I told Marina I wouldn't be going into work when she came to pick me up the next morning and I arrived at the hospital to find Sergey lying in bed. His lip was split, his jaw was black and he'd bruised his kidneys.

The muscles in his face twitched as he looked at me.

'What happened?' I asked.

'Well, you should know.'

'What do you mean?'

'Didn't you send them?'

'Who?'

'Your fucking Muslim lovers,' Sergey spat. 'The ones who did this to me. Men from the café you love so much.'

'What are you talking about?' I whispered. 'Of course I didn't send anyone. I knew nothing about it.'

'Well, we'll see about that won't we? I'll be home soon and then we'll know the truth about your customers.'

How could that be true? I didn't believe him. At work, I said to Aziz, 'My husband seems to think you sent some men to beat him up. Is he crazy?'

Aziz looked me straight in the eye. 'No, Oxana, he's right. I sent my men to teach your husband a lesson in respect. I will not tolerate him treating you that way, or making his scandalous accusations against my good name. Now he knows we're watching him and if he touches you then all you'll need to do is let us know.'

I gasped. So it was true! But this was terrible. Rage coursed through me. 'And then what?' I screamed. 'Are you going to feed my baby every day, look after him, put money on the table when you've killed my husband?'

Aziz frowned and said nothing.

'No? So how will I live? How will my baby eat without a man to bring home money or someone to look after my child while I work for you? Can't you see what you've done? I can never come back here now, and my husband will probably kill me for it.'

'No, Oxana, you're wrong. Stay here and you'll be safe. I promise.'

'I can't.' Shaking with anger, I turned around and slammed out of the café. Aziz might have thought he was protecting me but this wasn't an end – it was only just the beginning. I was sure of just one thing. The moment we were alone Sergey would have his revenge.

* * *

It was like waiting for a bomb to go off when Sergey came home after a week in the hospital. I didn't know what would trigger the explosion but knew it would come soon and so I became more and more scared when he was silent. It was as if nothing had ever happened and neither of us mentioned Aziz or the café. But the relief I felt each night when I went to sleep without a beating was replaced by fear as the waiting started once again the next morning.

I missed working at the café – the money I'd earned, the food we'd eaten, the friends I'd made – but couldn't go back. My door into a new world had slammed shut and I was as trapped as ever on the wrong side. I still saw Marina and she brought me bits of money and food whenever she could but we didn't talk about what had happened. Our lives were just too different and I wanted to forget mine when I was with her.

But as days turned into weeks, I began to wonder if Aziz had been right after all. I'd always known Sergey was scared of other men and maybe fear of what might happen again was enough to keep him away from me. I wasn't sure but, like an actress playing a role, I gave him sex when he wanted, didn't say a word when he went out drinking and never mentioned getting a job again. Things went back to how they always had been and, even though I couldn't believe that Sergey would forget so easily, I began hoping he might leave me alone.

A couple of weeks after he got back from hospital we finally moved from the summer kitchen into the main house with Sergey's sister Ira and her husband Alex. The tenants had left and Ira had decorated the house ready for us. I liked her. She and Alex worked on a market stall selling wedding dresses and, although they couldn't have children of their own, had taken in their niece Vica when her mother had committed suicide.

They had a good life and it was almost like being part of a family again. Our new home might not have had running water or an inside toilet, but it had a proper corrugated iron roof, white walls and maroon floorboards. There was also a living room where Vica slept and two bedrooms – one for Ira and Alex and another for Sergey, Sasha and me. But although I enjoyed sitting together with Ira in the evenings, I still wasn't sure whether I could really trust her or not. She was Sergey's sister after all, even if she didn't seem to like him much. But she was also kind – she gave Sasha and me food whenever she could and looked after her niece Vica when she could easily have put her into an orphanage just as I had done with Pasha.

I hadn't forgotten my little Pasha, of course. I thought of him constantly but even though I longed to see and hold him, I was too scared to go the orphanage. I was consumed with guilt for leaving him there, and terrified of what he might be suffering. I couldn't bear to think about his tiny body undergoing an operation and dreaded to think of how he might look at me when I visited him. So I was a coward and, despite my longing, I did not go.

He's better where he is, I told myself firmly. And he'll be coming home when his six months at the orphanage are up, and then I'll be a better mother to him.

Soon after Pasha left, I discovered I was pregnant again. I could not refuse my husband what he wanted and did not have the money for contraception. But even though I worried about feeding another mouth, I was also happy. I just knew everything would be different this time: I would be a good mother and this baby would be easy and healthy where Pasha had been sick and unhappy. I would prove that I could be a good mother and, when Pasha came home, he would have a new baby brother or sister to love.

Sergey didn't say much about it when I told him but I didn't care as long as he left me alone. I had done what he wanted – given Pasha to the orphanage and stopped working – and so he seemed happier now. All I could do was pray that he would continue to leave me alone.

This time though, God wouldn't hear my prayers.

Chapter Seven

A couple of months later Sergey asked me to go out with him one night. As darkness fell we walked down a dirt road towards a stone house with a big metal door.

We walked inside and into a dirty room with an old sofa and bed in it. In the half light, I could see four men and two girls listening to music. They all seemed drunk.

Sergey immediately started chatting but I said nothing as I sat down. The girls looked as if they were going to pass out and soon one of the men had pulled them to their feet.

'We're going,' he said and they left.

Soon Sergey got up as well.

'I've got some business,' he told me. 'I won't be long.'

Now I was alone with two men – one had dark hair and was tall and slim, while the other was shorter and a little fatter.

'So how are you?' the dark man asked. 'Would you like a drink?'

'No thanks,' I told him. 'I'll have to leave soon.'

He walked over to the sofa and sat down next to me. 'Come on, have one,' he said in a sing-song voice.

'No, thanks,' I said as I felt his arm move around my shoulders. I pushed him away.

'Just a friendly hug,' he laughed as he stood up and walked over to the table where he sat down again and started rolling cannabis into a cigarette. I knew what it was because Sergey sometimes smoked it. The smell was horrible.

I looked about anxiously. Where was Sergey? He had been gone so long, was probably getting drunk somewhere. I'd had enough. I wanted to leave.

The fat man got off his chair as I stood up. 'Where are you going?' he cried.

'Home.'

'No, no. Don't go.'

The dark man got up and walked towards me. 'No, don't,' he said. 'We're just getting started.'

'But I've got to,' I replied and turned away. Suddenly an arm twisted around my throat from behind. 'Let me go!' I cried.

'No,' a voice said. 'First we're going to enjoy you. You'll be okay. You'll like it too.'

I knew instantly what he wanted. This couldn't be happening – not with a baby inside me. 'No,' I screamed as I tried to break free. 'Sergey will kill you. He'll be back in a minute.'

'No, he won't,' the voice behind me laughed. 'He's very busy.'

I struggled as the arm closed even tighter around my neck. It was so strong that I couldn't breathe. Panic twisted inside as I was pulled towards the bed and pushed onto it before the dark man climbed on top of me – grabbing my hair and pushing his mouth onto mine as I screamed. Pictures of the beach flashed into my mind and the cold terror I had felt then filled me. 'Please, please leave me alone,' I pleaded as I started crying. 'I'll do anything.'

But the men didn't listen as they tied my hands above my head and something silenced me. There is only so much a soul can take before it freezes into nothing and that is what happened to me that night. My mind went blank as the men forced their way into the furthest corners of my body and I turned to stone.

They laughed and smoked when they'd finished, and I pulled on my clothes before stumbling out of the house into the darkness.

Sergey was sitting waiting for me.

'I need to talk to you,' I whispered. I had to tell him what had happened, otherwise the men might talk and he'd think I'd wanted them. Then he would kill me. Tears ran down my face as we started walking.

'What's wrong?' he asked.

'Your friends …'

'Yes?'

'I've been raped.'

Sergey stopped walking. 'Really?' he said slowly.

'Yes. They made me do it. I swear. I couldn't stop them.'

He looked at me. 'I know what happened. Those men are my friends. Nobody raped you, so why are you lying?'

Confusion rushed up inside me. 'But I'm not,' I shouted. 'They raped me while you were away.'

'I was outside all the time, Oxana.'

'Well, then you must have heard me screaming.'

'I didn't hear anything,' said Sergey, his voice like ice with a smile in it.

Suddenly my whole body went cold. He knew what had happened to me, had done nothing as he heard my screams.

'Did you think I'd let you get away with having your dirty lovers do your dirty work?' Sergey said softly. 'Did you think I'd just forget what those Muslim fuckers did to me?'

I turned away. 'I'm going,' I sobbed. 'To Mamma's, the police, I don't care if I have to live on the streets.'

'Are you sure?' Sergey called. 'Your mother wouldn't have you and I've got a lot of friends who'd want to fuck you so much that they'd find you wherever you ran. Besides, what will you tell the police? They'll never believe you. Everyone knows you're a whore.'

My head swam as we stood in the darkness. He was right. Who would believe me? What man would allow his own wife to be raped? Even Ira, who knew her brother's thieving ways, would not think he could stoop this low.

I had two babies, and another on the way. There was no way I could ever escape him. All I could hope was that his thirst for revenge was slaked and now he would leave me alone.

'Let's go,' Sergey said quietly.

I turned to follow him home.

I had been stupid to believe that Sergey had forgotten what Aziz's men had done. I wouldn't make the same mistake again, so now I watched Sergey and waited for what he would do next. I did nothing to provoke him, even when he came home drunk and pushed me out of bed, or slapped me without a word – he was just waiting to hurt me again and I knew it. It was as though he could no longer bear the sight of me and I felt my resilience in the face of his hatred begin to waver. Surely I must have deserved what had happened? Sergey was right. I was worth nothing.

Meanwhile his life was disintegrating. Sergey was becoming seriously addicted to drugs and one night I saw him in the kitchen with a friend. As he sat at the table, he put a band around his arm and flexed his hand while his friend injected him with a syringe. I watched him through the open door as he lay down in the half-light, his expression one of blissful oblivion.

So that was how he escaped this miserable existence, and how he condemned his family to hunger and poverty.

Sergey beat me regularly now, no matter how quiet and good I was. He'd wake up sweating and shaking and hit me, or I'd heat up his gruel too much and he'd beat me. We fought a lot about food because he often ate everything and left nothing for the children and me.

Bit by bit something inside me was breaking and I was becoming afraid of my own shadow. I believed Sergey when he screamed at me about how ugly, stupid and useless I was. Why else had my life turned out the way it had?

'All you can do is get pregnant and now you're fat as a cow again with another child,' he'd shout. 'You're useless.'

Life became so painful that I turned into a robot and switched off my thoughts and feelings. Wake, eat, wash, clean, cook, feed, bathe … My life was about physical details, and I didn't want to feel or see anything as I told myself again and again that what had happened was all just a movie.

'There will be a happy ending,' I'd whisper inside as I drew water up from the well with which to wash Sasha's clothes. 'This isn't real, just make-believe, and Papa is watching over you.'

After one bad argument Sergey took a washing line and tied my hands and feet behind me before leaving me for several hours lying on the floor. Punching, strangling or slapping, he didn't care what he did and it was almost as if I didn't either. This was my punishment.

'You're like a dog,' I'd tell myself. 'When he wants to eat and no one feeds him he gets skinny and helpless. You're just like him and Sergey is your master.'

I had two choices: either finish my life and leave my children, or wait for this one to end and a new one to begin. I just had to believe that the pain would end and love my children while I waited. They were the one good thing in my life – the only thing that could cut through my frozen heart – and, as Sasha lay sleeping beside me at night, my hands would stroke my round stomach. Whispering silently to the child inside me, I told it that one day we would be happy together.

Chapter Eight

Pasha looked like a new baby when he came home again in December 1994. I'd finally gone to see him just before his time at the orphanage had ended and was filled with shame when I saw how changed he was – where once he had been thin and sickly, he was now fat and healthy. He'd started eating as soon as he'd had his hernia operation and I was happy that he could sit, hold his head, laugh and grip my fingers like any normal eleven-month-old baby. Now he wasn't ill anymore I was released from my feelings of guilt and hoped I could love him the way I wanted to, like a real mother.

Sergey just ignored him when he came home and I did not mind. But it was as if the light in Pasha switched off from the moment he came through our door and he started crying once again for hours on end. Day after day his screams went on and it felt as if they would never stop. I was in despair – why couldn't I be a proper mother to my son and make him happy? Should I have left him in the orphanage, where he had grown and become healthy?

Pasha's unhappiness seemed to fill the room where we lived. I was six months pregnant with another baby and didn't know how I could cope. Ira and Alex were sympathetic, but they also found it hard living with Pasha's constant wailing. At least they could go into their room and close the door.

The noise drove Sergey mad.

'Shut the fucking baby up!' he would shout, then he'd punch me and I knew that if I didn't quieten Pasha it would just get worse. But no matter what I did, I could not seem to calm my son. He was so different to how Sasha had been as a baby. Where my eldest child had giggled as I spoke to him and laughed as we played games, Pasha seemed to be in a different world from me and I could not understand how to reach him. He cried and cried and, even when I managed to keep him quiet, Sergey would still come for me with beatings, slappings and whippings.

Early one morning, Pasha was screaming particularly loudly. Sergey was in bed, the pillow over his head, trying to sleep while I did my best to soothe the baby. Sasha was fast asleep, the only one of us who could shut out the noise.

'Make him shut up!' Sergey shouted as I ran to prepare some food which I hoped would quiet Pasha. 'Christ knows how the others manage to stand this noise! He's going to wake the whole house.'

The bedroom door was open and as I stood at the stove I saw Sergey get out of bed and walk towards the baby. He raised his hand, slapped him and I saw Pasha's head knock against the wall.

'No, no!' I cried, rushing back to the baby. He was momentarily silenced by the shock of the pain and his little face was dead white. I felt sick as I picked him up and cuddled him. 'Leave him alone!' I shouted. 'He's only a baby.'

Sergey grunted and shrugged, then turned away, while I hushed Pasha and took him back to the kitchen. I wept silently as I fed him. No child should be treated in such a way but how could I protect my son when I couldn't even protect myself?

As soon as Sergey had left for the evening, I bundled up the children along with some of our belongings and took them to the waiting room of Simferopol train station. It was the only place I could think of to keep warm and I told myself we'd spend the night there while I decided what to do. All I knew was that it was too dangerous for us to remain with Sergey any longer. He had hurt Pasha and I could not allow it to happen again. But we stayed the next night and the one after that – leaving during the day to walk around the park for a few hours before returning to the warmth of the waiting room – because I did not know what else to do. There were no shelters for women in Ukraine, no free housing for people in trouble, and so I almost stopped thinking about it as the days passed. We just had to survive.

I told myself we were better off than people living on the streets. At least we had somewhere warm to sleep – Pasha in his pram and Sasha on a bench – and there was a cloakroom basin to wash nappies in before hanging them over the pram to dry. We could also go to the canteen where the staff would give me spare bits of bread or heat up bottles of milk I'd taken with me. But soon Sasha began coughing and Pasha got diarrhoea.

On our fourth night in the waiting room, Ira came bursting in. 'I heard you were here! What are you doing? These children will catch their deaths! Come home at once.'

I stared up at her, terrified. 'I can't come home! You know what Sergey will do to me. You know how he treats me.'

She looked at me with pity. 'Yes, I know. He's a scoundrel, I can make no excuses for him. But that is what I've come to tell you. Sergey's not there. He's been arrested!'

'Arrested? What for?' I'd begun to think that Sergey would never be punished for his countless acts of crime and thievery.

'Come home. I'll tell you all about it.'

Back home, I was glad to be in the warmth, with the children tucked up in bed and Ira giving me a cup of hot tea and some soup.

'Sergey's been arrested and he's being kept in custody,' Ira told me as I ate. 'A man was set upon and robbed a few months back, and died as a result. The police think Sergey did it.'

'I can't believe it,' I replied. 'He's vicious but he's also a coward. He only beats women.'

'I know.' Ira looked sad. 'I'm glad our mother is not here to see how he turned out. But you know how he's been lately ...'

'The drugs.' I nodded.

'It's been getting worse, we can all see it. It's perfectly possible that Sergey was high on something and went too far when he robbed the man.' Ira looked at me. 'As it is, he's a thief and a drug taker. He's not likely to get off easily from the police if they decide to make life difficult for him. If I were you, I would enjoy the peace and quiet while he's gone. That baby of yours is due soon, isn't it?'

'Yes.' I looked down at my swollen belly. 'Only a week or two more.'

'All the more reason for you to be here, not in some draughty waiting room. Honestly, Oxana, what are we going to do with you?' Ira smiled kindly. She knew how desperate I had to be to do something like that.

'But without Sergey, how am I going to feed the children?' I said dully.

'Well, you know, I might just have an answer ...'

At Ira's suggestion, I began to work from home making flowers for the wedding dresses she sold. I would be paid \$2 for each one I made and the first took five days. But I quickly got faster at sewing the roses and lilies which would be worn by brides, and I thought of them as I sewed under a lamp after the children had gone to bed. I'd always dreamed of marrying my prince wearing a beautiful white dress and flowers in my hair.

'One day, Oxana, one day,' I kept telling myself as the house fell silent with sleep and I carried on sewing.

Most nights I worked until four o'clock and then slept for a couple of hours. But sometimes I'd only just be finishing as the children woke up and I could hardly see to make their breakfast. I didn't mind though. It was a relief to live without the fear of being beaten, and to earn the money I needed to provide food. I could almost begin to feel hopeful – if I wasn't so afraid of what would happen when Sergey came home.

On 9 March 1995 I gave birth to our third child, a little girl called Luda. Once again I was filled with love when I looked at my child's fat, rosy cheeks.

'Hello, little girl,' I cooed to her. 'I'm your mamma! And we're going to be very happy, I promise you.'

Ira and Alex welcomed us home with little cakes and wine, and Luda quickly became everyone's darling. I fed her, looked after the children and earned what we needed with the flowers I was making. I had my three children and I was providing for us all. That was all that mattered.

* * *

When Luda was about four months old, I was told I had to be interviewed by a police investigator about Sergey's arrest. I went into the police station apprehensive and nervous, and was taken to a bare room where a policewoman was waiting for me. She gestured to me to sit down, told me the details of the case and then stared at me coldly.

'The attack happened on 24 February. Can you remember that day?' she asked. 'Your husband says he was at home with you as usual, but we have a witness who was with him that night and says he was out all evening. Can you help us at all?'

My mind raced back over the past few months. How would I ever remember one particular night? It was such a long time ago now … then suddenly I remembered something and my breath caught in my throat.

'No. I don't remember that day,' I said quickly.

But I did. There had been a public holiday on 20 February and I knew that a few nights later Sergey had arrived home late at night with bloody and scraped knuckles.

'Darling,' the investigator said softly as I stared at her. 'Do you know that it is a criminal offence to hide evidence? You could go to prison for three to five years.'

I stared at the table. I could keep silent, protect Sergey and risk being taken away from my children. Or I could tell what I knew and perhaps there would be a life for me and the children away from his violence and criminal life … What choice was there?

'I do remember that night,' I said slowly.

The investigator looked at me and I felt my heart beat as I started to talk. I told her everything I remembered.

'Thank you. You've done the right thing,' she said, as she passed me a pen so that I could sign my statement.

A few weeks later Sergey was charged with robbery and manslaughter.

The news that he would face a trial and perhaps a prison sentence gave me mixed feelings. On the one hand, I was happy to think that soon he might be locked away, never able to hurt me again – maybe God had finally listened to my prayers just as I'd always hoped He would. But I was also scared of life without my husband. It's hard to understand but when you've been beaten for long enough you start believing you are as weak and worthless as you've always been told you are and, in a country as hard as Ukraine, sometimes just the few dollars that a violent husband brings home is what separates you and your children from starvation.

Besides, I'd loved him once, and he had loved me too. We had had three children together, including the daughter he had never seen. I couldn't help feeling grief for the joy we'd once shared and the chances we'd once had. Where had all that happiness gone? Why had it all turned so ugly?

Then in April 1996 came the news that Sergey had been convicted of manslaughter. He was sentenced to seven years in prison.

I went to see him in prison a few weeks after the court hearing. He was waiting for me as I walked into a cabin divided by a glass partition and picked up a phone to talk to him. I didn't feel anything as I looked at him.

Just four years ago I'd been at school, dreaming of a true love and never imagining what a man like him could do to me. But now it was as if a fog had been lifted from my eyes. Sergey was far worse than I'd ever wanted to see. He'd been stealing from me for years – everything from good dresses and a watch to Pasha's baby clothes while I was in hospital having him. I'd been blind, like a child believing in Santa Claus, and now I was growing up fast. I was twenty, a mother of three and had to look after my children.

'So is there anything you want to tell me?' Sergey asked as he stared from the other side of the glass.

'No. What do you want to hear?'

He leaned forward and put the phone closer to his mouth. 'I know what you did. You told the police I wasn't at home that night. It's because of you that I'm here.'

'That's ridiculous,' I said, keeping my voice steady as my heart raced. 'Who told you this?'

'Don't try and pretend,' Sergey snapped. 'I know exactly what happened and I promise you this – I will find you when I get out of here and you will die.'

I didn't say anything as I got up to leave. Seven years was a long time but would I be able to run fast enough to get away?

As I left the prison, I prayed that I would never see Sergey again.

Chapter Nine

A rush of sickness burned the back of my throat as the smell of rotting meat filled the air. It was thick, like syrup curling into my lungs, and I wanted to retch.

'Put your scarf over your face,' Klava said as she looked at me. 'It will help.'

I covered my mouth and stared down. I could see old meat, mouldy vegetables, broken toys, cartons, bottles, tissue paper, bloody rags – all the things people throw into their rubbish bins without thinking someone will ever make use of them. I pulled my scarf tighter. I couldn't breathe.

'Come on,' Klava said. 'Get started. You won't find anything if you don't look.'

'But I don't have any gloves.'

She reached into her coat pocket and handed me two plastic bags. 'Tie those around your hands,' she said and plunged hers into the bin beside me.

It was about 11pm and everything was quiet in the rich area of Simferopol where we had come to search for food. Earlier I'd left the children sleeping and pictures of their faces filled my mind as I looked down. I grabbed a rotting piece of meat, threw it to one side and started searching. I had to find food. We had hardly eaten for weeks and now I was afraid that we would starve to death if I didn't do something.

Just after Sergey was sentenced, Ira came to me and explained sorrowfully that she could no longer pay for me to make flowers for her. 'I'm sorry,' she said. 'We're not making wedding dresses any more, we can't make a living at it. You'll have to find something else to do.'

'What else can I do?' I asked desperately. 'I've got to look after the children, I can't go out to work!'

'Maybe another wedding dress maker will need you?' she suggested, but without much hope. Neither of us could think of who might need someone to make flowers for them. 'You can live here for as long as you need to,' she added. 'And I'll do what I can to help you. But you know how it is, it's hard for all of us, especially as I'm supporting Vica.'

'I know.' I nodded. 'And thank you, Ira.'

But when she left, I was devastated. I could hardly begin to think how I could make ends meet. Without a husband, however bad he was, I was in a terrible position. I was utterly helpless.

When my last bits of money ran out, I was forced to beg from friends and neighbours. Ira, Marina and Janna did what they could but, if they gave me a piece of bread in the morning, I couldn't go back to them again in the evening even though the children were hungry once more. It was agonising to see Pasha, who'd just started walking, with his big belly and tiny, weak legs or hear Sasha cry for food. Some days I could only give them hot water with bits of bread soaked in it or lumps of fried pork fat that Marina's mum gave me. But at least I still had enough milk to feed Luda. I hated asking friends for help all the time and so sometimes I'd go to see Mamma.

But any affection she'd had for me had long been replaced by her love of vodka, and she'd amuse herself by making me beg for half a potato. I would walk home with whatever scrap she'd given me, weeping hot, angry tears. How could she refuse her own daughter and grandchildren? I knew that I could never refuse Luda food, and that I'd share half of what I had with a starving dog.

One day I felt so desperate that all I wanted to do was forget. I left the children with Ira and went to get a bottle of vodka from Janna. I'd never drunk more than a glass or two before but I'd seen many times what alcohol could do. It seemed to make my mother happy despite her miserable existence – perhaps it could do the same for me. Glass after glass burned its way into my chest as I tried to run away from my life.

Ira came in to find me dead drunk, lying with my head on the table, barely able to speak.

'What are you doing, Oxana?' she cried, obviously appalled. 'What kind of a state are you in? Do you think I can look after your children while you get yourself into this condition? It's no kind of answer, you should know that by now.'

'Just leave me alone,' I slurred and turned away from her.

'You've got to stop this,' she said angrily. 'You can't take this path, you just can't! What kind of mother are you? Sergey might be gone but your children are still here.'

'Get away from me!'

'No!' Ira shouted as she started dragging me across the room. 'How can you sit here feeling sorry for yourself when you have three children who need you?'

She pushed me in front of a mirror. Staring back at me was a stranger. The woman I saw was thin and pale with black circles under her eyes. She looked so old. I did not recognise her. Surely she didn't have the strength for what lay ahead?

I started crying.

'You must be strong, Oxana,' said Ira softly. 'You have no choice.'

It was then that Janna's friend Klava showed me a way to help myself when she gave me a jar of meat in jelly. Klava had been a teacher but she'd lost her job and when you lose work in Ukraine you lose everyone around you as well. Now she was lonely, old and one of the few comforts she had was in a vodka bottle.

'Where's this from?' I asked as I held the expensive-looking jar.

'The bins.'

'What?'

'The bins. I go through them for food.'

I stared at her. I had no idea people did that. The most I'd ever done was pick up cigarette ends from the street and roll the bits of tobacco in newspaper to smoke.

'You'd never believe what some people throw out,' Klava told me. 'Packets of gruel, jam that's only a couple of days out of date, I even found red caviar once.'

My stomach turned as I looked at the jar.

'Open it up,' Klava said. 'You'll see. It'll be fine.'

So I did as she said and she was right. After that I went with her, pushing down the shame inside me. Papa would understand why I was doing this. We had to eat. What did I care if someone saw me? Searching through the rubbish, I quickly found an unopened tin of meat and rice.

'There'll be more at the back,' Klava chuckled as she heard me gasping to push down the sickness in my throat.

'People know we come and leave food they think we'll want. But they have no idea what we'll really use.'

I walked around to the back of the bins and could just make out a few boxes and bags lying on the floor. I kneeled down to pick something up – a small cardboard box which must be gruel. Then I reached inside a sack and pulled out a piece of toasted bread. The whole bag must be full of them! I could get some stock cubes and make soup for the children. It would feed us for days. Happiness rushed through me. Later, at home, I found tiny, white maggots wriggling in the bread and for a moment I was repelled – then I reached for a knife to pick them out. I couldn't waste such a find. I tasted a little of the tinned meat and rice before thinning it down with water to make a soup. If it hadn't made me ill by the morning then I could give it to the children.

'More, Mamma, more,' Sasha kept asking the next morning as I fed him.

It is hard to describe how it feels to see your once-hungry child with a full stomach.

The food I found in bins kept us alive for a few weeks until I found a cleaning job at an army base. I was so happy to be earning $30 a month – enough to feed us three times a day – but taking the job also meant leaving the children at home. I told myself I couldn't rely on dustbins and friends forever but fear lay like a sleeping snake in the base of my stomach for the next five months whenever I left home.

Soon the colonel who'd given me my job explained that he couldn't pay me because no one in the army was getting any money. The economic situation was still very hard in Ukraine and so he gave me $10 when he could – enough to feed us for a while. But then I arrived home one day to find Luda had had a terrible accident. Sasha had got out a small electric bar fire that I used in winter because he was cold, and she had fallen on to it. There were two scarlet burns on her buttocks which left scars after they healed and I knew I couldn't go out to work again.

I struggled to survive as I worried about my children and the life I couldn't give them. They at least deserved to have full stomachs and a good home. Sasha, who was nearly five, was always out playing, liked cars and planes and had a happy soul, while Luda, only one and a half and toddling about, adored her brother and did whatever she could to keep up with him. She was like me – a fighter. Pasha though was still different. Where his brother and sister were blond, he was dark; where they were rosy-cheeked, his huge eyes filled his pale face. He was still weak and even though he was nearly three years old, he hadn't spoken a word. He was a difficult child to look after at a time when just surviving took all my energy. I tried to be patient with him.

Then one day, I took Pasha to the doctor and finally we learned what was wrong with him. Pasha was deaf. It explained everything – the fact that he didn't speak and made groans and shrieks like an animal as he lay in his cot. I felt so guilty because I hadn't even realised. His behaviour had frustrated me and sometimes I'd wanted to scream as he lay there, banging his head or hitting a toy against the bars of the cot. Now I knew it was because he was locked inside his own strange and silent world, and he would stay there until he started at a special school for deaf children when he was four. I felt so ashamed that I'd failed him again. Was he deaf because of me? After all, I'd tried to rid myself of him when he was still in the womb.

Could I ever make it up to him? Life for a child like Pasha was very hard in Ukraine and I felt full of fear for his future but it was hard to know how to help him. Of course I knew him well enough to understand when he was hungry or tired but I couldn't speak to him, sing him songs or calm him with soothing words, and there was no one to help me understand his disability. It was like being on the opposite side of a river from my son as the water rushed between us.

If only I had more money, I could give him and my other children a better life. Maybe with a good roof over our heads and proper food on the table, I would at last be a proper mother, especially to little Pasha who needed me so much.

Ten months after Sergey went to prison, a woman I knew called Yula returned from working abroad. She was divorced and her parents had looked after her children while she had been away. Now she was back with money and everyone was very impressed by the new fridge and television she was showing off. But it wasn't her new things which interested me – it was her face. She was wearing make-up, had dyed her hair and there was a look in her eyes which said money had suddenly bought her a place of her own in the world.

I couldn't stop asking Yula questions about where she'd been, what she'd done, but she wouldn't tell me much. I wanted to know though because I'd heard she'd been working in a factory in Turkey and earning $200 some weeks. I couldn't believe what I was hearing. I'd always known Turkey was close to Europe and all the rich countries there but I had no idea it was like that. No wonder Yula looked so different.

I thought about it again and again. At night I lay in bed and thought of the rotting bins, my children's hungry faces and our cold, bare room. Was this what I'd been waiting for – a way out of this awful life? If Yula could do it, why couldn't I?

Chapter Ten

My trainers squeaked as I walked towards a metal staircase which was moving upwards. I was in Istanbul airport and it was a beautiful place – so light and clean. Stepping off the big, red modern bus which had collected us from the aeroplane, I'd even seen two men driving a small car which cleaned the floor. Earlier I'd wondered whether I was closer to God as I sat on the plane and watched my country get smaller and smaller. Now I followed the stream of people as they got off the staircase.

I could hardly believe I was really in Turkey. Before I left, it had almost seemed that Yula didn't want me to go – she wouldn't help me at all. But I forced her to tell me what I needed to know – she couldn't keep such good fortune all to herself! – and in the end she'd given me a scrap of paper with a scribbled address on it.

'That's where I worked,' she said.

I had borrowed the money for my ticket from a travel agent, but I knew I would soon pay it off with my new wages.

Now I was on my own. It hadn't been an easy decision to leave my children but, however much I didn't want to, there was just one question to ask myself: how could I turn down such an opportunity and leave us poor forever? This was a second chance at life, an open door that I just had to walk through. I felt scared and excited at the same time. Scared about being alone in a strange country but excited that finally I might be able to provide the kind of life for Sasha, Pasha and Luda that I'd always dreamed of.

Pictures of Sasha's face filled my mind. He'd cried when I'd pulled him into my arms as I stood at the door to leave earlier that morning. He smelled of sleep and I wanted to cry with him. But I just had to keep telling myself why I was leaving.

'Let me take him,' Ira said as she lifted him up. She was going to look after the children and I would pay her with my wages from my job in Turkey.

I couldn't say anything, didn't dare let myself speak as I looked at Sasha.

'Go now,' Ira continued. 'Don't look back. It's bad luck to look back.'

Now I wished I was safe at home again as I walked through some doors into a crowd of people. There were so many faces there.

Ira had lent me enough money to pay for a taxi to the factory and Yula had told me it wasn't far from the airport so I wanted to go straight there to ask about work. Getting into a cab, I couldn't stop staring out of the windows. Turkey looked like America did in films, with signs for burger bars, modern cars and many people. There was so much green outside, the roads were smooth and straight, and I kept seeing beautiful mosque domes silhouetted against the sky.

'Which road?' the taxi driver asked me after we'd been driving for about fifteen minutes.

I understood enough to show him the piece of paper with the address written on it. He stared at it and frowned.

'*Cumhuriyet caddesi?*' he said.

'Yes – factory,' I replied in the little Turkish I'd learned from Yula.

The man didn't say anything else as he started driving again. He just stared ahead and sighed. I looked at the sun in front of us. It was getting lower in the sky and I wished he would drive faster. I didn't want the factory to be closed when we arrived.

Soon we pulled into a long, dusty road. I opened the door and got out of the car.

I didn't understand.

There was nothing there.

'*Cumhuriyet caddesi?*' I asked as I bent my head back inside the taxi.

'Yes, yes,' the man said. '*Cumhuriyet caddesi.*'

He must be wrong. There was no factory on this road – just some small wooden houses and a couple of stalls selling fruit. What had happened? Why had he brought me to this place?

'*Cumhuriyet caddesi?*' I asked again, trying to stop the panic rising inside me.

'Yes, yes,' the man shouted and tapped his finger on the meter.

I looked at it.

Seventy Turkish lira.

I had just one hundred with me.

My heart hammered. Why had Yula sent me to a street with nothing on it? What should I do now?

Ten minutes later I was standing on a noisy street in the centre of Istanbul, holding a plastic bag with my clothes in it and my passport. The taxi driver had brought me here after I started to cry. The journey had cost all my money. I had nothing. My heart thudded with anxiety – what would happen to me now? I was alone in this strange city.

Weeping and shaking, I walked, faces and buildings passing in a blur as I went, not knowing where I was going or if I'd ever stop. Everything was so different to home – the writing on the signs, the clothes people wore, even the colour of their hair and eyes. This city was so full of noises, smells and people. I felt as if I was drowning.

Panic rose inside me. I'd been so stupid, was so far from home and now I might never get back. What would I do with no money and no friends to help me? I should never have come here or dared to think I could change my life. I didn't know which way to turn, where to go now.

Suddenly I heard Russian in the air. Someone was speaking my language and I followed the voice to a shop where a woman stood outside calling people in.

'Best discounts here,' she called. 'Come and look. No obligation.'

I stopped and looked at her. Tears and dust smeared my face and my breath came in gasps.

'What is it?' she asked.

'I don't know what to do.' I started crying. 'I was told I would work in a factory but it wasn't true. Now I'm alone and I don't know what to do.'

'Calm down,' the woman said as she stepped towards me. 'I can't understand you. Why don't you come inside?'

The shop was cool and dark as we entered and the woman took me into a small room at the back. I told her about life in Simferopol and my conversation with Yula and how she had lied to me. Now I was far from home and my children. The woman listened quietly as I told her what had happened.

'Wait here,' she said as she got up and walked to the front of the shop where she started talking to a man in Turkish. A few minutes later she returned and looked down at me. 'I can't lend you money for a ticket home,' she said. 'But you can sleep at my house tonight and maybe we can find you some work after that so you can start saving.'

I stared up at her. 'Thank you,' I whispered as I got to my feet.

'I'm happy to help you – I'd do the same for anyone,' the woman said, as she smiled kindly at me. 'My name is Zhenya.'

Chapter Eleven

When I woke the next morning, I thanked God for leading me to Zhenya. With no money, I couldn't go back to Ukraine yet and she said she would help me find a job. Soon I was working with her in the leather shop where I'd first met her. The hours were long and selling to tourists walking along the street was hard but I was being paid about $60 a week – the same as I'd make in a month in Ukraine. It wasn't as much as I'd dreamed of earning but so much more than I'd ever had before.

But I couldn't stop thinking about Yula and why she had sent me to a place which didn't even exist. But when I spoke to Zhenya about it, I realised that maybe she'd had something to hide.

'I think you asked too many questions and she had to give you an answer,' she told me one night. 'Yula just picked a street name out of her head and gave it to you to get you off her back.'

'But why would she do that?' I replied.

'Because she didn't want you to know the truth. I've heard of many women who say they're working in Turkey but in fact they're selling themselves.'

'To men?'

'Yes.'

'For money?'

'Yes – big money,' Zhenya told me.

The anger inside me against Yula died then. If that was what she had done then I pitied her. Soon I pushed her out of my mind. Maybe she did have something to hide, maybe she hadn't worked in a factory. I was just glad that I didn't have to do the same and was at last working towards a real future. I was so lucky to have found Zhenya. God had smiled on me at last.

Zhenya was thirty-two, eleven years older than me, and became like a mother to me. Organised and efficient, tall and slim with bleached blonde hair, a long straight nose and blue eyes, she had come from Moldova to work in Turkey after getting divorced. Now her parents looked after her son back at home while she earned her own money because she didn't want to be a burden to them. Like me, she dreamed of one day owning a house to live in with her child.

Soon my life had fallen into a pattern and I was happy to be earning money each week. I worked twelve hours a day in return for $60 a week, which meant I earned $240 a month – $150 to send to Ira, $50 for my rent and $40 for myself to live on. I knew I should start saving more but first there were things my children needed like clothes, proper leather shoes, heaters for our room and bed linen.

Nothing had prepared me, though, for how much I would miss Sasha, Pasha and Luda. My children flitted in and out of my thoughts like dragonflies dipping into water – when I ate I wondered what they'd had that day, when I watched a cartoon on TV I imagined the sound of their laughs – and each morning I'd open my eyes and feel an ache deep in my stomach for them.

'When are you coming home, Mamma?' Sasha would ask on the phone and I'd try to sound happy as I told him it wouldn't be long. The sound of Pasha and Luda babbling in the background made me want to burst into tears.

Sometimes I'd cry as I walked along the streets and saw young children working and not going to school. It made me sad to see them and, with their dark hair and eyes, they reminded me so much of Pasha. Of all my children, he in particular filled my mind. I knew he needed me most of all and that life would be hardest for him. I longed to be with him, to help him through his own challenges.

Zhenya would sit with me as I cried for them.

'You must try to carry on. They need you,' she would say. 'Now calm down and try to rest. You'll get ill if you don't. Then what good would you be to your children?'

As the months passed, I began to accept my new life and discover new things. I went to a nightclub, bought new clothes, wore make-up for the first time, plucked my eyebrows and cut my hair. When I returned home for a two-week visit in June 1997 after three months away, everyone could see how well I was doing thanks to my leather skirt and shoes. I went to find Yula, to give her a piece of my mind about the job in Turkey, but couldn't find her at the house she'd lived in. I was told she no longer lived there and that she was abroad working again, so I shrugged and went home. I was too happy to see my children to think about her anymore. I'd brought them new clothes, games and toys – all the things I'd wanted to give them before but couldn't. It made me so happy and in particular I was glad to see Pasha again. I had missed him so much and we spent a lot of time together during the visit. But one evening, Ira talked to me about the children as we sat at the kitchen table after supper.

'I don't mind looking after Sasha and Luda,' she said. 'They're lovely children and they get on well with Vica. She likes mothering them. You're sending me enough money to support them. But Pasha … he's a different matter.'

'What do you mean?' I asked, panicked.

'He's just too difficult,' she said. 'He's not like the others. He doesn't understand what I'm saying, he isn't strong. I'm sorry. I'm fond of him but I'm letting him down. He needs more than I can give him. He'll have to go somewhere else.'

I couldn't be angry with Ira. I could see how hard it was for her. If she could no longer care for Pasha, I didn't have a choice – he would have to go to live at the school in Simferopol for deaf children.

I knew it was for the best, but it broke my heart. I will never forget the day I took him there. I knew he didn't want to go, could see it in his eyes though he couldn't tell me so, but I had to harden my heart against my own child. He wept as I handed him over, holding out his arms to me, begging to be taken back as the tears poured down his stricken face. But I couldn't take him back. I couldn't give up working in Turkey to look after him because then we'd never have a better future and at least he would be cared for properly. Soon, just as I had when he was a baby, I would come back for him.

As I left, I was weeping bitterly, hardly able to believe that I was leaving my son for a second time. 'It's for the best,' I told myself, wiping away my tears. 'You'll earn enough money to buy a house and then you'll take him home to be a family once again. Here they can help him understand his world.'

I would visit him soon, I told myself. I would never let any of my children forget me. One day they would understand why I'd had to leave them.

Chapter Twelve

All too soon, I was working in Turkey again. It was hard being away but at least I was making some money. I was trying to save as much as I could so that I could start our new life. I lived for my visits back home and the time I could spend with my children.

My trips home lasted anything from two to twelve weeks and the longest I was away from the children was seven months. But, as the months turned into a year and then another and another, I started to worry more and more. I could see in Luda's eyes that she was beginning to forget me and it hurt when she called Ira 'Mummy' by mistake. I was also worried about Pasha. I had not seen him for a long time after going to the school to visit him one day. I had been so looking forward to seeing him but when I arrived he'd hidden behind his teacher's legs – shy and uncertain at seeing me as I bent down to smile at him. My heart turned as I looked at his dark eyes staring out from behind a stranger and, taking him into the garden, I tried to play with him. But he kept crying and in the end his teacher had had to comfort him. I felt sick inside as he clung to her. This woman, a stranger, knew how to enter Pasha's closed world and I did not. Once again, it seemed as if I had failed. I knew that as much as I wanted to take him home with me, I would not be able to give him the same chance to learn and develop that the school offered. He needed whatever they could teach him for his uncertain future. But I was sure that during every day we were apart another of his childish memories of me slipped away. I promised myself that I would leave him to learn what he needed but return for him as soon as I left Turkey.

The only one of my children who truly remembered me was Sasha but in the first year I was away he had a bad accident. He and Luda were being looked after by a new babysitter when he hit his head in a fall. I felt as if I would die when Ira phoned to say he was in a coma. It was seventeen days before he woke up again and the hospital bill was $600. I couldn't go home for months as I paid it off but when I finally did, I found a serious boy who seemed so much older than the happy little one I'd left behind. The injury had made Sasha aggressive and forgetful in a way I didn't recognise and, although the doctors told me he would recover in time, he needed expensive medicines to keep him well.

And so I was trapped in the cycle of working, saving and spending. I continued to live with Zhenya but kept changing jobs to get a better wage and save more. Outside work I went out with men, craving companionship and hoping I would meet someone rich enough to look after me and my children. But I never met anybody I felt anything special for. All my money got swallowed up paying for trips home and the children's babysitters. However hard I worked and prayed to God for a better life, it seemed as if I'd never get it. I was like a rat on a wheel. All I needed was the $2000 that Zhenya had told me would buy a house in Moldova. I dreamed of being there with her. But the years were passing. Now Sasha was nearly nine, Pasha was six and Luda was five. They had stopped living at Ira's as she no longer had enough room for them. Sasha and Luda were now staying with Tamara, my friend Marina's mother, and I sent money to her for looking after them. I knew I had to get home soon or they'd forget me forever. Sergey was also going to be released from jail one day and I needed to have left Simferopol far behind by then – I hadn't forgotten what he'd promised to do.

One night in April 2001, I met a woman called Marianna. She was the friend of a friend of Zhenya's and was visiting from Moldova for a while. I warmed to her because she always seemed upbeat and cheerful and she liked a good night out, with some drinks and lots of funny chat.

That night, I'd been thinking about my dilemma and couldn't summon up the smiles and chatter that Marianna liked.

'Hey, what's up with you?' she said, at last. 'You're in the dumps tonight.'

Her kind smile loosened my tongue and I told her all about my troubles.

'Simple!' she said. 'I've got your answer. Why not do what I do? When I'm not at home in Moldova, I work in a nightclub in Bosnia. I only have to work half the year to earn enough to live comfortably at home for the other half.'

'What do you do?'

'Oh you know, serving drinks, working behind the bar. Honestly, Oxana, it's easy money. Pouring vodka, talking to customers, and all the tips I get are my own.'

'How much do you make?'

'Four hundred dollars a month.'

'Four hundred!' My eyes opened wide. A few months of that, and I'd have enough to buy a house for me and the children.

'You could do it too, if you liked,' she said casually. 'There are many rich people in Bosnia and there's always a demand for pretty girls to serve them drinks in expensive nightclubs. I'm sure you could do it easily.'

'Do you really think so?'

I thought for a second. Turkey had once seemed so strange but I was comfortable here now. I did not know if I wanted to leave here for another foreign country.

'I'm not sure,' I said. 'I've got a good job and I'd hate to leave Zhenya.'

'Zhenya's going to leave herself before too long. Tell you what … you're going on a trip to Ukraine soon, aren't you? Well, I'm going back to Moldova before I return to Bosnia for work. Why don't you come back through Moldova, and you can let me know then what you've decided. If you want to join me, we can go to Bosnia together. If not, you can come back here. That should leave you plenty of time to make up your mind.'

The idea rooted itself in my mind and when I got home, I told Zhenya all about what Marianna had said.

'I don't know,' she said doubtfully. 'It doesn't sound like a very sure plan to me.'

'Why not? Think of it – four hundred dollars a month for serving drinks behind a bar!'

'But I don't like the idea of you working in a nightclub.'

'Why not? I'll be able to buy a house near yours, we can be neighbours and our children can play together!'

Zhenya looked at me thoughtfully.

'I don't think that this is the way to do it. Maybe one day your fortune will come but this isn't that day.'

I was annoyed that Zhenya was stamping on my dreams so I said no more about it to her but I couldn't stop thinking about this new opportunity. On my trip to Ukraine, I thought about it constantly and had almost completely made up my mind to take Marianna up on her offer. When I said goodbye to the children, it was with more hope and optimism than I'd had for a long time. Surely we would soon be together permanently if my plan worked. I told Ira that she might not hear from me for a little while but that I would soon be in touch, and able to send as much money as she needed for the children. Then I made my way to Moldova.

Zhenya was also making a visit home at the same time and I went to see her at her parents' house before meeting Marianna in a local café for a cup of coffee.

'You really should come,' she said. 'I've talked to my boss and he'd be happy to employ you. It's guaranteed money. How can you turn it down?'

'Okay,' I said, taking a deep breath. 'I'm almost certain.'

'Better make your mind up quick. I'm leaving tomorrow. I'll see you at the bus station at ten if you want to come along.' Marianna smiled. 'Why on earth not, Oxana? Huh?'

Later that night I told Zhenya that I had decided to go with Marianna to Bosnia.

'No,' she said. 'I don't trust her. Don't go.'

'But why not?' I cried. 'Marianna isn't a stranger to us. She knows your friends, they say she's trustworthy, so what is there to fear? We know plenty of people who work abroad and they're fine. I need to do this.'

'I'm telling you, Oxana, she's up to no good.'

'I don't understand why you're being so pessimistic. Everyone here knows you and your family, Marianna wouldn't dare get up to anything here or cross you, would she? It's fine. I want to go.'

Zhenya suddenly became furious. 'No! It's not that simple. You mustn't go, Oxana, please. I don't trust Marianna. There's something about her I don't like.'

'So how long am I going to stay in Turkey?' I asked her angrily. 'Another ten years until my children have grown up? I'll just need to do this for six months to earn enough to go back to them. Can't you see it's my only hope of being with my children? They forget me a little more each day. I must get home to them. I can't go back to Turkey! I just can't.'

I stormed out, ran back to the café and found Marianna, where I gave her my last $300 to buy the tickets that would take us from Moldova to Romania and then on to Bosnia.

'You're doing the right thing,' she said with a warm smile, and I felt relieved that I had finally made the decision that would take me back to my children.

I was still cross the next day so I didn't go and see Zhenya, but as I climbed onto the bus to leave, she came running towards me.

'I had to say goodbye,' she whispered as she hugged me. 'Be safe.'

But I couldn't bring myself to say sorry. Despite everything I'd said, I knew that doubts were flickering at the back of my mind. Somehow this all felt too easy. Maybe Zhenya had been right all along? But what could go wrong that I wouldn't be able to put right again?

All too soon I would know one way or the other.

Chapter Thirteen

Marianna and I laughed and chatted happily as the bus trundled across Moldova. Hours later, we stopped at the station where we would continue our journey into Romania by train.

Marianna left me on my own for a few minutes and returned looking miserable. 'I can't come with you across the border,' she said. 'I've just been to check at the ticket office and there's a problem with my passport. I can't travel until it's sorted out.'

I gasped. 'Oh no! What will we do?'

'You go on without me. My boyfriend Leo will meet you at the other end. He'll look after you and I'll join you in a few days.'

I didn't know what to say as we stood there in the cold station, people swarming about us, hurrying to catch their trains.

'But I don't want to go without you,' I said at last. 'I'm supposed to be starting my job with you. I can't go on my own.'

'Hey, we'll be together,' Marianna said gently. 'Just as soon as I get this problem fixed. But the train tickets are booked and you don't want to waste yours, do you? Otherwise you'll have to buy a new one.'

I hesitated. I didn't want to go alone but couldn't afford to wait and pay for new tickets.

'What are you worried about?' Marianna asked. 'Don't you trust me?'

I looked into her eyes, remembering Zhenya's words of advice. This was my last chance to turn back if I didn't trust her. But Marianna looked back at me with a clear, open gaze and I pushed my worries to the back of my mind. 'Yes,' I said, 'I trust you.'

'Good!' she said with one of her big smiles. 'We are going to have so much fun together! Bosnia won't know what's hit it. Now, I'll see you later. You'd better get on the train. Bye, darling.' She gave me a kiss.

I got on the train.

After a long, dull train journey, I finally arrived in Romania. Marianna's boyfriend was waiting at the station. He spotted me at once.

'Oxana? Hi. Marianna told me to expect you. She'll catch us up as soon as she can. Now, we'd better hurry, we don't want to miss our connection.'

He took me to a bus which travelled for a few hours until we reached Bucharest train station and got onto a night train to Timisoara near the Serbian border. We spoke very little as it was so late and I was tired. By the time we arrived in the city, I could hardly keep my eyes open and only wanted to sleep. Marianna's boyfriend got us a taxi and after a short trip we arrived at an apartment where an old man was waiting. I had no idea where I was but I was too tired to care and fell asleep as soon as I was shown into a bedroom. It wouldn't be long before we reached Bosnia and this awful journey would be over.

When I woke up, it was daylight. I wandered out of my bedroom to find Marianna's boyfriend had gone and I was alone with the old man.

'Get your stuff,' he said in Russian. 'We've got to go.'

Fear pricked once again in the back of my mind but I pushed it down. Marianna would be here soon although I wished her boyfriend was still with me instead of this old man. There was something in his eyes – foxy eyes they were – which I didn't like.

The old man said nothing as we walked in the front door of an apartment building surrounded by trees and knocked on a ground-floor door. It was opened by one of the biggest women I'd ever seen in my life – she was about six foot tall, wore a navy skirt and blouse, and had dark wavy hair and skin like a child's.

She started talking rapidly to the old man until he cut in: 'She's Russian – you can talk to her.'

The woman turned to me. 'Hi,' she said in a low voice like a man's. 'My name is Olga. We need to have a quick chat so can you wait for us please?'

'Sure,' I replied as she ushered me into the flat and towards a door.

'Just wait here for a few moments,' Olga said as she opened the door and closed it behind me.

I heard the click of a key turning in the lock and tried to stop myself from panicking as I looked around. The light in the room was dim, blocked by thick trees outside a window which had bars covering it. I could feel dirt all around me – in the heavy air, the worn carpet and the stained cover stretched across a large bed. Lying on it were three teenage girls who stared silently as they smoked cigarettes. One was blonde with blue eyes, the second had short, dark hair and a beautiful face like a Barbie, while the third had long black hair and a long face. All of them looked very young. Suddenly they started speaking in a language I couldn't understand.

Shaking, I reached for my cigarettes to try and calm the thoughts rushing into my head.

'This isn't right,' a voice in my head said. 'Look at these girls.'

'No, no, no,' another voice replied. 'You know Marianna, trust her, it couldn't possibly be what you think.' But I felt afraid and started crying as thoughts of home filled me. What was happening?

As I sobbed, the blonde girl got off the bed and came towards me. Putting her arms around me, she made soothing noises as I continued to cry.

'Eenglish? Eenglish?' she asked.

'No, small, small,' I said, pinching my thumb and forefinger together, trying to explain that I only knew one or two English words.

The girls gathered silently around me as I carried on crying and one started dabbing at my face with a tissue to try and clean away the tears.

'Bosnia?' I asked in Russian, walking my fingers along in the air like a stick figure. 'You go to Bosnia?'

Maybe they were just like me. Maybe they too were on their way to Bosnia and Olga was helping lots of people to get in – visas, passports, it was complicated.

'No, Italy, Italy,' said the blonde girl.

Italy? What was she talking about? Smoking cigarette after cigarette, I tried to force down the panic rising inside me as I sat and listened to the low murmur of voices in the corridor outside. It seemed like forever until the door opened and Olga gestured for me to follow her.

We walked into the corridor where there was a small table and chairs and, after disappearing into the kitchen, she returned with two coffees for us. Her hands holding the mugs were covered in huge gold rings and around her neck was a thick gold chain like a dog's collar.

'Where am I?' I said in a rush. 'When will I get to Bosnia?'

'Have a cigarette, drink your coffee,' Olga replied in a voice soft as honey. 'Do you know where you are?'

'No.'

'A halfway house.'

She sounded so friendly, so kind, but I didn't understand what she was saying. 'So when will I reach Bosnia?' I asked.

'Bosnia?'

'Yes, to work in a nightclub,' I said in a rush. 'I've given Marianna three hundred dollars for my papers and we're going to work together.'

A smile flooded over Olga's face as she stared at her coffee cup. 'You're not going to Bosnia,' she said, drawing her chair closer to the table. 'You're not going anywhere.'

I looked up at her. The hardness in her eyes warned me against disobeying. I didn't understand what she was saying.

'Yes, I am,' I whispered. 'Marianna has arranged it.'

'No, she hasn't.' Olga carried on smiling, even though her words were terrible. 'Don't you understand? You've been sold. You belong to me now.'

As I heard those words, fear, despair and horror rushed through me like a whirlwind. It was like standing on the edge of a cliff and feeling my feet slip into nothing, or staring at a gun and knowing I was going to die. Inside I began to scream but I couldn't speak, couldn't say a word

as my life rushed in front of my eyes – everything that had
brought me to this point, the faces of my children – while
Olga smiled at me as if it was an ordinary day.

'How can I have been sold?' I finally whispered. 'I've
paid money to get to Bosnia. I'm going to work there.'

'Oh, come on – how old are you?' Olga sneered as she
leaned back in her chair.

'Twenty-five.'

'Well, then how can you be so stupid?'

'But why are you saying this?' The tears rushed to my
eyes and I sobbed. 'My friend is going to help me. I trusted
her.'

'In this business you can't trust anyone,' Olga spat.

'But can't I go home? I'll give you my address, pay you
back the money you paid for me.'

'No way. I don't need you to tell me your address – I
know it, I've got your passport and I've seen the pictures
of your children in it. The people who brought you here
spent money, I've spent money and now I'm going to get
it back. I paid seven hundred dollars for you and I'm
going to sell you on to somewhere else – maybe Italy,
maybe Albania, maybe Germany. I don't care – as long as
I get my money it makes no difference.' She sat back in
her chair and sighed. 'Anyway, maybe it's good you're
here because you can make a lot of money and help those
children of yours. Think of all you'll make on your back.'
She got up and looked down at me. 'Do you want something to eat?'

I shook my head as Olga handed me a cigarette and
returned me to the bedroom. Hearing the lock click shut
once again, I turned and stared at the bars on the window.

* * *

I don't know how many tears I cried that day. I cried until my body was dry but still the sobs came. All I saw was Luda begging me not to go when I'd left her days before and me telling her that I had to earn the money for a better life as I promised her I'd be back from my next trip soon. Luda had held on to me and I had to pull away from her. Why had I been so stupid? Why hadn't I listened to Zhenya? I had been such a fool to ignore my fears, telling myself that if anything happened then I could get away just like last time.

But look at me now, locked in a room with no way to escape.

Memories of home cut into me as I sat in that filthy room and the girls tried to stop me crying – cuddling me, wiping away my tears, speaking to me in words I could not understand. Eventually I pulled out some photo albums I had packed and stared at the pictures, hoping that by wishing I was back at home, I would get there like magic.

But all I could do as the darkness came was stare at the pictures – me with the children dressed in the good Christmas clothes I'd brought from Turkey; Sasha singing at a concert and the only picture I had of Pasha – taken just before he'd gone into the orphanage when he was a baby. I didn't have any other photos of him. In our culture we believe that if your child is sick it is bad luck to take pictures of them. I stared and stared at the pictures. They were real – not this nightmare.

Late in the evening I was allowed to use the bathroom and I'll never forget standing under the shower as my eyes searched for a way to escape.

High up to my right was a window and, with the water running to hide the sound, I tried opening it. Pulling as hard as I could, I tugged and tugged but it wouldn't move.

'Keep looking around you,' I told myself as I walked into the kitchen to make myself a packet soup. But I soon realised that every window had bars on it and the flat had not just one but two locked doors leading into it. There was no way to escape – everything was locked and barred to keep us from running.

'Just wait,' I told myself. 'They can't keep you here forever and when you get outside you can run.'

I walked back into the bedroom to find the girls on the bed. Pulling a cover over myself, I lay down on the floor but sleep didn't come to me that night.

How was it possible to go from being free to being a prisoner in one day? How could I have been bought? I was not a thing, I was a human being – surely I could not be traded like a sack of grain, or kept against my will?

I was living in a nightmare. Soon I would wake up or find a way to get out of this terrible place.

It was the same the next day – we were locked in the room and only allowed out to go to the kitchen or bathroom. This time, though, there were men in the flat who watched everything. There was no door on the kitchen so they could see us and we could only close the one to the bathroom for a few minutes before they started banging on it.

Once again I was silent but the girls carried on trying to speak with me. With a few words and by pointing to things or making gestures, I soon learned their names and ages. Christine, the blonde girl, was sixteen and told me she'd been a nightclub stripper. The girl with long dark hair was called Sabrina and she was also sixteen. Later I would find out that she was a thief who'd been in trouble with the police. Finally the beautiful Barbie girl told me she was called Vera and was just fifteen.

'Me Oxana. Twenty-five,' I told them as I lifted my fingers into the air. Their eyes widened. I was so old.

Time passed slowly. A second seemed like an hour and an hour like a day as we sat and waited. I couldn't stop thinking of home. What would Sasha be doing now? Would he be helping Tamara wash up the dishes like he did with me? He'd soon worry if I didn't phone home. Everyone thought I was back in Turkey and I usually rang at least once a week.

It was late afternoon on the second day when Olga opened the door and gestured for me to follow her into the corridor. Two men were waiting for us.

'Take your top off,' Olga said.

I stood still.

'Take your top off,' she repeated, her voice hardening. 'They want to see your body. They need to see that you look nice – no marks, no stretch marks, nothing. Show them.'

I stared back at her. My breath stopped. I was just an object now with a price. Nothing more. Slowly I lifted my T-shirt and pulled up my bra as I looked away. My face burned red hot as shame rose up in me while those strangers stared – how did I look? Good tits? Sagging arse? Any fat? Good for a fuck?

'No, not like that,' Olga snapped. 'Take your whole top off.'

She stared at me angrily as I refused to move but she knew she had a choice – either to force me and maybe put the men off me because I was a troublemaker or let me win this time. Olga turned and spoke softly to the men in a language I couldn't understand. They looked me up and down once again. I could see they didn't like me.

'Stand at the side,' Olga said brusquely, gesturing. I went and pressed myself against the wall. Christine was called in next. I watched as she stood in front of them. She obviously understood what the men said because she answered their questions as she obeyed Olga's commands. The other girls were the same. Laughing, they stripped off their clothes and pushed out their breasts before turning around and thrusting their bottoms out. It was as if they had no fear, like it was all a game to them. Disgust crept over me as I watched. I felt dirty. This was a slave market. Why were these girls doing this? Why were they laughing like it was all a joke?

I hated them in that moment – hated that they obeyed Olga so happily, hated that they had no self-respect, hated that they laughed as they showed themselves off. And I hated the men for looking at them.

All I can think now is that they were too young and stupid to understand what was happening to them, instead believing all the promises they'd been given about a better life. All those girls, I'm sure, had had hard lives – growing up in orphanages, drinking, sleeping on the streets – and for them going with a man meant shoes and food. It was about survival. They had no idea what was really waiting for them.

'Think of Sasha, Pasha and Luda,' I kept telling myself. 'You must be strong. Whatever happens you must carry on, no matter what. You'll get home to them soon.'

Chapter Fourteen

Early the next day Olga came to see me.
'Can you make me a Turkish coffee?' she asked. 'Do one for yourself as well and sit with me.'

Five minutes later I carried two cups of thick, black coffee back to Olga who looked at me with her hard eyes.

'You need to get used to it, you know,' she said. 'Men are going to come for you and you'll need to show them your body. You were no good last night. You must smile, say hello, play with them a bit like the others do.'

'But I can't,' I said slowly. 'I won't.'

'Well, it's up to you,' Olga replied casually. 'You can live with me as long as you want but it won't be a good life. You'll be locked up in the room and never get away. You should help me. I need to sell you quick. The men last night thought you were fat.'

I looked at her. It was true – after three children I was bigger than the teenagers.

'You must diet,' Olga continued. 'For breakfast you'll have a cup of coffee, salad for lunch and an apple in the evening.'

'But I won't ever be like the other girls,' I replied. 'I've had children.'

'Well, you're too fat. You know, you don't have a choice anymore. Just do what I say.'

I knew now that this was no bad dream from which I could wake up. Marianna was not going to arrive, laughing and telling me it was all a big joke. This was real. I began to lose track of the time as hour followed hour in that miserable bedroom.

Then the men would come to look at us – sometimes two, sometimes four. I didn't know where they were from.

'Mmm, soft like pillows,' they'd say as they grabbed at my breasts and buttocks, feeling my flesh between their fingers. I was not a person to them, I could tell that.

'But can't you smile?' one asked as he stared into my face.

'Yes,' I replied – forcing the corners of my mouth upwards.

'You look like you want to kill me,' he said laughingly as he turned away.

He was right. I hated them all. Over and over again I stood in front of them wishing I could kill them just as they were killing me. I didn't feel sad as the men looked at me – just angry. It was as if my brain couldn't allow my heart to realise what was really happening to me.

'She's fat but she has a nice figure and beautiful eyes,' Olga would say as they looked me over. 'She'll please a lot of men.'

It was obvious that she would still sell me however angry I was. She was a professional and no one would get in her way. Christine and Sabrina had gone, now it was just Vera and me left, along with another girl who'd just arrived.

'Men will love those eyes,' Olga continued. 'They'll see those and won't need anything else. She's on a diet but she'll be perfect soon. Look at her breasts ...'

No one seemed interested in me though and as the days passed I started hoping that Olga would give up and let me go. But each time the thought entered my mind, she seemed to see it.

'You know that whatever happens, I'll sell you,' she told me every day.

All I could do was cry as I sat and waited. I didn't fight. I didn't scream. What was the point? I couldn't go anywhere, do anything, I was a prisoner and knew I couldn't escape until I was taken outside. At times I thought about finding a razor in the bathroom, seizing a knife in the kitchen, hurting myself, killing myself to make it all end. But the voice kept whispering inside me, telling me to be strong for my children.

'Stop crying,' Olga would say angrily as she put make-up on me to try and hide my red cheeks and eyes. 'You're supposed to be used to it by now, you've been here long enough now to understand, so stop crying like a child. Remember, you can make big money and then you'll leave this business.'

After a week or more, I finally went outside. We were told roughly to gather our things and prepare to leave. Hope lit up inside me when I smelled fresh air. Olga seemed nervous as she took us out of the apartment and I dragged my heels as sunlight flooded into the dark corridor leading to the front door. Maybe the police were coming.

'Get a move on,' she hissed as she dug me in the back.

But just as I reached the threshold I saw that a car had been pulled up close to the door and a man was standing watch over us. There was nowhere to run. We were pushed inside, the car doors slammed shut and we sped off.

About ten minutes later we arrived at another apartment building and were taken to a flat on the ground floor. It was very different from Olga's place – clean, light, the living room was filled with men and girls sitting on sofas and watching TV or chatting. It was more relaxed than Olga's home but the bodyguards here looked like real gangsters – muscly and tall with bald heads. I saw that one had a pistol hidden inside his coat as he took it off.

'Hello,' said a blonde woman as we walked into the room. Dressed in fashionable foreign clothes, she looked about forty and smoked a long, expensive-looking cigarette. She was obviously wealthy. 'Would you like something to eat?' she asked, gesturing towards the kitchen. 'Go through and help yourselves. There's food on the table.'

I went towards where she pointed.

'Don't eat too much,' Olga shouted after me.

'No, no, she's okay,' I heard the blonde woman say. 'She just needs clothes and make-up.'

As I ate hungrily in the kitchen, I heard conversations and then the front door open and close. Olga was gone. Was that the last I would see of her? I felt panicky – I had been trying to forge some kind of relationship with her in the hope that she would allow me to leave and repay her for what she'd paid for me. Was that plan worthless now?

A little later, the elegant blonde came and took me into her bedroom where rows of dresses hung in a perfect line in the wardrobe. She gave me a pair of white trousers and a white top to wear, and later, when some men came, I had to take part in the now familiar ritual of parading in front of them. This time I wasn't asked to take my clothes off. Instead they chatted and ate as I stood before them. But however different this woman was from Olga, I knew that she was still a pimp and we were for sale. She was the one in charge now.

Olga came back that night, and in a way it was a relief to see her. At least she was someone familiar in this strange new world I found myself in, even if she didn't give a damn about me. It became clear that Olga would be guarding us at night, while the blonde pimp did the selling during the day. Soon I started learning about prices: I was only going to fetch $1000 but some of the other girls would sell for as much as $3000.

I also learned the name of the girl who'd joined us at Olga's flat a few days before we left. Her name was Anna-Maria and she was a seventeen-year-old Romanian. Tall and slim with short ash-blonde hair, she had a long face and a big nose and mouth.

The hours ran into each other as Vera, Anna-Maria and I sat and waited, watching TV and smoking. There were other girls there too from time to time but I didn't speak much to anyone. Instead I shut myself down just as I'd learn to do in the past. It was only at night when I looked at my photo albums while everyone else slept that sadness choked my throat. It was then that I let myself cry.

'My babies,' I would whisper to the photographs of the children. 'When am I going to see you again?'

On the third morning, a man arrived to look at Anna-Maria and me. He wore a suit and looked about thirty-five.

'How old is she?' he asked Olga, jerking his head towards me.

'Twenty,' Olga lied.

'Mmm. She doesn't look it, she looks older.'

'It's just the light in here,' Olga insisted. 'She's beautiful. Look at her breasts – the best out of all of them here. I won't charge much for her – say $1000?'

They started arguing about money and it seemed Olga was refusing to be knocked down on the price. After all she'd paid $700 for me, there had to be something in it for her. She was a professional.

'But I want that one,' the man suddenly said, pointing at Vera.

I knew he couldn't have her. She'd already been sold. Beautiful Vera, she looked so young, so scared, like a little cat who sat quietly all day long, and I wanted to protect her from it all. She was just another little girl who believed she was going to a better life.

Later I returned to the bedroom and was sitting smoking when Olga opened the door once again.

'Get your stuff packed,' she said. 'You and Anna-Maria need to get ready. You're leaving.'

I had been sold.

Chapter Fifteen

The yellow glare of car lights swept through the trees where Anna-Maria and I were hiding. We had been waiting for about an hour in a pitch-black forest as frogs croaked and mosquitoes buzzed around us. The car came to a stop and two men got out. They came over, shining a torch in our faces. Without a word, they pulled us to our feet and over to the car, throwing us onto the back seat and covering us with a piece of tent canvas. The engine started and we moved off.

Rage filled me. Earlier as we'd driven along the motorway, the man who'd bought us from Olga had stopped the car and disappeared into the darkness to make a phone call. Anna-Maria and I were alone. It was the chance I'd been thinking about every moment since I'd arrived at Olga's.

But, as lights from the road filled ours with a split-second glare, something had stopped me from pulling the door handle open. I'd felt so afraid and confused as I stared down at the handle – fearful that something worse might be out there waiting for me, almost numb inside. I did nothing.

Now anger wrestled with shame as I lay under the canvas. What kind of mother was I? Why was I so scared? Why hadn't I run when I got the chance? It was the same as it always had been – I let people hurt me and did nothing to stop them.

Soon the car slowed to a halt and the doors opened. It was completely dark as we got out but I thought we were in some kind of barn. Yet another man stood before us and, with a gun at his side, gestured for us to go into a small outhouse where we were put into a room containing a single bed, table and cupboard as the door was locked. Without a word, Anna-Maria lay straight down on the bed and fell asleep. I was glad for her but couldn't relax myself. After all those days of waiting, I was fearful now that my journey had actually started.

A couple of hours later the man returned and threw a black tracksuit top on the bed for me. I was wearing black trousers and high heels and he put a finger to his lips as he gestured at me to put the jacket on and get my things together. We were obviously pressing on with our journey. I picked up my precious suitcase and prepared to follow. The man seemed nervous as he led us out of the room and we walked out onto a road. Although it was very dark I could see that we seemed to be on the edge of a village because, after passing a few houses, we came to outbuildings and barns full of hay and sunflowers. The man made us walk very quickly, almost run, before stopping from time to time to listen. His nervousness infected me – I ran when he ran, rested when he rested, and once we got out into open countryside it felt like we were never going to stop again. My suitcase was small but it soon began to feel heavy as I hauled it with me, but there was no way I could leave it behind. Soon I realised that I wouldn't be able to keep up in my heels and took them off. Running barefoot, I could felt the wet grass hit my shins like knives while stones and roots dug into my feet. But I didn't feel any pain – all I could hear was my heart bursting in my ears as I ran to escape my enemy.

It felt like hours later when we reached a barbed wire fence. The man's nervousness seemed to reach a height and I guessed that this must be the border, probably into Serbia. He held the wire open for us as Anna-Maria and I pushed our bags through and then scrambled after them. Once the three of us were safely beyond the fence, he led us a few yards away and we all sat down in the darkness, catching our breath and surrendering to our exhaustion. Our escort sat cross-legged beside us, still alert, holding tightly onto his gun as he looked about him into the night.

Then, suddenly, a scream and a crack like a hailstone filled the air. I looked up at the sky to see what had made the sudden noise as the man leapt to his feet.

'Move,' he shouted as he hauled us up and started running.

Once again I heard a crack and realised it was a gunshot. I clutched my suitcase to my chest and began to run wildly after our guard, but panic swept over me and I stumbled. Anna-Maria reached out to pull me up as bullets started whistling in the air around us and a bright light circled above our heads. I didn't know where it was coming from and didn't stop to look behind me. Anna-Maria was so quick, so strong, and I kept stumbling behind her as I tried to keep up.

I saw my children's faces as I ran. I had to live.

We reached a field of sunflowers where we threw ourselves down onto the earth as the light swept over us before getting to our feet again when it moved away. The sunflowers scratched my face as I ran through them and

the weight of my suitcase made me almost lose my balance
again and again.

Gunshots whistled as the light circled and my heart
thumped. I didn't think anymore, just ran – desperate to
escape the guns – and it seemed like forever until I saw
the sky lightening. Running out of the other side of the
field, I suddenly realised the noises were fading and gradually we slowed to a jog and then to a walk until we
reached a line of trees where we sat down.

No one spoke as we rested. I had no idea where we
were but I guessed I was now in Serbia. It was the next
stage of a journey whose ending I didn't even want to
imagine.

Chapter Sixteen

My eyes widened as the bodyguard walked into the room. Minutes earlier I'd been trying to open the window and wondered if he'd heard anything.

'We can run,' I'd hissed at Anna-Maria. 'Help me open it.'

She'd smiled at me, not understanding what I was saying as she helped pull the handle. But it was no good. The window was fixed shut just like every other. Seeing the look on my face, Anna-Maria realised what I wanted to do and seemed surprised. It was as if she didn't even think about escaping.

After being picked up in the forest, we'd been brought to a deserted hotel and a waiting bodyguard had showed us to a room. I could hear footsteps, cars and voices on the street outside but once again we were trapped, in the keeping of yet another strange man.

Now I looked him as he walked into the room with a Kalashnikov gun strung over his shoulder.

'Do you want to eat something?' he asked.

'OK,' I said, looking quickly back at Anna-Maria as he let me out of the room and locked her back in.

We went downstairs to a bar. In the middle was a pole with a small round stage around it and about fifteen tables. The smell of stale wine and beer hung in the air and the floor was sticky under my feet. Above the bar was a huge picture of women wearing corsets and stockings with feathers in their hair grouped around a man.

'They dance here,' the bodyguard said as I looked at it.

'But where are they?' I asked.

'We're closed.'

He took me into a kitchen which was as dirty as the bar had been. I found a towel and a piece of soap and cleaned a space on the work surfaces before turning to the fridge. The smell of rotting meat hit me as soon as I opened the door. I threw a piece of slimy steak into the bin before grabbing two tomatoes, a cucumber and some feta cheese.

'Is that all?' asked the bodyguard when I put his share in front of him.

'That's all there is.'

He grunted and ate the meagre lunch. I sat opposite him and ate my own, eating slowly to savour the taste of the tomatoes and salty cheese on my tongue. Olga would be pleased, I thought grimly. I was losing plenty of weight on the amount of food I'd had lately.

When we'd finished, I took some food back to the room for Anna-Maria. She was sitting on the bed staring into the distance when I walked in, hugging her knees as she rocked herself. She hadn't spoken to me much but I knew she had an old sick mother and a younger brother to look after. The more I knew Anna-Maria, the more it also became clear that her mind was a little like a child's.

I got into bed next to her and pulled out my photo albums.

'Your children, your eyes,' Anna-Maria said as she lay beside me. 'Beautiful.'

I stared at the pictures in the half-light and tears rose up in my throat. I felt so tired, so far from everything I knew as I started to cry. I gulped the sobs down, stuffing the pillow into my mouth to try and stop the noise.

'I love you,' I whispered to the photographs. 'You're the only happiness I have had.'

Anna-Maria's arms wrapped around me but I couldn't stop thinking as I tried to sleep. I remembered it all: kissing my children goodnight, cuddling them as they slept, listening to their breathing and watching their smiles during their dreams; their tiny legs, their feet, their fingers, the moles on their arms and freckles on their faces. Every memory cut into my heart and deep down just one question kept repeating itself to me: how can you be rescued if no one knows you're lost?

'Hellooo,' a voice said as the bedroom door opened.

It was our second day in the strange, quiet hotel. Earlier, we'd been looked at by three men and I'd felt uneasy about them from the moment I saw them. They were all in their late twenties or early thirties but two in particular looked like little boys – laughing and joking as they stared at us. Now we looked up to see the same three men standing in our doorway. They were obviously drunk.

'We want you to come with us,' said one of the men, looking at me.

I'd noticed him earlier because he had a face like a film actor but he'd disgusted me as he picked his nose while he stared. Now I looked at him, unsure of what to do. I could see a pistol tucked inside his belt.

'Come on,' he said and pulled me with him.

The men took me into the corridor where they opened another door to a bedroom. In the middle was the biggest bed I had ever seen. I stopped in the doorway, not wanting to go in.

'Move,' a voice said, as a fist dug into my back and pushed me.

'I want to talk to you,' the beautiful man said as the door closed behind me. His voice was low as he looked at me with his fine features and the manners of a pig. 'My friend is a cameraman and we're thinking of doing a film.'

He opened the wardrobe where two video cameras stood on tripods inside. The man took them out and put one in front of the door and one in front of the bed.

'Okay,' he said, breathing out. 'Take off your clothes slowly.'

I looked at him and felt myself begin to shake.

'We're going to have sex with you and you'll be famous,' he said with a smile.

'No,' I shouted. 'I won't do it!'

I started crying, begging them not to make me, but suddenly they were forcing my arms behind me and pulling at my clothes. I struggled against them. But no matter how loudly I screamed or however hard I kicked against them, they wouldn't let go.

'Stop it,' a voice said suddenly and I looked up to see the third man sitting in one of the chairs.

'Do you want a cigarette?' he asked as his friends suddenly stopped grabbing me.

'What?' I replied, my breath coming hard after the fighting.

'I said, do you want a cigarette? Come on. Come and sit with me.'

The hands slid off me as I walked towards him and took a cigarette. I shook as he lit it.

'What are you doing?' he said, looking up at his friends. 'You can't be like that with women. If you want her to do something you have to ask her. You can't rape her – you won't enjoy it.'

I sat down beside the quiet man, hoping that if I stayed close the others would leave me alone. They seemed to listen to him, he must be in charge.

The men started talking together in a rush as I stared at the cigarette I was holding. I wished it was a knife. I wanted to take a blade and run it across my throat, or throw myself out of one of the huge windows in front of me – into the night and onto the hard blackness of the concrete below. I wanted to die. But I couldn't move.

'The children,' a voice inside me said.

The beautiful man turned and walked towards me. 'Come on, we're going to leave you,' he said with a smile on his lips. 'It was only a joke. We didn't mean it. It was just for fun.'

Silently, they led me back to my bedroom and opened up the door again.

'Here,' the quiet man said as he gave me a packet of cigarettes and the door locked behind me.

Chapter Seventeen

The next morning the bodyguard came to our room to tell us we were leaving. Anna-Maria had nothing to pack but I started gathering the few things I had into my suitcase. Finally I took the photo albums from beside the bed.

'I'll take those,' the bodyguard said as he moved towards me.

'No, please,' I replied. 'I need them. I must have them.'

'It's your guarantee,' he told me. 'We have your passport and now these to make sure you don't escape. You'll get them back later.'

I sobbed as we were taken outside and put into a car where a small, fat man with grey hair and blue eyes was waiting. He looked at Anna-Maria and me as we got in but I didn't see him. All I could think about was my pictures. I needed them to remind myself of why I must be strong. I had to see Sasha, Pasha and Luda's faces to know there was another world waiting for me which I just had to get back to. The only thing that kept me going was the idea of escape, of returning to my babies.

Roads sped past the windows for several hours until we arrived at an apartment building and the man took us up to a dirty flat on the seventh floor. There was a filthy mattress in the corner of the open-plan kitchen and living room and another in an empty bedroom off the main corridor.

I asked to have a bath and the man showed me where to go. Anna-Maria was lying on the mattress watching TV when I returned.

'Where's he gone?' I asked her.

'Out,' she told me.

Blindly, I walked to the front door – knowing it would be locked but just wanting to check for a miracle. There wasn't one. Yet again locked doors surrounded me and, just like the rest, this man probably had a gun tucked somewhere. Anyway, what would I do even if I did escape? I didn't know where I was and had no money or passport – I'd never be able to get home and the police wouldn't do anything for someone as stupid as me.

I lay beside Anna-Maria staring blankly at the TV screen until the man arrived home a couple of hours later. 'Come with me,' he said as he came to the foot of the mattress.

'Why?' I asked, looking up at him.

'Because I like you.'

I stared back at him.

'I don't like skinny girls,' he said, smiling. 'I like them like you – big breasts, big bum.'

'Please, I don't want to,' I whispered as I started crying. But I knew very well that he was going to take what he wanted.

'But I'm going to be nice to you,' he said, as he leant down and took my hand. 'Don't worry.'

He pulled me to my feet and into the corridor where he pushed me into the bedroom and shut the door. I stood in front of him, unsure of what to do, how to get away.

'Come on,' he almost shouted as he pushed me onto the mattress.

Standing above me, he started to strip off his clothes – dirty trousers, underwear, T-shirt – before leaning down to the pile on the floor and taking a condom out of his trouser pocket.

'Don't worry, we'll be quick,' he said as he bent down towards me. 'Now take your clothes off.'

Sickness washed over me as I tried to sit up.

'Please leave me alone,' I begged. No matter how much I knew that it was inevitable, I couldn't stop myself trying to fight him.

'Stop it,' he shouted. 'Just come on.'

Pushing me back down, he started ripping at my T-shirt and bra. He was so heavy on top of me, and I could feel hair everywhere as I pushed at him – on his chest, on his back and on his arms.

'No don't, I don't want to,' I begged, feeling tears run down my face.

But still he pulled at me – grabbing at my trousers again and again as I tried to get out from under him and stand up. Suddenly his fingers dug painfully into the soft skin around my mouth and he drew close to me. I could smell alcohol.

'It's better for you if you don't move,' he said in a husky voice. 'If you move you'll hurt yourself, if you stay still you'll be okay.'

Once again he forced me back down and pushed my thighs apart. His tongue was everywhere as he licked at my face, neck and shoulders. I could see strands of white spit hanging between his lips like a dog, and smell his dirty, sweaty body as he pushed me down.

Suddenly he stood up and started putting the condom on. I tried to get onto my knees, my half-undone trousers making me unsteady and slow.

'Just relax, calm down,' he shouted as he grabbed my hair. 'You're going into this business so you're supposed to be used to it. Everyone is going to fuck you and they won't all be reasonable like me.'

He threw his weight on top of me again – holding my hair tightly in his hand to stop me moving as he pushed me on to my stomach and pulled me on to all fours. He knelt behind me before pushing himself hard inside. I felt pain deep in my stomach and clenched my teeth together. He said nothing as he breathed hard, panting like an animal and stinking like one too. Afterwards he knelt up on an elbow and looked down at me.

'Thank you.'

I felt a kiss on my forehead as he got up and left the room. Silently I stood up and walked back to the bathroom. Turning the shower onto cold, I got in and started scrubbing at my skin. I wanted to rip it off, tear it from my body because no matter how hard I washed I knew I would never be clean again. Looking down I saw red bite marks on my skin and the first traces of bruises where the man had held me down. My stomach hurt where he had forced himself inside me. But I could hardly feel it as I replayed what had happened in my head – his hands, his hair, his lips. It was the same as it always had been. How stupid I'd been to think I'd left that life behind when Sergey had gone. Now I knew I never would.

Chapter Eighteen

It's hard to remember all the faces of the men in the chain through which we were sold. Instead there are snatches of conversation which stay with me. For instance, I remember that the grey man who raped me sold us on to another two men the following day. Those men took us to a train station.

'Can I have my passport and photo albums back now?' I asked one. I'd seen my sad little suitcase handed over by the grey man.

'No,' he replied. 'They're security to stop you from running because you know we have your address and children's names. We can't kill you because we need to sell you but we could punish them. Do you understand?'

A chain locked around my heart in that moment. Whatever I'd been hoping, I now knew I could never run because of what might happen to my children if I did. Fear is like a cage which traps you with invisible bars and, even though I was surrounded in the station by ordinary people on another ordinary day, I didn't dare scream or run. I was just too afraid. I felt as though I no longer had any rights over my own body. All my life people had done to me whatever they wanted and it was happening again.

* * *

Soon Anna-Maria and I were put onto a train where the conductor hid us in his van while we crossed another border. In the darkness and rhythm of the moving train, the man had sex with me and I let him. I couldn't fight anymore.

'Think of your children,' the voice kept whispering inside.

I had no idea where we had come from or where we were going to. When the train finally stopped, we were picked up and taken to a hotel where another man arrived to move us on to a house. I felt almost relieved when I arrived there. It was a village house but there were rugs on the floor and an old woman inside who smiled at us. There was also a younger woman, the man's sister perhaps or wife, and two small children – a girl of about three and a boy who looked eight.

'Nothing bad can happen to us here – this is a family home,' I thought as he showed us to a bedroom and I looked out of the window to see a garden with yellow flowers and fruit trees.

But later when Anna-Maria went to wash, the man came in and locked the door before taking off his trousers.

'No,' I said.

I didn't know what language he spoke but everyone knew that word.

'No, no, no,' I kept saying but the man didn't listen as he pushed me onto the bed. I cried out but he just put his hand over my mouth. It was like a knife in my heart as I thought of the two women on the other side of the door who did nothing as I cried out.

From the village house we were taken to a barn in the countryside, where a Romanian gypsy girl joined us. We were kept there for several days and it was there that Anna-Maria's luck ran out. So far everyone had been interested in me – now they took a piece of her as well. One night two men took her away and when she returned, she was silent and frozen. She curled up like a little cat on the bed with her knees pulled to her chest. She didn't cry and I understood why.

After almost a week, more strangers arrived, this time in an expensive car. We were given black clothes to wear and then put in the car and driven up into the mountains. When we finally stopped, we were chivvied out of the car and told to walk down a steep hill. By now it was night and so dark that I could hardly see Anna-Maria as I followed her. Behind me was the Romanian gypsy girl.

After a long walk, we reached the edge of the forest where a small shingle beach bordered the edge of a river. A boat was waiting and we were told to sit on the floor as we got in. I heard more men's voices but couldn't see their faces – it was too dark and my eyesight was too bad.

How many more of these strange, bewildering journeys would I make? Where were we going now? I had the strange feeling that if we just kept on going for long enough, I would eventually arrive back home, but that was crazy. Watch out, I told myself. Don't let them drive you mad this way. Only by staying clear-headed will you have a hope of getting back to the children.

After travelling along the river for about half an hour, the boat docked at a jetty. We got out and into a waiting car. Three hours later, after driving through mountains and along motorways, we stopped outside a big hotel. We'd reached a destination of some sort.

Inside, the hotel was richer than anywhere we'd been before, with nice pictures on the walls and thick carpets.

But even though I saw no one as we were taken upstairs, I could sense other people nearby. The doors to the rooms had peepholes in them, the kind you can look through from the corridor. I was sure there were people behind those doors.

But who was on the other side and why?

We were taken to a room and at last we were able to sleep.

Chapter Nineteen

'Get up,' a voice said and I opened my eyes to see three men standing at the bottom of the bed where Anna-Maria, the Romanian gypsy girl and I were sleeping.

Two of the men were young with the same cold look of power in their eyes that I'd seen so often on this journey. But the third was old, tall and slim, with short grey hair and green brown eyes. He was wearing a dirty vest top and black trousers which were grey with dust. Around his neck was a gold chain with a Muslim moon and star on it and a tattoo of a girl covered his right upper arm.

'Come on,' he said as we all stared up at him. 'Time to get up.'

As Anna-Maria and the Romanian sat up and rubbed their eyes, the old man sat down and started flirting with them.

'So how old are you? Where do you come from?'

The younger men stood next to him and smiled as he talked – occasionally reaching out to touch the girls like objects in a shop. The three of them made me sick and I got up to go and wash my face in the bathroom. I'd been getting bad headaches and hoped the cold water would help.

'Hey,' the old man said as I walked back into the bedroom. 'Who are you?'

'My name is Oxana, not hey,' I said coldly.

I was sick of these men treating us like village idiots. I didn't care what they might do. Why did it matter to me? What else could they take?

The old man laughed. 'Oh, really, Oxana? And where are you from?'

'Ukraine.'

'Languages?'

'Russian and Turkish.'

'Well, I'm Serdar,' he said before firing a stream of questions in Turkish at me: how old was I, where had I lived in Turkey, did I know Istanbul well and so on. I felt that he was trying to test me somehow so I answered them all and my answers seemed to tickle him. He grinned at me and the expression in his eyes was the kindest I'd seen on my long and terrible journey. I decided to try and ask one of my own, the question I was longing to know the answer to. I felt that if I didn't know soon, I would truly go mad.

'Where are we?' I asked.

'Albania.'

My stomach turned. It was so far from home.

Serdar looked at me. Something in my face seemed to rouse his sympathy. 'Do you want any food?' he asked.

'Yes, please.'

He translated a menu for us. 'Have whatever you like,' he said.

We ordered our food and I could hardly wait to gulp down the lamb and rice I'd asked for. But as the food was brought in, the door to our room was left open so that we could see into the room opposite, and suddenly I forgot my hunger.

The room across the corridor was full of girls – fat, thin, small, tall, blonde, dark – some sitting on the beds eating fruit while others smoked and talked. They all seemed to be speaking the same language, could understand each other, and fear mixed with loneliness inside me as I looked at them. So this was what the peepholes were for: so that the goods could be selected.

I felt afraid as I stared at the girls but at the same time longed to be with them. Perhaps someone among them was a friend. I kept looking into the room hoping that just one would look up and catch my eye, give me a smile or a nod to tell me that I wasn't alone. But no one did.

We ate our meal, the first proper food we'd had in days, and I felt strength returning to me.

'Good, you are eating well,' said Serdar with a smile. He got up to leave, his companions stepping to his side protectively as he stood. He looked at me, staring straight into my eyes. 'I'll be back,' he said.

The door was shut and I could no longer see into the room opposite. Instead I could only lie on the bed and wonder what would happen next.

A few hours later Serdar returned in clean clothes, smelling of soap. 'Come,' he said.

I went with him downstairs into a bar where two bodyguards armed with guns stood waiting for us. It was a beautiful room with ornate metalwork and black tables with red cloths. Next door was a restaurant full of men. We sat down at a table where Serdar ordered coffee and cigarettes to be brought to me. I felt nervous that he had picked me out like this. He must have hundreds of women to choose from. Why pick on me?

'I can see you don't want to be here,' he said softly. The bodyguards were sitting a little way away from us, unable to hear our conversation. 'I understood that from your eyes the first moment I saw you.'

'Yes,' I said slowly. I had to be careful. I could see that Serdar was important and I didn't want to offend him.

'But you're not like the rest,' he continued. 'They all want to be here, know where they're going, no one's made them do anything. All of them have problems which they need to solve.'

I looked at him. I didn't believe what he was saying. Even if some of the women thought they knew what they were going to do, they couldn't have known about the guns, locks on doors and peepholes to watch them. They were prisoners. Who would want that for themselves?

'You've come from Turkey,' he said. 'I have family and friends there. Let's talk about Turkey.'

Was that why he seemed to bond with me? I wondered. Did I make him think of a better life, where no one knew what kind of work he did? Perhaps a tiny part of him feared that I had once had coffee with an aunt or a cousin, and for a moment he realised that they were women, like the women he traded in. Perhaps he needed to separate me from the herd to help him pretend that he wasn't doing anything so bad.

We talked of Turkey for a while and then Serdar beckoned some other men over to join us. While he talked to them, I stayed silent, sipping my coffee and smoking a cigarette. It was almost as though life was back to normal for a moment – an evening out in a nice bar with some friends, like an ordinary woman living an ordinary life.

An hour or so later, Serdar got up to leave. 'Thank you, Oxana. It's been a pleasant evening. Do you want anything? Clothes, toiletries?'

I smiled. 'That would be nice.'

'I'll get you something then,' he said. A bodyguard stepped forward to take me back upstairs. He had a pistol in a holder over his shoulder. 'Good night, Oxana. I'll see you tomorrow.'

'You're very lucky, you know,' said my guard as he unlocked the door to a strange room.

'Why are we here?' I asked. 'What about Anna-Maria and my old room?'

'That's what I mean. You've been given this room to yourself. Because Serdar likes you and that's good.'

'But why …?'

'Don't you understand? He's a mafia pappa, our boss, the boss of everything here in his hotel.'

Coldness spread across my chest as the door closed. I didn't want to be in this room alone, picked out by Serdar and separated from the other girls. I wanted to be invisible like them.

The next day I spent alone in my room. I had one visitor during the day, a bodyguard who brought me a bag full of cosmetics, soaps and shampoos, along with some clothes and shoes. Most of the clothes and one pair of shoes fitted me.

'Serdar's coming later,' the bodyguard said with a leer. 'So get yourself ready.'

It felt strange to be preparing myself and making myself as beautiful as I could. I had gone in what felt like a few minutes from a dirty barn, no food, filthy clothes and sore feet to a comfortable hotel room with a bath and a bed of my own, getting ready to spend an evening with a mafia boss.

Serdar arrived with the bodyguards who never left his side.

'Very nice,' he said, gazing at me. 'Now we are going out to eat.'

We drove to a restaurant not far from the hotel and ate our dinner like a normal couple, except that two bodyguards with guns were watching over us from a nearby table. Serdar made me tell him all about myself and I started to loosen up with the warmth of his attention and the obvious pleasure he took in my company. I realised quickly it would be a good idea to be nice to him. He obviously had power – perhaps he would be able to help me to get home to my children, if only he liked me enough.

Late that night, we went back to the hotel. The bodyguards were dismissed at last, and he came into my bedroom with me. As he pulled me to him and began to kiss me, I shut my mind off, as I had so many times before. He could do anything he liked with me – better that it happened this way than with force and violence. If I appeared to enjoy myself, I knew it would please him and if I pleased him, he might be my ticket home.

The next morning I awoke to find Serdar gone. When I'd washed and dressed, I discovered that the door had been left unlocked and I walked out into the corridor.

Where is Anna-Maria? I wondered. I wanted to find her, but I couldn't remember where the other room was. I could hear bodyguards down the corridor and I didn't want to run into them.

Then I found another open door and inside I could see other women sitting about, like the ones I'd seen on the night we arrived. I walked in tentatively. There were about six girls sitting about, one curled up almost asleep on one of the beds. A few were talking quietly to each other while they chain-smoked cigarettes, another was leafing through a tattered magazine. No one looked up at me as I came in.

I sat down. Smoke hung heavy in the air and no one appeared to notice me, let alone talk to me, but I felt pleased to be among people again. I soon noticed a woman sitting alone. Her eyes were red as she sat smoking and pity filled me when I realised she was pregnant. As I looked at her, she glanced up and caught my eye. I smiled.

'How many months?' I gestured as I held my fingers up.

'Four,' she replied in Russian.

I tried to be friendly. 'I know how you feel – I've had three babies. It's the early days that are the worst, isn't it?'

She smiled back weakly and put her hand on her stomach. 'I was horribly sick – really terrible! It's not so bad now.'

Slowly, as we talked, the girl told me that she had arrived here at Serdar's hotel some months ago knowing full well she was going to work as a prostitute.

'My family is very poor,' she explained. 'My mother is sick. We need money desperately. So I decided that this was the best thing I could do to earn money. They were going to send me to Italy to work – but then I got pregnant by Vlad. He is one of the guards, do you know him? And now Serdar can't sell me.' Her eyes filled with tears. 'I'm terrified that they're going to send me home. The shame would kill my family. I'm unmarried and pregnant, it's a terrible disgrace. But there's nothing I can do.'

'How old are you?' I asked gently.

'Nineteen.' She began to sob. I went over and put my arm round her, not knowing what to say to comfort her. How many sad stories there were in the world. Probably every woman here had a tale of poverty and abuse to tell.

* * *

'Hey, hello. I'm Tasha. What's your name?'

It was a woman I'd seen hanging about with the body-guards. She wasn't like the rest – she seemed comfortable with them, not as numb as the other girls with their young faces and blank eyes.

'Oxana.'

'Well, I've come to make friends. It looks like you and I might be here a while together.' The woman smiled at me. She was wearing lots of make-up and seemed quite at ease.

'What makes you think that?' I asked warily. Was this another clue to my fate?

'The guards told me that you're Serdar's woman. I've heard he likes you a lot. Lucky for you! It was the same for me. I came here a while back and one of Serdar's sons took a fancy to me. So he took me for his own and I've never left.'

'So how long have you been here?'

'Two years. I don't think I'll ever leave now. I'll stay with him forever.'

I stared silently at her. Is that what's going to happen to me? I wondered. Am I destined to live here for the rest of my life, a guest in a strange hotel, the woman of a mafia boss?

But life was about to change again.

Chapter Twenty

'Into the buses!' shouted the guards. 'Come on!' They hustled all the women out, loading them into a minibus and two jeeps. I was sent to the front seat of one of the jeeps and a few minutes later Serdar climbed into the driving seat.

'Where are we going?' I asked, as we roared away from the hotel.

'Into the country,' Serdar told me. 'There was a police raid nearby last night. We want to clear out until things have quietened down a little. 'Here.' He pulled a gun out of his pocket and passed it me. 'Can you hold this for me?'

I stared down at the weapon in my hand, feeling the cold metal in my palm. Serdar trusted me enough to hand me his gun, even though he'd known me only a few weeks. Shall I shoot him? I wondered. I imagined holding the barrel to his temple and squeezing the trigger, feeling the recoil as the bullet exploded into Serdar's brain. But he was driving fast – no doubt we'd all die in the crash that followed. Anyway, I knew I could never kill anyone: it was a sin to take to a life. Besides, I had another plan. I was going to do all I could to win Serdar's love and trust – then he would give me more freedom and eventually I would escape.

Sasha, Pasha and Luda filled my thoughts. I saw
them when I shut my eyes, stared at food on my plate
or felt Serdar's hands pull my body to his. Now I thought
of them again as I sat next to him and we drove into
the countryside. I had to make my plan work and get
home.

Soon the cars came to a stop on a dirt track and Serdar
got out.

'We've got to walk,' he shouted, and the bodyguards
and women started following him down a steep ravine.

He led us to the bottom, along a gorge, and then out
again to a place where a large house stood. We went
inside, where there was a big sitting room, three bedrooms
and a kitchen. Below was a huge cellar.

'It's basic here. There's no running water, no bathroom.
You'll need to draw water from the stream,' Serdar told
me as we walked inside. 'Make sure the girls understand
that they can't go alone. I want you to take charge of them,
do you understand?'

I nodded. 'You can depend on me.'

Serdar smiled. 'Good. And I'll need you to start organising the cooking and cleaning. Just tell the guards what
you need.'

We spent the day settling in. The change of scene, the
fresh country air and the novelty of the old house gave
everyone a burst of energy and we dusted, cleaned and
sorted out our things. Serdar said we'd be here for perhaps
a few weeks, so we needed to be comfortable.

Later that evening Serdar came to me. 'I want to show
you something.'

We went outside, down the steps and towards the huge
doors leading to the cellar. Serdar opened them and
gestured to me to look inside. I peered in and saw rows

and rows of guns with boxes of bullets lying around. I snapped to attention but tried not to show my shock.

'Do you sell them?' I asked casually.

'No, they're for my guys,' Serdar replied. 'We need to protect ourselves.'

'From what?'

'Our rivals.'

'For what?'

'You and women like you. Sometimes men bring women to me and they're sold to me cheaply and I sell them on to people across the border. But things can get difficult at times. The women don't have the money to get across but they want to go to earn good money and I can't do it for nothing.'

So that was the story that Serdar told himself: the women wanted to go. They all chose to work as prostitutes. There was no force or imprisonment involved. Why all the guards then? Why the threat of being shot if we tried to escape? I stared silently as Serdar picked up a large triangular frame and walked towards the cellar door.

'Let's go outside.'

Darkness was falling as he set up the frame and locked a gun into it.

'I own the hotel where you've been staying,' he told me. 'I've earned good money you see but I have no one to share it with. My wife and daughter died in a car accident many years ago and I've been on my own ever since.'

Sadness washed across Serdar's face for a moment before he took hold of the gun and stared into the distance. Suddenly the still night air was split open by the sharp sound of bullets as he started firing the gun, laughing.

'See?' he shouted. 'All this land is mine and I can do what I want with it.'

I said nothing as he continued shooting into the darkness. Serdar was showing me how strong he was and, with a gun in his hand, there was nothing he couldn't do.

There were about a dozen girls in the house, including Anna-Maria and me, and we soon got into a routine. As Serdar's woman, I was seen to be in charge and each morning I gave each girl a job to do – two went to draw water from the river, two more cleaned and two more helped me cook as I taught them Russian songs and they taught me Romanian ones while the bodyguards watched over us. I was so much older than them that they didn't seem to mind me organising the house and I managed to keep the place in some sort of order and provide decent meals for all of us.

Serdar and his men would arrive at around six in the evening and we would all eat our evening meal together. Then Serdar and I would retire to one of the bedrooms while the others discreetly made themselves scarce. The bedrooms were all very hot and stuffy, and Serdar's sweaty weight heaving on top of me made me feel sick, but I never let him see it.

'That was wonderful!' I would lie when he finally rolled off me.

Serdar would smile with pleasure and hold me tightly for a while, often talking a little about himself and his life.

'I like you,' he told me once. 'Since my wife died, I have missed a woman's touch. I have my sons, of course, and I'm proud of them but it is good to feel soft skin against mine again.'

It seemed that my plan was working.

Afterwards we would rejoin the others. Most evenings we all sat outside, talking and smoking, watching the long summer evening turn to black above the trees. At about 10pm Serdar and the men would leave again for the hotel, leaving a different pair of men to guard us the next day. Before he left, Serdar would ask me what I needed and I'd give him a list of things like knickers, shampoo and the long, thin cigarettes that I smoked, which he'd bring for me the following evening.

Most of the luxuries he brought me I gave away to the girls. Soon they were calling me Mamma and I hated the word, knowing that my children were so far away while I was like the madam in a brothel. But the girls were young and feared me because I was Serdar's so I didn't say too much. When two of them had a row one day and I asked them to stop, they came to me later and begged me not to tell him. I told them that I never would.

Some days men came to see us and once we were driven into the forest to be looked at. The prices for us now were in Deutschmarks and we would be sold for anything between four and eleven thousand – between about one and four thousand pounds. If you were young, slim and new to the job then you were expensive; if you were pregnant, tattooed, already experienced or old, you were cheaper.

At first I thought that the girls didn't care but then on about the fourth day some of them rushed up to me and started pulling me with them. They took me into a corridor which was so dark we had to use a candle to go through a door leading off it.

'There's something nice in here,' they giggled and I looked around to see blocks of brown resin wrapped in plastic bags and big sieves with newspaper underneath to catch a kind of green flour. There were also poppies in the room whose petals had been picked off and the girls laughed as they stole some of the green leaves from the tables.

'Be careful,' I warned them. 'I don't know what Serdar will do to you if he finds out.'

But I was glad when they smoked the leaves and came back smiling and happy. I didn't try it though. I was too old for drugs, had seen the damage they did. I wouldn't find an escape, however much I wanted to forget what was happening to me.

Chapter Twenty-One

A few days later Serdar arrived at the house, looking angry.
'What's wrong, my love?' I asked him gently.

'Your fucking friend! What's her name? Anna something?'

'Anna-Maria?' I felt suddenly frightened. Earlier in the week Anna-Maria had been sold and I'd kissed her as we said goodbye. I'd felt sad to be losing her but she seemed almost happy to be going.

'Yes, Anna-Maria. Why didn't the stupid bitch tell me she was pregnant?'

'Pregnant?' I was astonished. I'd had no idea.

'Yes. The men who've bought her have asked me for their money back. She's damaged goods now!' He paced about furiously. 'Fucking bitch!' he shouted. 'I'm trying to help this stupid teenager and look what she does. If she'd told me I could have fixed the problem.'

'Where is she? In Italy?'

'No. She's been sent back to Romania.'

I stared at him, fearful. Was he telling the truth? He might talk of how he 'helped' girls, but I knew he was ruthless. He wouldn't let a poor, terrified girl who'd angered him stand in his way.

* * *

The girls came and went as usual, part of the mysterious trade that was never explained to us. Sometimes someone would disappear without warning and a bodyguard might tell us that she'd been sold and was on her way to Italy or Germany.

One morning we woke up to find a new girl at the house, sitting by the window staring out at the sky. She said nothing and answered no questions, so we had no idea where she had come from. She ate some breakfast, but otherwise sat all day by the window, gazing at the sky. I could see how scared she was, like a frightened mouse. Serdar took her back to the hotel that night and I never saw her again.

On another day an older girl arrived at the house and I immediately noticed her because she looked about the same age as me. Soon she told me her name was Claudia and she was twenty-eight. She was from Romania but we could talk because she'd learned Russian at school and I could see from her eyes that she was clever. Claudia had grown up in an orphanage where she'd been abused and hadn't been able to find work when she left. She'd ended up living in the cellar of an apartment block but was kicked out onto the streets when she was discovered.

'I had no choice but to do this,' she told me. 'I want children and a home one day and I can make money like this.'

She spoke bravely but she was so broken, sad and weak. I could not see how she would survive this lonely and difficult life.

It is women like those who I often think about now. What happened to Claudia, Anna-Maria and the little mouse girl? You need good people around you to survive in life and they had no one.

* * *

As the days passed I became more and more hopeful that my plan with Serdar was working. By now he let me go to fetch water without a bodyguard and had started telling me how lonely he was and how tired he had become of his work.

'One day my sons will take over and I will buy a house far away from all this,' he said.

'And you will deserve it after all your hard work,' I replied as I smiled inside. I was sure that I would soon be able to get Serdar to do what I wanted, and I decided to test my power. One night I asked him if I could go back to the hotel with him.

'I'm tired of life out here in the middle of nowhere,' I said as I cuddled up to him. 'Can't I go back with you? Surely the police are no longer watching, it's been over two weeks since we got here.'

Serdar kissed my forehead. 'You've done a good job here. Perhaps you are owed a treat.'

'I want to be alone with you,' I told him. 'Can't we be together properly?'

'All right,' Serdar said with a smile. 'Tomorrow night you come back with me. Have your things ready and get dressed up. I'll take you somewhere nice.'

I was excited as I waited for him the following night and grew happier with every passing mile as he drove me back to the hotel. Serdar had done what I'd asked. He truly cared for me. Surely I would soon have the opportunity I needed.

My treat was a visit to an ice-cream parlour and I gasped at what I saw. There must have been fifty different ice-creams in every colour of the rainbow and I'd never seen anything like it.

'Do you like it?' said Serdar, grinning at my pleasure.

'It's amazing!' I cried, thinking how my children would have loved it. Serdar bought me strawberry, vanilla and chocolate flavours, and I smiled at him as I ate. Pictures of Sasha, Pasha and Luda played in my head as I looked at him. Soon I'd be with them. I almost pitied Serdar for being so stupid, but I needed him to believe in my love for him, so I was glad he was so gullible.

We ate our ice-cream giggling and happy as the ever-present bodyguards looked on. I felt confident and strong, and it was a strange but pleasant feeling.

'I've fallen in love with you,' I told Serdar that night. 'I don't want to leave you.'

'You won't be going anywhere,' he said, and he hugged me.

That night as always he left his trousers on the floor by the bed and I lay in the dark picturing the money and keys I knew were in his pockets. Soon they would be mine.

The next day Serdar and I were watching television when a beauty contest came on. I started laughing as I looked at the women in thick make-up with their orange skin. They looked like funny birds with their long noses and strong features.

'In Russia there are beautiful girls everywhere,' I giggled. 'But is this the best you get in Albania?'

'What do you mean?' asked Serdar quietly.

'They're ugly, poor things! Maybe you don't get enough decent food in Albania,' I teased.

Serdar looked at me. 'But everyone knows what Russian girls are like.'

'What are they like?'

'Whores. Look at every country and who are the women selling themselves? Russians.'

I felt anger boiling up. 'What are you talking about?' I snapped. 'There are only Romanians and Albanians here. If Russian women are so easy, then how come I'm the only one in this hotel?'

I saw instantly that I shouldn't have spoken back. Serdar's face changed and he looked suddenly like a stranger.

'I was only joking, my love ...' I began, and tried to hug him, but he pulled away and stood up.

'Just shut the fuck up,' he said. 'Don't say another word.' He walked over to the door and slammed it behind him.

I sat there frozen, staring after him, while the Albanian women still paraded up and down the television screen. What had I done? Tears sprang to my eyes and I started to cry. Serdar had turned icy cold on me, as though my words had broken a spell. Could I really have destroyed everything I had so carefully built up? How could I have been so stupid?

I'd have to make it up to him, I decided. I'd be sweet, loving, tender and eager for sex. He'd soon forget those foolish words of mine.

He was gone for hours and eventually I gave up waiting and went to bed. Much later, I felt him climb into bed next to me. I pretended to be asleep as relief washed through me. He was back. I'd find a way to sweeten him tomorrow. All this would soon be forgotten.

The next morning I was woken up as he shook my shoulder in the early light.

'Get your stuff,' he said. 'I want you downstairs in fifteen minutes.'

'Why? Where are we going?'

'Someone wants to meet you.'

I felt scared as I got up out of bed and dressed in a tight white T-shirt and black trousers. Was Serdar still angry with me?

When I got downstairs he was sitting next to a young man with short gelled hair like a little boy's and blue eyes. He was slim and didn't look older than sixteen.

'This is you new boss,' Serdar said quietly. 'His name is Ardy.'

Shock filled me as I looked at the boy. He couldn't be buying me! He was too young. I looked at Serdar, wondering why he was making such a bad joke. But his face was frozen. It was as if he'd never met me, taken my body, talked to me or confided in me.

'You're going to Italy,' he snapped. 'Now get upstairs and change your top. You can't travel with your tits hanging out like that. Everyone will know you're a prostitute.'

In that moment, I saw what I should have seen all along. Serdar felt nothing for me. I had angered him last night and now he was bored with me. He had been playing a game all along just as I had and all I was to him, like everyone else, was just a commodity to be sold.

I'd never stood a chance.

Chapter Twenty-Two

'You know your daughter is very beautiful, isn't she? I've seen her picture and she'll grow up well, I think.' Ardy spoke softly as we sat in his bedroom. I'd been with him for several weeks as we waited for a boat to take us to Italy and, although he hadn't told me anything, I knew that was where I'd finally start working. I had been locked into this nightmare for more than two months now. It was such a short time and yet it felt like a lifetime, an imprisonment without end. My hunger to see my children, to speak to them, was overwhelming. I craved them.

I'd been wrong to think that Ardy was too young to buy me. He was twenty-one in fact and, just as Serdar had told me, I belonged to him now. He'd taken me from the hotel by car to his parents' house and, although it had no running water or proper kitchen, there were grapes, peaches and figs in the garden, and crystal ornaments on the shelves in the sitting room – a family home.

'Hello,' a plump woman had said as she walked up to shake my hand as I arrived. 'Would you like something to eat?'

She was Ardy's mother and I saw in that moment that she knew exactly what her son was doing. I wasn't a person to her – just a bag of money. Ardy, who spoke a little bit of English and Russian, told me that she had been a teacher for thirty-five years. But while she cooked me food, taught me Albanian words and bought me clothes for a trip we'd soon be making, her husband never once spoke to me. In fact he hardly looked at me, as if he couldn't bear to see such a dirty creature in his home.

In the weeks since leaving Serdar, I'd stopping thinking about running away. Where once I'd been kept prisoner with guns, Ardy didn't threaten violence because he didn't need to. Instead he simply planted new seeds of fear in my mind every day and slowly I realised that, however brave I'd tried to be, I would never escape now.

'We'll find you if you run,' Ardy told me. 'We know everyone in this town and you wouldn't get more than a mile. We also have relatives in the police and politics and do you think they don't need to eat? Everyone does, everyone needs money, so just think of your daughter and be a good girl.'

It was words like those which caged me in. I knew Ardy had paid a lot of money for me which he'd make my children repay if I ran and I believed him when he said I wouldn't get very far – as well as Ardy's aunt and cousins coming to look at me, one of his policeman relatives had even visited. What hope did I have of getting away if even he knew I was here? And so I didn't beg or even try to escape when I was left locked in the house for a few hours at a time. There was no point at the moment. For now, I had to bide my time, accept what was happening to me and see what the future held.

At least the time I spent alone allowed me to think of my children in peace. I dreaded the sound of the front door opening as Ardy arrived home to demand sex. It was horrible. At night I couldn't see him and he couldn't see me as I stared into the blackness and he took what he wanted. But in the day his face wasn't hidden and it sickened me to see my body and his joined together.

A couple of times I'd fought against him as he asked me to do something I'd never done before – like putting him in my mouth. But then he'd push my head into a pillow and the next morning I'd feel ashamed as his mother walked in to open the bedroom window as the smell of sex hung in the air. I learned not to fight but, however much I begged Ardy to use a condom, he refused.

I felt as if there were two people inside me. One who on the mornings after those nights hated herself. She deserved what was happening. She wasn't supposed to let Ardy take what he wanted, she should have screamed and clawed at him, done anything to protect herself. But then there was the person who knew she was alone and had never, however hungry she'd been, done anything as bad as what was being done to her.

'It can't be like this forever,' I'd tell myself as I prayed to God. 'After the bad will come the good, you just have to be patient.'

It was hard to know exactly how long I was in the house, though I guessed it was almost a month. There was a calendar on the wall but I couldn't bear to look at it. It was August now and Luda's first day at school was getting closer. I didn't want to think about it, picture her buying a dress and pencils, wondering when Mamma would be home to take her just as I'd taken Sasha to school on his first day. My body kept reminding me of time passing because my period arrived on the 13th of every month but I tried not to think about it. I was sure Ira and Tamara would know something had happened to me by now because I hadn't phoned home for so long. They knew how much I loved my children, that I'd never leave them unless I had to.

It was late one night when a man arrived to speak to Ardy. When his mother started packing our clothes into plastic bags, I knew that the weather was finally good for the boat to sail. I was told to dress in a black cardigan, sports trousers and trainers and then I was taken outside to meet Ardy's policeman relative who put us into his car.

He drove us to his home where we stayed the night before Ardy took me down to the nearby beach the next morning.

'I want to see that you can swim,' he told me. 'Get in.'

It was a blazing hot August day, so hot that I could feel my skin burning as I waded into the water. It was a pleasure to feel the cool water on my body, and all my summer trips to the Black Sea as a child had made me a good swimmer. Ardy seemed happy with what he saw. Soon we went back to the house where the waiting started once again. We ate, we sat, we smoked.

It must have been about midnight on the second day when the policeman came to fetch us and we were driven back to the beach where Ardy gestured towards a long spit of stones stretching out into the water.

'This way,' he said and I followed him in the dark.

A boat was waiting some way ahead by the side of the spit. It looked like a big lifeboat and there was a wheel in the middle with a man standing behind it. Beside him was a big light.

'Get in,' Ardy said as I looked down.

There were so many people, young and old, crouching silently on the floor of the boat that there didn't seem any space left for us.

'Come on,' Ardy hissed, and pushed me as I started to climb down the spit.

I pulled myself over the side, got in and crouched down in the darkness like everyone else. Opposite me was a woman with a little girl of about five.

'When do we go, Mamma?' she asked but the woman stayed silent.

Suddenly I heard a scream as a shot rang out in the air and I lifted my head to see a person in a white sash running down the beach. Police. Another shot rang out and the sharp smell of fear filled the air.

'Let's go,' a voice screamed.

'Come on, quick,' another pleaded.

The little girl started crying as Ardy pushed down my head. My heart thumped and the deep roar of the boat engines vibrated in my chest. What we were doing was wrong. Would the police catch us and kill us?

The boat lurched forward beneath me and soon the noise of the shots faded as we reached open sea. But my fear didn't disappear so easily. All I could hear was the roar of the engine as cold water soaked me each time the boat hit the water with a loud thump. Fearing I would be thrown over the side, my hands reached out to cling onto whatever I could find as an elbow dug into my back, the little girl cried and a person near me started to vomit. Later I would realise that my bleeding nails had been ripped in two as I held onto the side but now I could feel nothing as my body went numb with cold and fear.

I don't know how long the journey lasted – it might have been one hour or several because time stopped. I stayed crouching down, holding on for my life as everyone around me did the same. I could hardly see anything in the blackness as the boat moved fast and I prayed that I might live.

But all of a sudden everything went quiet and the boat came to a stop. No one spoke. In the silence I could hear the sound of waves lapping around us and then the sound of another engine far away whispered in the air. It got louder and louder. Someone was looking for us.

Suddenly our boat turned sharply to the side as the engine sprang into life and we started moving again.

'Stop! Police!' shouted a voice through a microphone, and lights started flashing above my head.

Without a word, the people around me started moving like a wave as they jumped off the side of the boat and into the water. Ardy tried to pull me up but people were climbing over me. I felt a foot on my head and tried to stand up as I fought to move. But I couldn't.

Suddenly I was lifted up and thrown into the sea. In the split second before I hit the water, I held my breath before it closed cold around me. I opened my eyes. Everything was black. I could feel myself starting to sink. I clawed for the surface but my clothes, shoes and the bag on my back were too heavy. A foot kicked my shoulder and I felt myself drop even lower. I couldn't die, couldn't let the water suck me under and hide me forever. I couldn't die now. No. No. No. Tearing at my clothes and bag, I tried to get them off as my chest felt like bursting. I was going to die.

A hand pulled the back of my neck and air exploded into my lungs as I broke the surface of the water.

'Put your feet on the floor,' a voice said. 'It's shallow enough here.'

But I was too short for my feet to reach the bottom and had to pull myself forward with my hands as I gulped down air. The water was alive with people. I could hear dogs barking and see lights flashing brightly across the water. I clawed myself forward until I felt sand underneath my feet and started crawling through the water on my stomach. I didn't look back. I just had to keep moving. I couldn't let the police catch me.

Ardy was ahead of me on the beach. As the lights moved above us, he grabbed handfuls of wet sand which he smeared over his light jumper to make it disappear in the darkness. My breath came in gasps and there was grit in my mouth as I started moving up the beach. People were running into the bushes just ahead of me and I followed Ardy as he crawled towards them. We were like ants scattering as people disappeared into the night, the police pursuing us.

I crawled through the bushes and out the other side. In front of me was a track with trees beyond it and Ardy grabbed my hand as he talked quickly to another man. They seemed to be discussing where we should go as people ran in opposite directions. Soon a group of about nine of us were walking through the trees and bushes as the noise of panic slowly started disappearing. When it was finally quiet we stopped so that everyone could change out of their wet clothes. Now I understood why Ardy's mother had wrapped everything in plastic.

We were in some kind of forest. There seemed to be trees all around us but it was so dark I couldn't see properly. We walked silently together until the men pointed to a ditch they'd found and we all got in. Time passed, the sun came up, still no one spoke. A dog barked in the distance and we all crouched down even lower. We were there all day and no one said a word or moved. We had nothing to eat or drink, and no one even went to the toilet.

I was like a statue, so scared that I couldn't think of anything. I kept remembering the darkness of the boat journey, the cold water as I fell into it. How would I ever survive what was happening to me?

People only started moving again when it got dark. Ardy whispered that I should move quickly as we started walking once again with a small group of people through trees, bushes and grass. Soon we came to a dual carriageway where cars rushed noisily past as Ardy pointed us into more bushes and left to go to a little roadside café in the distance. He could speak Italian, and came back a few minutes later.

'I've called us a taxi,' he said and sat down beside me.

There was a newspaper in his hand and I felt cold as I saw the date. 1 September 2001. Luda's first day at school. Pictures filled my mind – of hands putting her hair into plaits and pulling her brown school dress and white pinafore over her head before helping her into her sandals and white knee-length socks. The weather would still be warm enough to wear summer shoes and, just as every Ukrainian child did on their first day of school, Luda would be holding some flowers for her teacher in her tiny hand. Memories of Sasha's first day at school filled me. I'd come back from Turkey to take him and felt so proud as I dressed him in a dark-red school blazer, black trousers and shoes and white socks. I knew I'd be the youngest mother at the school and wanted to make him proud of me so I'd made sure his hair was cut and put on my best long silver dress for the day. Then I'd walked him to school where all the other children were gathered and watched as the oldest ones each took the hand of a youngest before giving them an alphabet book. I closed my eyes and saw Sasha in front of me again, his worried face looking up at me before turning to go into this strange new place called school.

Today it would be Luda's turn and I wasn't there, her own mother wasn't there. I ached for her. Tears slid down my face as I sat in the bushes.

'Come on,' Ardy said as he stood up. 'There's a car here. It's time to move on.'

Chapter Twenty-Three

Three days later I was put to work for the first time in a town called Venezia Mestre – a suburb of the famous city of Venice that I'd never even heard of back then. We were living in one room at a small, shabby hotel and earlier Ardy had watched me get dressed in clothes he'd bought for me – trousers and a short leather jacket. He'd also picked out a mini skirt but I didn't want to wear it and look like the girls I'd seen in American films. The jacket was a size eight. I'd lost weight. Olga would have been pleased.

'But how will I talk to the men?' I asked.

'You only need to know a few things,' Ardy told me. '*Mi chiamo Oxana* means I am Oxana and *Io sono Russa* means I come from Russia. A fuck is *una scoppa* and it will cost them *cinquanta mila lire*; a blow job is *boccino* and it's *trenta mila*; to tell them no bum just say *no culo* and fuck off is *vaffanculo*.'

'But what if they don't give me money?'

'Just make sure you get the cash first. You've got what they want.'

'What if they beat me?'

'I'll be watching. If you get in their car, I'll follow, and if you try to run, I'll be there. You'll never be alone so you won't get hurt.'

Ardy had an answer for every question I had. There was no way out. But even though I felt afraid, I was also strangely still inside as I got ready to go out. Only my body told the real story of how I felt. I was cold, tense, like a robot while Ardy seemed almost excited, as if he were going to be a big man now he had a woman to make money for him.

A cousin of his who lived nearby was going to drive us and earlier in the day I'd heard him telling Ardy that if I were good then he'd be a rich man in just one year.

'We'll go fifty fifty on whatever you make,' he kept telling me.

I did not get my hopes up. He'd also said that the eleven thousand Deutschmarks he'd paid for me – the equivalent of about four thousand pounds – was a debt I'd have to pay back with my wages, as well as paying for my travel, the share of the hotel we were staying in and money to his cousin for his petrol and time. I guessed that it would take a long time before I saw any of the money I earned; it would all be sucked into my endless debt to him.

Soon we left the hotel and drove to a long stretch of dual carriageway with dirt tracks on either side and a bar in the distance. Girls lined the road but I didn't talk to them.

'Keep it on,' Ardy said as he handed me a mobile phone.

I didn't get any customers that night. Plenty of cars came by and some stopped next to me, the drivers winding down the window to look at me. But they saw the fear in my eyes as I whispered, 'Would you like a fuck?' in the broken Italian I'd been taught.

'What the hell are you doing?' Ardy shouted down the phone as another car drove away. 'You won't make money like this and then I'll have to sell you and your next boss won't be as understanding as me.'

I felt freezing as I stood in the darkness and watched the car lights flashing past. Where were all these people going? Home to their families? What did they think as they saw me standing at the side of the road? Was I just another whore living in the shadows where she deserved to be?

I stood on the roadside for nine hours before Ardy picked me up and I was almost smiling inside as we drove back to the hotel. Maybe he'd let me go if this happened again and again. But the next day he was full of rage when his cousin refused to drive us.

'He thinks you're stupid, that you won't make us any money,' he screamed. 'Do you see what you've done? How will I pay for the hotel now?'

And on the third day he shouted again when my period arrived early. Then he became menacing.

'You need to think about your children. Or don't you want to make enough money to get back to them? Don't you care about your children? Maybe I'll have to use them to teach you a lesson …'

Of course Ardy would not let me off so easily. I couldn't escape forever and a few nights later he took me to the corner of a crossroads near Venezia Mestre's busy station. I got there about 10pm, stood beside a traffic light and it wasn't long before a car pulled up beside me.

'*Quanto?*' a man said as he looked out of the window. 'How much?'

'*Cinquanta milla,*' I replied and he beckoned me into the car. Panic exploded in my chest as I opened the door and a hard metallic smell filled the air around me. The man was half bald with blue eyes, white skin and pink cheeks.

He looked slow, stupid, like a pig, and said nothing as he drove me to some nearby waste ground before pointing at my clothes as he pulled at his. I knew what he wanted. Slowly I took off my jacket, trousers and underwear.

The man stared silently before taking himself in his hand. I wanted to look away, I'd never seen a man do such a thing before and had always been told it was wrong. But his fingers dug into my cheeks as he pulled my face towards him. I held my breath as he stared at my body and the car filled with the sound of him – half pant, half groan. He said something I couldn't understand as he pulled at my legs. I opened them for him.

'Don't think,' my mind told me. 'Don't feel. You are a thing now to do with as he wants. Don't think of your children. They must never be with you when you are in this world. They must never touch it, come close to it. You are here to protect them.'

'*Boccino. Quanto?*' the man said suddenly. 'Blow job. How much?'

I told him the price and he gave me the money before I put a condom on him and he pushed my head up and down roughly. I couldn't breathe, I wanted to be sick but I concentrated on thinking of nothing at all.

When I'd finished and dressed myself, I knew I was almost glad that Ardy was somewhere close by. It was a strange feeling as I sat in that stranger's car surrounded by the night and my heart betrayed me. However much I hated Ardy, at least he was out there. I wasn't completely alone.

I saw up to five men during the eight or nine hours I worked each night. There were no hugs, no kisses and I never touched anyone without a condom on or got into a car with more than one man inside. I froze myself more and more as I became an object for men to use as they wanted – shoving their fingers inside me, pulling my hair, pinching me, ripping off my underwear, biting me. So many of them were angry and I learned to see the signs within them. Each one was different and I had to know how to calm him down or he might hurt me. But by the time I finished for the evening my body was filled with pain and all I wanted to do was go back to the hotel to try and wash the stench of sex off me.

'Are you sure this is everything?' Ardy would ask as he looked at the money I gave him.

'Yes, I'm sure,' I'd reply as I stripped off my clothes.

I had to undress in front of him and, although he pretended not to, I knew he checked my clothes when I went to have a bath. Sometimes I'd fill it with water so hot it almost burned me and lie there for hours smoking cigarettes – anything to delay the moment when I got into bed next to Ardy and he asked for sex. I always said no and sometimes he listened but sometimes he didn't. He sickened me, I hated him and he knew it. It was like an odd dance between us as I pretended to hide my feelings and he pretended not to see them.

I had to. If I let Ardy do what he wanted then at least he wouldn't hit me. He'd slapped me a few times but I didn't want him to beat me. I'd had enough of that in my life. Ardy was just like every other man. He thought sex was just sex and didn't care what I felt. I was as much of an object to him as every customer who saw me. All he cared about was money and soon he was wearing a new leather jacket, Dolce and Gabbana jeans, a thick gold chain and carrying a Valentino wallet. He looked more and more like a rich man.

'That's good,' he'd say as he took everything I'd made that night.

I never saw any of the money I earned. During the day Ardy would go out to eat and lock me into the room before bringing back burgers or pizza. I hated the food. But sometimes he'd want me to go with him and I hated that as well. I didn't want to go outside and see people being happy. Mostly though Ardy left me alone and as the weeks passed I shut my mind down more and more. I couldn't think about either my future or my past as I slept, watched TV or stared into space while I smoked cigarette after cigarette.

I learned quickly: how to find the right words to calm a customer down, how to put a condom on with my mouth to make sure they finished easily. I also worked hard at improving my Italian and customers laughed at me when I wrote down words I didn't know in a book to learn later on. But I didn't care. It was the only way I could learn the language and the more I did that then the more I could do what many men wanted – just talk.

Sometimes they'd had a bad day at work or lost money or trusted a partner who betrayed them but, whatever it was, the words would pour out of them as they sat with me. That was why it was important to learn as much of their language as possible. Most of the men who talked were older and gentle, they asked before they touched, they were good customers – if there ever can be such a thing. But for every one of those, there were far more who fucked me like an animal before kicking me out into the street. I was threatened with a gun before being dumped in the middle of nowhere by one man while another tried to run me down with a car. My life was almost worthless now and the men using me knew it.

* * *

I stared down at the stick I was holding as a thin blue line appeared on it. For a moment I felt afraid but knew what I had to do. Emptiness filled me once again.

'It's positive,' I told Ardy as I walked out of the bathroom.

'But what are we going to do?' he said, like the little boy he was. 'You've got no documents so I can't take you to a public hospital.'

I didn't care what he did. I just wanted his baby out of me. I knew it was his because I'd used a condom with every customer but he'd refused. He was an animal and so was his child.

Ardy took me to see a doctor who didn't ask any questions about who I was or where I was from. It would take a couple of weeks to arrange the abortion, and the cost would be added on to what I owed so I had to go back out to work again while I waited. A couple of customers noticed my stomach and breasts were rounded, unlike the rest of me, but others probably didn't think as I retched while they pushed into me. I refused to think about the pregnancy even though I was sick every morning: it wasn't a baby growing inside me and it had nothing to do with me or my children. They were the only thing which kept me going in the quiet moments while Ardy slept and I unlocked the love I had for them inside me and allowed myself to think about them before wrapping up my feelings safe again. This thing inside me now was made in hate and when, a few weeks later, I was taken to a clinic for the operation, I was numb.

I bled for weeks afterwards, often feeling drunk and dizzy. I didn't want to eat or think about anything. I was broken inside. I couldn't even let the bright-coloured pictures of home come into my mind like I once had.

Before they had comforted me but now they made me feel crazy. Sometimes my head felt as if it might burst and I'd pull out my hair as I scratched at my scalp. I wanted to hurt myself, mark myself, make the deadness inside me show on the outside. Night after night I sat in scalding baths as I tried to make myself bleed even more in the hope that I might die.

But Ardy would always pull me out and two weeks after the termination he made me go back out to work again.

'You owe so much money,' he told me. 'And I've got nothing left.'

I put a sponge inside me to stop the bleeding while I worked and soon I was even weaker.

'You look good now you've lost some weight,' Ardy told me admiringly one night.

But looking in a mirror, all I could see was a thin, sad young woman with porcelain white skin, dark circles under her eyes and hate within them.

Chapter Twenty-Four

Soon after I went back to work, a car stopped one night beside me. It looked expensive and so did the man in it. He was wearing jeans, a chunky woollen cardigan and had blond hair and a square face. He must have been about forty.

'How much please?'

'Fifty thousand.'

'And how much is a blow job?'

'Thirty.'

'Anal?'

'I don't do it.'

'Why?'

'Because I don't.'

'Okay.'

I got in the car and the man started driving.

'So how old are you?' he asked as he turned to me. 'Where are you from? How long have you been here?'

I didn't mind answering his questions – at least he was polite. Soon we stopped between two lorries in a big car park. I couldn't see anyone around. The drivers must all be asleep.

'So what do you want?' I asked as I turned towards the man.

'A blow job and then sex.'

'Okay. Money first.'

'No problem.'

The man put his hand into his pocket, took out a lump of folded-up notes and handed me one hundred thousand lira. Twenty thousand extra. It was a big tip.

I felt so tired as I put on the condom and bent down towards him. The bleeding had stopped but I still felt weak. I just had to switch off my thoughts, get through the night and wait for the moment when it finally ended.

I worked quickly and the man was soon ready for sex. He folded back the seats and climbed on top of me. But it was clear that he would never be able to finish like that and suddenly he stopped.

'Can we change the position?' he asked hesitantly.

'No,' I told him.

I only ever had sex with the man on top of me. If anything changed then he'd have to pay for it. Ardy had told me again and again that if a client wanted to change position they had to pay, if they wanted my clothes off then they'd have to pay, if they asked to kiss my body they'd have to pay.

But as I looked at the man, I remembered he had given me twenty thousand lira extra. He had been kind.

'Okay,' I told him.

We moved to the back of the car and I knelt in front of him as he went inside me once again.

'How about the other way?' he whispered as he leaned into me.

'No. I've told you I don't do it.'

'Oh come on.'

'No. I mean it.'

This time I wasn't going to feel sorry for him. I never did that, never would and I wouldn't change my mind however much he offered to pay.

The man said nothing more as he grabbed my hair and pulled my head back. Suddenly his hands closed like iron around my hips as he withdrew from inside me. For a moment he steadied himself before pushing violently inside the place that I'd refused him. I screamed.

'You fucking whore,' the man shouted.

I tried crawling forward on the seat. I had to get away from him, couldn't let this happen to me. This was the one thing I wouldn't sell, the one place no one had ever touched me. But the man's hands just dug deeper into my skin as he rammed himself inside me again and again. My body was filled with terrible pain.

'You fucking bitch,' the man screamed as he hit me. 'You love this.'

I tried biting his fingers but couldn't get hold of them and the man pulled his hands away as he started hitting my bottom.

'You've been fucked before like this and you just want to get the price up, don't you?' he panted. 'All that pretending you did not want it was just an act, wasn't it?'

When he'd finished, he turned to me and smiled. 'You enjoyed that, didn't you?'

Later that night I went back to the hotel and told Ardy what had happened.

'You should have taken more money from him,' he screamed. 'Anal costs one hundred thousand.'

I felt cold as I stared at him. 'Did you hear what I said? He raped me.'

'Pah,' Ardy exclaimed. 'You've been in this business for months. How can anyone rape you? Sex is your job and that money you lost will go on to your debt.'

I think there are some men who think that if a woman says no she's really saying yes and if she's a prostitute she's just trying to get a higher price. They believe you can sell everything and that nothing you have is private. But they are wrong. Prostitutes are actresses and all the men who believe them when they tell them how much they love their work are fools. A few might but most women don't enjoy selling themselves – they do it because they have to and they close their hearts to it. But when someone beats and rapes you it's impossible to ignore those feelings anymore.

It's hard to describe how I felt after that night. I couldn't forget the pain, the word 'whore' as the man screamed at me. Strange as it sounds, I felt almost as I had when I lost my virginity all those years before. The violence, the violation of the part of me that no one had ever touched before, were the same and all those feelings I'd buried returned.

In the days that followed I had to stay in bed a lot during the day because of the pain but my mind kept moving even as I lay still. Again and again, I thought about killing Ardy, smothering him as he slept, pouring acid onto him or cutting him into small pieces – each one representing one of my customers, all the men he'd made me sell myself to. Only then could he know what I knew.

I tried to hide my thoughts when I opened my eyes and got out of bed but some days I couldn't and Ardy would slap me.

'Don't look at me like that,' he'd shout. 'You're just a fucking whore.'

But mostly I lay in bed until it was time to get up again and go to work.

'Make-up, clothes, work, make money, come back to the hotel, take a shower and sleep,' I'd repeat to myself as I prepared to go out.

It was as if I didn't have a heart or soul anymore. I was empty.

'This should make you feel better,' the old man said as he held out a glass.

He'd picked me up earlier off the street and taken me to his house. It was December and I was freezing cold but now the warm smell of spices and wine filled my nose.

'Be careful. It's hot.'

The old man had agreed to pay six hundred thousand lira – or one hundred and eighty pounds – for a night with me and, although Ardy wasn't happy about it, he knew it was good money. Anger flickered inside me as the wine warmed my stomach. The old man had no idea that I had a pimp – he had made the arrangement with me after all – so he didn't know that Ardy was sitting outside spying on us. I didn't understand why: I was completely docile, I never argued with him, lied to him or held any money back. As far as he knew, I was a sheep who would follow him forever and he had long stopped waiting and watching while I worked.

Perhaps he guessed that this customer was different.

The old man had told me his name was Roberto. He was tall and slim with bad teeth and the smell of wine on his breath, but his house was warm and he was cooking me food. This was far better than being on the streets. If I closed my eyes for long enough I might almost believe I was safe.

'I'll just go and check the stove,' he said as he got up. My Italian was getting better and I had no trouble understanding him.

It felt strange to be in someone's home and stranger still that the old man was treating me like a friend. But I didn't say anything as I ate the pasta and cheese he made before bringing me a cup of coffee. Later he showed me around his house – there were three bedrooms, a sitting room, a kitchen and a cellar full of wine bottles.

Finally he opened the door to another room, a study with a camp bed in it.

'Come and lie down with me,' he said gently.

I realised that he did not want me in the room he'd once shared with his wife who he told me had died many years before – and, as soon as we lay down together, I realised too that we wouldn't be having sex. All he wanted was to be close to me and to touch me as I complimented him on how soft his skin was. He just wanted the comfort that a night with me could give him.

When I woke in the morning, I wondered for a moment where I was and then remembered. Roberto was still asleep and I dressed quickly and prepared to leave. At the door, I looked back at him. He was kind, his house was comfortable, he had given me a sense of peace. I knew he wouldn't hurt me. He was just lonely and wanted to feel as if he had someone in the world. I could understand that.

I slipped back and left the number of the mobile phone that Ardy had given me to take calls from him next to Roberto, hoping that he would ring me. I couldn't use the phone to contact home but it would be nice if just once I picked it up and someone other than Ardy was on the other end.

'Well?' Ardy snarled when I climbed into the car he had borrowed. He was cross from the cold, uncomfortable night he had spent. 'What was it like?'

I shrugged. I wasn't going to tell him the truth – it would only make him more suspicious. 'The usual. He wanted sex.'

'Where's the money?'

Ardy's irritation seemed to evaporate as he held the notes. 'Excellent,' he said. 'The old donkey is good for something, then.'

I was pleased when Roberto called me again, and made another arrangement for me to spend the night with him. This time Ardy didn't bother waiting outside. It was easy, eating his food, talking to him and then sleeping the night with him. Soon Roberto suggested that I stay the entire weekend with him, from Friday night to Monday morning and, although Ardy didn't like it because I was gone for more than two days, he couldn't refuse the money it earned him.

'What did you do? Where did you go?' he'd ask each time I got back to the hotel.

His nervousness hung in the air between us. He didn't want anything getting in the way of the power he had over me.

'We just stay inside. What do you think?' I would reply.

'Just remember that if you make any trouble then I can burn you in your bed with him,' Ardy would tell me. 'I have friends everywhere so don't get any ideas. We'll know what you've done and where you've gone if you run.'

I realised he was worried that I was making a companion who might help me to get away from him. It hadn't occurred to me that Roberto might be a way out – I had seen him simply as a small source of kindness in a life that was utterly without affection.

'I won't run,' I replied. 'I like being here with you, Ardy. You know that.'

I knew that it was important Ardy believed in my loyalty.

My time with Roberto did not make me happy – it simply made me less miserable. I was glad that at least I wasn't standing in the cold street and Roberto respected me – he said thank you after he'd touched me, cooked for me and never let me wash a plate. After a few weeks, he began to take me out. Sometimes he took me shopping for clothes or to a restaurant and one day he even took me into Venice. It was so beautiful – the big square with a huge church looking down over it, the shops selling masks, the boats floating on the water. It was like a magical place and, as I stared at it, I looked at other young women in the crowd. Were any of them like me? It was hard to believe that anyone else was as alone as I felt.

As the weeks passed, Roberto started asking questions. 'So who do you work for? Most of the foreign girls here work for Albanians.'

'There's no one,' I told him often, but I was sure that he'd guessed I was lying.

Roberto never pressed me though, and perhaps that was why I found myself telling him a little of my story as we sat together after dinner one evening.

Roberto didn't seem shocked. I think he'd met other girls like me. 'You mustn't be scared,' he said. 'You could live with me, I can help you.'

'No,' I replied. 'It would never work. Ardy knows who you are, where you live. He has many friends – they would never leave you alone and he would never let me go. He would sooner kill me than do that, I'm sure of it. Besides, I owe him money and he has threatened to hurt my children if I don't pay him back.'

Roberto looked sympathetic. 'I didn't realise you had children. Where do they live?'

I told him a little about Sasha, Pasha and Luda.

'You must miss them very much. How much do you owe?'

'Four thousand pounds.' As I said it, it seemed an impossible sum, more money than I could ever dream of.

Roberto sighed. 'I can't afford that. But at least let me send something home for your children. How long has it been since you spoke to them? You can use my phone to call your family.'

I gasped, speechless.

He smiled at me. 'Let me do this little thing to help you, Oxana. You've brought me a great deal of happiness and comfort since I've met you – you can't know how much. I'd like to repay you a little, not your boss. Okay?'

I looked at him. Money for the children would be wonderful but Ardy would kill me if he found out. I would also have to phone Ira to tell her the money was coming. It had been five months since I left Ukraine. What would I tell her?

'Will you let me do this for you?' Roberto asked quietly.

'Yes, thank you,' I managed to say at last. How could I refuse?

'Good. We'll do it tomorrow.'

The next day Roberto took me to the train station where there was a shop to transfer money. I didn't dare go in with him but sat in a fast-food café while he went. If

Ardy was watching and asked me what we were doing, I'd tell him we'd had lunch and Roberto had gone to the toilet.

'Here's the receipt,' he told me when he arrived back.

I stared at it. He'd done what he said. Two hundred dollars had been sent to Ira. Enough to feed my children for two months.

'Thank you. I'm very grateful. But you should take this,' I said as I handed back the receipt. 'I can't keep it. Ardy will find it.'

For the first time in months I felt happy as we drove back to Roberto's house. But I was also terrified. Not only was I scared of Ardy discovering what I'd done, but now I had to phone Ira and tell her the money was on its way. What would she say?

My hands shook slightly as I picked up the receiver and dialled the number. There was silence, hissing and finally a long beep, the sound of ringing.

'Hello?' a voice said.

Ira.

'It's me,' I whispered, but my voice could hardly be heard.

'Hello?' Ira said again.

'It's Oxana.'

There was silence.

'Where have you been?' Ira said at last. Her voice was so cold. 'Why haven't you called? The children have asked and asked after you. What's happened? It's been months and no word from you. We've been so worried.'

I held my breath for a second before swallowing. My mouth felt dry. 'I'm sorry,' I said. 'I've had some problems. I can't talk much now but I'm not in Turkey any more and I didn't have any money to call before.'

'But where are you, Oxana? What's happened?'

'In Italy.'

'Where?'

'Italy.'

'Oh my God.'

I swallowed hard again. 'I've found work as a cleaner. I'm earning good money. I sent you some today.'

'You're like a travelling frog – jumping from one place to the next,' Ira said, her voice softening a little. 'But why haven't you been in touch? We were so worried. We've missed you. Sasha has asked for you almost every day.'

Tears choked my throat as I thought of him. 'How is he?'

'Fine. They're both fine. Luda is doing well and Sasha doesn't like maths. But I didn't know what to tell them when they asked after you.'

I tried to speak but couldn't. It was as if a stone was weeping blood inside me.

'Are you really all right?' Ira said softly.

Still I couldn't speak as I tried to calm myself.

'Don't cry,' she whispered.

I took a deep breath and said quickly, 'I'm fine. I can't explain it all but I'm going to send money from now on. I promise you, Ira.'

'Do what you can,' she said before pausing. 'There's something I need to tell you, Oxana.'

'What?'

'Sergey is out of prison. He came and asked after you. The children weren't here so he didn't see them and I wouldn't tell him anything but he was asking a lot of questions.'

Fear clawed at my stomach. I shivered as I thought of Sergey and the promise he'd once made to find me.

'Don't let him see Sasha and Luda. Please keep him away from them.'

'I will. I promise you. But I don't think it's them he wants to see – it's you.'

'I know. Don't tell him anything.'

'Please don't worry. I told him you'd gone away and taken the children with you. I don't think he'll be back.'

Time was passing so quickly.

'Ira, I have to go but I'll call again as soon as I can. Kiss the children for me. Tell them I love them.'

'They're at Tamara's. You can call them there if you have some more money.'

She gave me the number and I put down the phone before picking it up again. I couldn't phone Pasha at his school but if there was a chance I could speak to Sasha or Luda then I had to take it, even for just a moment.

'Hello?' a child's voice said as the phone picked up.

'Sasha?'

'Yes.'

Suddenly I came alive again. After all those months of being dead, my heart started beating and I thought it would break. I wanted to reach down the phone line and hold my son close to me, remind myself that I really did exist, that I was Sasha's mother and not just a faceless whore.

'It's Mamma here,' I said.

'Mamma?'

'Yes, darling. It's me.' I could hear shouts in the background. 'Is that Luda?'

'Yes, she's playing outside. Where have you been, Mamma?'

'I've been working, darling. I'm sorry I haven't phoned you. But I've been very busy.'

'When are you coming home? Will you be here for New Year?'

'I don't know, Sasha. I've just started a new job and need to work to keep you warm, buy you food and presents.'

'But I want you to come home, Mamma.'

'I will, darling. As soon as I can.' I held my fist tight in a ball. I had to stop myself from crying. 'Darling, I must go now. I haven't got enough money to talk for long.'

'But will you call again?'

'Of course. Next weekend.'

'I love you, Mamma.'

'I love you too.'

The line went dead and I wanted to scream. All around me were the ghosts of Roberto's life – his wife, the love for her that he had to use a whore to feel – and, even though my children were living, they were just as unreachable.

I felt a hand on my shoulder.

'You can phone again next time you come,' Roberto said softly. 'And we will send more money too.'

'Thank you,' I said, trying to gulp my tears away.

My heart felt heavy as I walked into the living room to get my coat. Roberto's home was so warm – he was the one person who'd treated me like a real woman in all these long months. I felt sick as I thought of Ardy waiting outside and the streets I would soon be walking again.

But as I closed the door to Roberto's house, I forced myself to cling onto the glimmer of hope inside me now. Roberto had said he would help me again. His promise was like a warm flame glowing inside me as I got into the car.

'Where's the money?' Ardy snapped as I sat beside him.

'Here,' I said and handed it to him.

He didn't speak as he counted the notes and put them into his pocket before starting the car.

I closed my eyes and put my head back against the seat. I wanted to remember every moment of Sasha's voice, the sounds of Luda playing. In just a few days I would hear them again. Roberto had said he would help me and I knew he would keep his promise. The flame of hope flickered a little higher inside me. I had a secret now, something Ardy would never know and I would count the hours until Roberto called for me again.

We got to the hotel and climbed the stairs to our room. I wanted to lie down in the darkness so that I could taste my memories once more. But as I opened the door to the room, I saw it was bare. Our suitcases were standing next to the bed. I felt cold inside.

'What's going on?' I said as I turned to Ardy.

'We're leaving,' he snapped. 'There's been a police raid. It's too dangerous for us here now.'

Instantly I felt scared. I'd only seen police officers once soon after I'd arrived when they asked me what I was doing as I stood on the street. I'd told them I was waiting for a friend and they'd left me alone but Ardy had told me I would face prison for years on end if I were caught.

'Don't you know what they do to illegal immigrants in rich countries?' he'd said. 'If you're caught by the police I'll tell them you were a willing party and you'd be put in prison. Do you want to get a record as a prostitute? For everyone at home to know what you really are?'

It was my worst fear but I also knew I had to try and stay here – near to Roberto and the help he offered.

Surely you can handle some police?' I said in a rush. 'Business is good.'

'Shut the fuck up and do what you're told,' Ardy shouted. 'Now get moving.'

Fighting down the scream inside me, I walked to pick up my suitcase.

Another promise to my children broken – and Sasha waiting by a phone that would never ring.

Chapter Twenty-Five

Ardy gave me a hard look as he left the coffee shop opposite where I was standing in the snow. He'd been in there all night keeping watch on me as usual but now it was 11pm and the place was closing. He walked to the end of the road before turning the corner. I knew he'd be back soon to check on me.

My legs felt almost numb and I stamped my feet a couple of times. I was wearing red trousers and a jacket with black high-heeled boots but the soles were thin and it was so cold.

A car slowed down and I stared into the window.

A teenage boy shouted in my face: 'Dirty whore! How much for a fuck, huh?'

Laughter burst out from the car. The boy was with friends who enjoyed the way he shouted at me.

'Filthy slut!' he screamed as he drove off.

It happened a lot now that we'd moved to a town in the Dolomite mountains called Cavalese. We were staying with two of Ardy's friends. Their house was tiny and Ardy, one of the men and I shared a bed while the other man slept on the sofa. That wasn't the only change. It was clear that with other people around to watch us together, Ardy felt he had to show who was boss more than ever before. He puffed out his chest, acted the macho man and treated me like dirt in front of them, giving me scraps of food as an afterthought or ignoring me completely.

When we were alone, it was a different story. He was jealous and protective, as though worried that I would go off with one of the other men.

'Just remember that you're my woman,' he kept saying and had even started telling me sometimes that he loved me. 'When we've finished working we'll be together and I'll look after you and your children,' he'd say.

I would smile and try to hide the hate in my eyes. Why did he say such things? Did he want me to trust him, to believe in him? Or did he really think that I would want to be with him after everything he'd done to me? The idea that this man could come anywhere near my children made me feel sick inside. But while I longed to scream the words 'pimp' and 'whore' at him, I couldn't. I knew that I needed him until I could find some way out of this.

More than ever, he disgusted me. I could see how pathetic he was and I loathed the way he thought he was playing the man by treating me badly. I thought of Roberto, a gentleman who'd treated me decently, and knew that Ardy was a wretched human being, a cruel little boy with nothing good about him. When he asked for sex now, I always told him to move behind me. I didn't want him to see my face as I cried in the darkness.

'You're so good,' I'd say to try and make him finish even quicker.

I never took any pleasure from our intercourse, in fact I didn't know what an orgasm was – but neither did Ardy and, as I gave him compliments about what a man he was, I could see he was starting to believe I really had feelings for him. All I knew was that it was better for me if he did.

He had to. Once I'd believed that somehow Roberto would be able to help me but now I knew that no one ever would.

Cavalese was turning out to be a mistake.

It was not a place for women on the street and there were not enough customers. I only saw two or three men a night and the rest of the time had to stand silent as teenagers screamed insults.

I tried not to listen but it was hard. If people hate you for long enough then you start believing they are right. Ardy, the men and even just the ordinary people who passed me all said the same thing with their eyes: 'It's your fault you're here, no one else's. You're stupid, disgusting and ugly inside and out.'

Here in this small town, I began to feel as though I were really going mad. Ever since the rape it was as if I lived two lives every day – one inside my body and one outside it, the storm which I hid and the calm which I showed the world, the woman and the robot.

Most of the time, my feelings were shut away, hidden as far as I could put them, where they couldn't hurt me. But when I was alone, guilt and grief filled me. How had I let this happen to myself? When would I see my beloved children? Was I being punished by God for something I had done? Was I truly a terrible person who deserved this life?

Alone in the bathroom, I would turn on the shower before clenching my hands into tight fists and stuffing towels into my mouth as I screamed and screamed. Staring down at my body, I'd cry in disgust as I thought of all the men who'd taken it. I took shower after shower to wash away the dirt but it never went. This was my punishment.

There were moments now which almost scared me. I felt like I was losing my mind as I turned off the water, sat down on the floor and just stared into nothing, or talked to myself, trying to hold on to the person I once was.

'You need to be strong. You're a grown-up woman. Just another step, another day and soon it will end. You've got to keep going because you need to be ready when it does.'

At other times, I'd stare silently at the mirror – pulling my mouth into shapes, hitting my skin so I made bruises, pulling my hair or scratching myself. I felt almost as if I was on drugs, I just wanted to fall asleep and finish everything. Never wake up.

One day I was in such great despair that I did not see how life could be worth living when it was so full of pain, so I tried to kill myself by wrapping tights around my neck and tying them to a light socket. But the tights didn't hold after I kicked out a chair from underneath me and I laughed as I crashed to the floor. I was so dirty that even God didn't want me.

'Think of your children,' a voice would say when I thought like that. 'You must get home to them. Be a proper mother to Pasha again. How will they live if you leave them? You must be strong.'

Then Ardy would knock on the door and I'd know that I had to go back out to him again. Pulling on my clothes, I'd look in the mirror to calm my face, smile at my reflection and switch myself back off, like turning a button inside to become dead again.

The weeks went by. I'd been working for more than six months now. When Christmas came, and the Italians celebrated, I couldn't stop myself thinking of home. We didn't do that in Ukraine but I knew it was a time for children and it made me sad.

Now it was 13 January 2002 and I was standing on a deserted street. There was no one around and the town was quiet except for the bar across the road. My breath came out in white clouds as I stamped my feet to try and get some blood into them. Would there be any more customers tonight? It was getting late and everyone was probably in bed by now. It was so cold.

Tonight I could only think of home. Ukraine would be celebrating New Year tonight. It was our biggest celebration of the year and in three days it would also be my 26th birthday. I ached as I thought of Ira and the children. Would they remember me as they lifted their glasses to mark the New Year? Would they have made me birthday cards but wonder why I wasn't there to open them?

I put my hand into my pocket and felt the fifty euros lying there. The new currency had just come into use and my one customer had given me the note. I pictured having a drink as I stared at the door to the bar. Ever since coming to Cavalese, I'd been stealing wine from Ardy's friends because I liked the soft, warm buzz which filled me when I had it and now I wanted a drink as I thought of home. But I couldn't. Ardy would kill me if he found out I'd spent his money.

But as the minutes went by, I began to feel angry. Why shouldn't I have a drink when all my family were celebrating? Why should Ardy make me stand on this freezing street yet again when no one even wanted me? I'd had enough of following him like a shadow, doing everything he told me. Fuck it. I was going to have one drink and think of my family as I tasted it. If I was quick then he would never know.

Fear made me run and I burst through the door of the bar. It was quiet inside and there were just a few customers sitting drinking. The familiar voice of my favourite Italian singer filled the air and my heart beat a little slower. I'd come to love Eros Ramazzotti since being in Italy – his music was romantic, his voice lovely and he was so handsome. Just hearing him sing made me feel better.

The barman smiled at me as I walked towards him and sat down on a stool.

'Double whisky. No ice,' I said in a rush. I had to be quick.

The man said nothing as he poured my drink. I gulped it in one and immediately wanted another as the whisky burned my stomach.

'Again please,' I said.

Smoking cigarette after cigarette, I drank my next whisky and soon forgot Ardy as my head started to roll. 'Happy New Year,' I said to myself as I pictured Sasha, Pasha and Luda. Would this be the year when I'd finally pay off my debt and get back to them?

Suddenly Ardy was standing beside me looking furious. 'What the fuck are you doing?' he hissed in my ear.

I turned to look at him.

'Fuck off,' I said. 'There's a celebration in my country tonight. It's New Year so I'm celebrating it here.'

'Get out of here or you'll pay,' Ardy replied in a low voice and took my arm.

The cold air hit me as he dragged me outside and my head spun even more.

'How fucking dare you?' Ardy screamed. 'Are you trying to be clever?'

He reached out to slap me and I started laughing. The whisky had made my head feel so light, my heart so brave.

Why shouldn't he know I wasn't always going to be his sheep?

'Don't hurt me too much,' I said. 'If I go to work with bruises tomorrow then no one will want to take me. But if you don't mind that then you're welcome.'

Ardy's eyes blazed as he reached out and slapped me again. I laughed once more.

'Well, I won't be working tomorrow because I'll be bruised. Is that what you want?'

'You're drunk, you fucking whore,' he hissed. Then he said nothing as he grabbed me and dragged me home.

The next day, I woke up with a pounding head, terrified at what I'd done. All my bravado was gone. Everything inside me was shaking. I had never disobeyed Ardy before. What would he do? Sell me to his friends as he was always threatening?

My face ached where he'd hit me as I got out of bed to have a shower before sitting down to light a cigarette.

'How do you feel?' Ardy asked as he walked into the living room.

'I've got a headache,' I told him.

'So what happened last night?'

'What do you mean?'

'I mean, what the fuck were you doing? Don't you remember?'

'No.'

'Liar.'

'I'm not.' I opened my eyes wide and looked innocent. 'I don't. What happened?'

'You told me to fuck off.'

I stared at him, looking shocked. I had to make Ardy believe that I couldn't remember what I had done. He mustn't know that even for a moment I could remember disobeying him. 'Ardy, that's awful. I'm so sorry,' I whispered. 'I should never have said that. I don't know what happened but I'll never do it again.'

Ardy looked at me coldly. 'Do you mean it?'

'Yes.'

'Well, make sure you do,' he said. 'Because otherwise you'll regret it. Just think of your children and the trouble they could be in. I often think of that beautiful daughter of yours, Oxana. Maybe she could work for me as well. I'm sure she'll make a wonderful whore when the time comes.'

I turned my face away, sickened but trying to hide it. I must never lose control again.

Chapter Twenty-Six

'Come on, we're leaving.' Ardy threw my jacket at me one morning. 'Get packed.'

'Again?' I said, sitting up.

'This place is a shit hole. Business is terrible. We're not making enough. We're going somewhere better.'

'Where?'

'Wait and see.'

It was the end of January, and the countryside was cold and bare as we drove through it. We got a lift to a nearby city where we met Ardy's brother-in-law. He drove us for hours, passing signs for Austria and then Germany. Was that where we were going this time?

No one stopped us as we crossed the border into Germany. We were going to stay with Ardy's sister who lived in an apartment block near Frankfurt. She answered the door to us but looked less than pleased to see her brother and beckoned us in without a word. The flat was warm and homely, and I saw toys lying on the floor of the living room as we walked in. There was no sign of the children, however, as we sat down to eat. Ardy's sister banged dishes of food down in front of us. She looked angry, cold and I could see that she was unhappy.

'Why don't you take a shower?' Ardy said as soon as we'd finished eating, and I got up to go to the bathroom.

Without a word, the woman followed me and handed me some bleach. Silently she made it clear that I was to wash everything down once I'd used it.

I climbed under the hot water, washing away the day and the long journey. Then over the noise of the water, I heard shouting.

'Dirty whore!' I heard the woman scream. 'What the fuck is she doing here? I don't want her in my house. How long will you two be here?'

I couldn't make out any other words, and stayed in the bathroom until the voices had stopped. When I emerged, there were two little girls in the living room who smiled at me as I sat down. They looked about three and six, and soon the older girl walked up and started speaking in German. I didn't understand what she was saying and just smiled at her as she spoke but when Ardy's sister walked in and saw her daughter, she took both girls out of the room.

Later Ardy took me downstairs to the cellar of the apartment block and unlocked a door to a small room filled with boxes full of old clothes, tools and weights for training.

'This is where you'll sleep,' he told me and pointed to a camp bed lying on the floor. 'Use that. There's a duvet and pillow in the bag next to it.'

I stared at the damp, dark room. It had just one tiny window and was very cold.

'Sleep well,' Ardy said.

I stepped through the door and breathed in the smell of wet stone. Behind me the door closed and Ardy turned the key in the lock. I couldn't sleep that night as I lay on the camp bed. The duvet was so thin, I was cold and couldn't stop crying as I lay there. I knew I couldn't go on letting myself feel. I had to close myself down even more, become like ice inside and feel nothing. Only then would the pain stop.

I knew that Ardy's sister would not tolerate me in the flat, so it was no surprise when Ardy packed me into the car the next evening.

'You may as well earn some money while we're waiting,' he said roughly, though he didn't explain what we were waiting for.

He took me to a pub. I walked inside to see a stage with a pole on it and mirrors all around. There was also a bar with a staircase beside it leading upwards and a glitter ball hanging in the air which sent tiny squares of light dancing across girls lying on leather sofas in front of the stage. It was about 8pm and the place was empty so they were sitting chatting and smoking. They all wore sexy nightdresses – some with strips of material over their breasts and others with a deep V in front, no back and a diamond G-string peeping out. I couldn't hear what they were saying because the music was so loud. Ardy chatted to a woman who seemed to be in charge before turning to me.

'You're staying here for a while. Marya will tell you what to do. She knows you're not to be let out, so don't even think about it, okay? I'll be back in a few days.'

Then he walked off, leaving me staring after him. Much as I hated the sight of him, he was the only constant thing in my world and I was terrified as I saw him disappear.

'Come with me,' the woman said in Russian and I followed her.

She took me upstairs to a corridor with doors leading off it.

'This room will be yours,' she said as she opened one. 'You'll share it with another girl and if it's busy you'll have to use a different one.'

The room was small and clean with pink walls, a big bed and pictures of naked women on the walls.

'Do you have any clothes?' the woman asked.

'Just this,' I replied, gesturing to my trousers and coat. Ardy had kept my bag back at the flat.

'I'll get you something.' The woman left and returned a couple of minutes later with a red nightdress. 'Put this on,' she told me. 'Do you have any condoms?'

'No.'

She sighed and turned to leave again.

Alone, I took off my clothes and put on the nightdress before sitting down to wait. It was perfectly obvious this was a brothel and I'd be entertaining clients here. I felt a little nervous. This was all new to me. The woman hadn't said anything about money. Maybe we charged what we wanted and the customer gave it to us when we were alone. A tiny flame of hope flickered inside me – perhaps I might be able to keep some for myself.

The woman returned and gave me some condoms.

'You should go downstairs and meet the others,' she said and I followed her once again.

I felt nervous as I sat down with the women on the sofas. I hadn't really talked to anyone working like me before. I'd kept my distance from other girls in Venezia Mestre and there hadn't been any others on the street in Cavalese. I wondered what they would be like but soon I realised they were like those I'd met at Serdar's – young, Eastern European and nice enough. I began to relax as we chatted in the mixture of languages we had learned on our travels, smoked and waited in our nightdresses.

I was dreading the first customer but there was no one that first night. It was so quiet that only one or two of the girls had any business at all. The next night was the same. Ardy was furious when he came back to find that I had earned nothing in the two nights I'd been there. In the daytime I simply waited for the evening – I was not allowed out as some of the other girls were and had to stay in my room.

The evenings were not so bad. There was one thing I liked about the pub – we were allowed to drink and dance during the hours when we waited for customers and, as the music beat inside my head and vodka filled my veins, I could almost forget where I was. Just for a second, I'd close my eyes and remember being with Zhenya when I was free. But then the music would stop, I'd walk upstairs to my dirty room and know I was in prison again.

Business was very slow and I saw just a few customers. Ardy got more and more angry as he came to pick up my earnings and found there was little for him to take home.

'What are you doing here you fat cow?' he'd shout as he waited for me in the bar. 'All you need to do is sell yourself and you can't even do that. You're useless.'

A few days after I arrived, a new girl appeared with two men who spoke Turkish to the manageress as they discussed her. I understood them, and I realised at once that she was like me.

'Don't let her leave this place,' one said. 'Don't let her make phone calls. All her money comes to us.'

Later that day, I found the girl crying in the toilet.

'What's the matter?' I asked in Russian, but she didn't understand me, so I tried Italian. She spoke a little and managed to tell me that her name was Anna and that she was from Romania.

'I don't want to talk,' she said, burying her face in a paper towel but unable to hide her sobs.

'Why are you crying?' I asked. 'Maybe I can help.' I knew how it was. I could see how scared she was, how trapped. She was like an animal in a cage just like me. 'You're not the only one in this situation, you know,' I said softly.

Anna looked at me with fear in her eyes.

'I heard your pimp talking about you. I know you're a prisoner.'

'He's not my pimp,' she said in a rush.

'Don't worry, you don't have to pretend with me. I know what's going on.'

'Don't,' she hissed, looking terrified. 'You'll get in trouble if you talk to me. I'll be punished if they find out I've told you anything.'

'There's no one here and who will know what we've said to each other? All I'm saying is that I'm the same as you. I trusted a friend, and now I'm here and I can't escape because I have children, and they'll be in danger if I do. I know you're unhappy but you have to keep going. Try and talk to the other girls, make some friends. You won't be okay here if you don't make friends and it's better than being on the streets. At least we're warm and safe.'

'Couldn't we escape?' she said, her eyes huge and hopeful.

I almost wanted to laugh as I looked at her. She hadn't been beaten into submission yet, as I had. 'We've got pimps,' I said. 'And they won't let us go anywhere. Don't you know that by now? There's no point in fighting. You've just got to accept what you are and hope that one day it will end.'

That night Ardy arrived to take his money. He came over to me, folding the notes into his pocket. 'It's your last night here,' he said casually. 'We're ready for the next stage.'

'The next stage?' I echoed. 'What's that? Where are we going?' I wondered what new tortures Ardy had in mind for me.

'Didn't I tell you?' He smiled gleefully. 'We're going to England.'

I was speechless and could only gaze up at him in astonishment.

He nodded, obviously pleased with himself. 'Yup. That's where we'll get rich. I've spoken to people there and they say there are lots of illegals. There's big money to be made. Everyone says it's the easy way to go.'

England. I knew of it, but very little, and almost didn't care where I was going now. I wouldn't see the country I was in. Once again, I'd be locked in a room or on a street with Ardy watching me and all I'd know of it was the men who paid for me. It was just another place for me to be in prison.

'When are we going?' I asked. A shudder ran over me but I tried to hide it. Most of my journeys over the last year or so had been ordeals and I feared another perilous voyage, chased by police, caught in lights and a hail of bullets, or tipped overboard into icy black water.

'Relax.' Ardy saw my expression. 'We're going tomorrow. It'll be fine. It's all arranged.'

After he'd gone, Anna came over to me. 'Was that your pimp?'

I nodded. 'He's taking me to England tomorrow.'

Anna looked stricken. I was her only friend here and now she was losing me. 'Can't I come with you?' she pleaded. 'Can't you ask Ardy? I don't want to stay here without you. I'm scared.'

'No way,' I exclaimed. 'If you come with me then you'll just swap one pimp for another.'

'But I can't stay here alone. I'll kill myself. He beats me. I can't stand it anymore.'

I looked at Anna. She was so young and afraid and, while I hated Ardy, at least he didn't beat me too often. 'Okay, I'll see what I can do.'

The next day I was ready for Ardy when he arrived, and Anna was with me, also ready to travel.

'Who's this?' Ardy said suspiciously.

'My friend Anna. She wants to come with us.'

He stared at her. Anna smiled and looked eager to please him. 'Why?'

'She hates her boss. She wants to escape him.'

Ardy frowned. It was a dangerous business to take someone else's woman but I could see his mind working. Later I learned that a buyer in England sent him money for Anna which he used to pay off her pimp. The rest he kept to pay our fares. All I knew then was that Anna was happy when he told her she could come with us.

'Thank you,' she said, delighted.

What a world, I thought, where a woman is grateful to be taken to a foreign country where she'll be forced into prostitution.

'Come on,' grinned Ardy. 'Next stop, England.'

Chapter Twenty-Seven

The car park was quiet as we walked towards the lorry. We'd been hiding in a ditch near a motorway service station just outside Brussels for hours and neither Anna nor I were carrying anything with us – we'd had to leave it all behind. About fifty people had waited in the darkness as two men led groups of six away. Then it was our turn.

'Money,' the man said when he came to get us and the other men in our group handed him five hundred euros each.

'It's a thousand for them,' he said as he pointed to Anna and me. Ardy handed him some money.

He led us into the huge car park where lorry after lorry was parked. Everything was still and silent as the men lifted up a tarpaulin covering the side of one and jumped in.

'Come on,' Ardy said as he dug me in the back.

I looked up and saw one of the men holding out his hands towards me. I took them and he dragged me upwards. Once inside, all I could see was the outlines of huge wooden crates. Each one came up to about my waist. Anna was pulled up behind me.

'Come,' a man said as he climbed up beside us and started moving forward, squeezing in between crates to get to the front.

We followed him without a word until the men stopped, took off the lid of a crate and started unpacking it. Staring down in the darkness I saw it was full of car hubcaps.

'Get in,' the man said.

My heart started pounding as I looked down but Anna didn't seem worried as she climbed over the side so I had to follow. The man gestured for us to lie down and we curled up like babies in a mother's womb – nose to nose, forehead to forehead, as he started reloading the crate.

Panic rose in me as we were packed in. It was so dusty. I couldn't breathe and I moved my head a couple of inches to bury my nose and mouth in my jacket. But I felt more and more afraid as the weight of the hubcaps pressed down. I could feel Anna's breath on my face, was sure that soon we'd run out of air in this tiny space. I was finally going to die here. The blood beat louder and louder in my ears as I started crying. I would never get out of here.

Sometime later I heard the lorry's engine start up and the sound filled the air. We were on the move. We were going to England. But would anyone find us hiding in our wooden tombs?

The journey was the most terrible I had yet endured. It seemed to go on for eternity. There was nothing to eat or drink, no way to go to the toilet. We could only lie in our tiny prison, hoping that we would let out before we died. The roar of the engine and the smell of fuel and metal were sickening, and the only way to cope with it was to sink into a kind of unconsciousness, a half-sleep. Vivid dreams passed through my mind, stories of horror and confusion from which I would wake suddenly, realise where I was and then sink back into the strange world of my mind. All I could be sure of was that I was going yet further away from my children.

At one point I woke suddenly and realised that the engine had stopped. I heard muffled voices and I was sure I could make out the sound of water nearby. Were we on a ferry or a boat? Now I wondered if we would be tipped overboard to drown in our tiny coffin. How long had I been here? Would I ever see daylight again?

There seemed to be no space at all between Anna and me. The air was fetid and damp as we were pressed together, our clothes hot and sticky with sweat. We didn't speak to each other. I didn't even know if she was awake although I could feel her breath on my face. What could we say? After a while there was another engine sound, except further away, and that lasted several more hours. Then, with a roar that made me jump, the lorry spluttered into life and we were moving again.

I had lost all sense of time and place. I had even begun to lose faith that this journey would ever come to an end, when the engine abruptly stopped. There were voices and loud noises that came closer and closer until the lid of the crate was lifted off, the hubcaps unloaded and we climbed out of a hole cut into the side of the lorry tarpaulin. Once again we found ourselves standing in a service station car park at night.

'We're going to Birmingham,' said Ardy.

I stared at a girl standing in a shop window as we stopped at traffic lights. She had a ring in her lip, black eye make-up and tattoos covering her arms. Her hair was blue, red, yellow and green.

'What kind of shop is that?' I asked Ardy.

'A tattooist.'

'A whole shop just for that?'

'Yes of course. This is England.'

I couldn't take my eyes off the world outside as the car drove on. Houses standing side by side with no space between them, old men with walking sticks, women pushing prams and people who looked as if they'd come from Bollywood films. Then there was the girl in the window. She was like a cockerel with her multi-coloured hair. I stared out at the huge red buses, supermarkets so big they could fit an army inside, and beautiful buildings including a church and a restaurant with a red and gold roof like the tiers of a skirt.

Anna sat beside me – as silent as she had been during the whole of our journey to England.

We'd arrived two days ago and now we were staying with three of Ardy's Albanian friends. Valdrim was a builder, Florim worked in a garage and then there was Defrim, the man in charge. I didn't like him from the moment I saw him: there was anger in his eyes.

'You girls are going shopping,' he had told us roughly. 'You're starting work tonight. You need some clothes.' He looked over at Anna. 'I'm your boss now, okay? So do as I tell you.'

I'd felt my heart sink. I knew Ardy would sell Anna as quickly as he could, to get some money. I had a feeling he owed money for our trip here to England. That was probably why we were going to start working immediately, with no time to recover from the nightmarish experience we had undergone.

Defrim drove us into a huge car park before we all got out and walked into a shopping centre. My mouth gaped open and I stared as we went inside. It was incredible, I'd never seen anything like it – it was so big and bright.

Lights and noises filled the air as we walked past shops filled with clothes, shoes, cosmetics, books, food, televisions, ice-cream and sweets. I could not believe my eyes: I'd never seen so many luxuries and such abundance in one place. The people in England must be very rich, I thought, if they could afford to shop here every day. Surely it was expensive! But ordinary people were walking about holding bags full of shopping.

Now I could understand why Ardy wanted to come here.

My eyes were caught by all the hundreds of beautiful things I could see. There was even a shop that sold only perfume, and I longed to go into it and luxuriate in the wonderful scents, but Defrim hurried us on. He shepherded us into a brightly lit dress shop.

I couldn't stop myself from gasping as I walked inside. It was like a dressing room in a theatre filled with wigs, feather boas, dresses covered in sparkles and stones. It was beautiful. Anna and I stayed in the changing rooms while the men brought us dresses to put on and watched critically as we stood in front of them. I knew that these clothes were investments for them, simply to make us more attractive to customers, but nevertheless I got some pleasure from trying them on. For a moment I could pretend I was an ordinary girl on a shopping trip with her boyfriend, being treated to a pretty dress because it made her look gorgeous.

The dresses were beautiful, and so were the shoes Defrim bought me. They looked like they were made of glass and had huge heels with a platform sole and straps around the ankles decorated with flowers. Later I found out that they cost £95 – more than many people in Ukraine made in four months.

'Now you're ready to start work,' Ardy said as we left.

My pleasure vanished. Just for an instant, as I gazed around the shop filled with colour and light, I'd almost forgotten what I was here to do.

'Do you speak English?' the woman said, staring at me.

I was in a sauna somewhere in Birmingham city centre with Ardy and Defrim. They'd talked to the woman behind reception before leaving and now she was looking at me.

'Small,' I said. I had picked up a few words of English during my travels but it was hard to understand what the woman was saying to me.

'What is your name?'

'Alexandra,' I lied.

'Here are the prices,' she said and handed me a piece of paper.

It read: '30 minutes = £45; 60 minutes = £80.'

'Jacuzzi?' the woman asked and smiled brightly at me.

I didn't understand.

Without a word, she led me out of reception and down a corridor where she opened a door to a room. There was a big bath in it which started bubbling after the woman pressed a button.

'Jacuzzi,' she said, pointing at the water before writing on another bit of paper. She showed it to me.

'30 mins = £55; 60 minutes = £100'

I nodded to show that I understood. 'Okay.'

'Now here's what you do in the time they pay for,' she continued. 'Shoulder massage.' She flexed her hands in front of me and laughed. 'Blow job.' She bobbed her head up and down. 'Sex.' She pulled her elbows to either side of her waist. 'Always condom. Money before sex.'

'Okay.'

After showing me the three rooms where I would take clients and a book that I had to fill in each time I did, the woman took me back to reception. By now it was full of girls speaking English. Five were white, two were black and one looked Asian. Later I found out she was from the Philippines but for now all I could see was that she thought she was the boss. She laughed too loudly as she spoke to customers, looked at the other girls out of the corner of her eye and, even though I didn't understand English, I knew she was talking about me as I sat and waited for somebody to choose me.

'Freak,' she said.

I didn't know what the word meant but it sounded like the Albanian for scared. Anger filled me. I wasn't scared. Who was she to say that about me? She didn't know me at all.

'No freak,' I said as I looked at her.

The woman turned around and stared at me. 'Oh yeah?' She started laughing and turned to the man beside her. 'She's a freak all right.'

Twenty minutes later a man arrived and my new job began. I could tell that this was different to my work on the streets. The men here seemed to want something more than the ones in cars who took five minutes getting what they wanted. My first customer was an American in a suit.

'You don't know what you're doing,' he'd snapped as I took him in my mouth.

I'd soon learn how to make them feel like they were getting their money's worth, even if men like him had taken too many drugs to finish what I started for them.

* * *

Anna didn't come with me to the sauna that first night because she had her period but it soon finished and we worked together. Our shifts lasted about twelve hours, and Ardy and Defrim would always be waiting in the car when we walked outside into the dawn. Anna was much more popular than me because she was younger, prettier and slimmer. I understood that but Ardy didn't and rang reception at least three times a night to see how many customers I'd had and again at the end of the shift to find out exactly how much I'd made. After a quiet night I'd walk down the stairs knowing he would be angry with me.

I knew customers didn't like my attitude. As each day passed I could feel a new emotion uncurling deep in my heart – an anger so powerful that I forgot everything else. I hated all the men who came to buy me. Night after night they walked into the sauna – young, old, fat, thin, rich, poor – and hot, liquid rage twisted my stomach. At first it was just one rebellious piece of my heart which felt like that but it quickly got worse and soon only a few customers wanted me. A couple even walked out seconds after I took them into the room.

'She can't speak fucking English and she's a miserable cow,' they shouted as the other girls laughed.

I had some regulars of course – a young Pakistani man who stank of smoke and a man so fat that he couldn't lie on top of me to have sex – but I wasn't earning as much as Anna. She was popular with customers and the girls didn't like it. Anna didn't care and she didn't try to fit in. I wanted to make friends and knew we had to be careful because the English girls had rights in their country which we didn't have, and they could make trouble for us. But the atmosphere just got worse as the girls disappeared in groups together to take cocaine and smoke cannabis.

'Don't tell me the fucking Queen of Romania actually bleeds?' they shrieked if Anna was off for a couple of days but I said nothing.

Things exploded one night when the Filipino girl ordered me to open the front door when the bell rang. I might not understand much English but I knew what she was saying.

'No,' I told her. I wasn't her servant.

'Just go,' she screamed as she walked over to push me.

I pushed her back but another girl quickly stepped in between us and I sat down again. Aggression made my hands shake as I lit a cigarette but I did nothing. Suddenly, though, the Filipino girl was shouting at Anna and no one stopped them as they started clawing and hitting each other.

The problems, however, didn't end at the sauna. Anna had changed as the weeks passed in England and, where once she'd told me her dreams for the future as we whispered in bed at night, she now hardly talked to me. I knew she liked Defrim and, like a spider in its web, could see that he was drawing her to him. I was worried for her because I knew that the last woman he'd owned had ended up dead. Ardy had told me after I'd found a photo of the two of them one day when I was cleaning. He'd said Defrim had come to England with the woman and she'd worked in the same sauna as Anna and me, but she'd died in a car accident when Defrim was driving and he'd never got rid of his sadness and anger at losing her. A cold feeling spread in my chest as Ardy talked. If Defrim would even sell a woman he truly loved to make money, then he could never be trusted.

But Anna just got angry when I tried to warn her that Defrim only wanted her to make him money.

'Oh, look who's talking,' she snapped. 'You're no better. You and Ardy used me to get here. You sold me to get the money to reach England.'

'But you know I had nothing to do with it,' I cried. 'He's just using you like Ardy uses me. Is it love to sell someone like he does every night?'

Anna said nothing as she walked out of the room and I knew that our friendship was at an end. I could never trust her now that she'd fallen in love with her pimp. She'd crossed a line which would separate us forever.

Chapter Twenty-Eight

Ardy and I never spoke about my debt even though I gave him all the money I made. I'd started writing everything down and knew I'd paid him about £2000 – nearly half of what I owed – but a few weeks after arriving in Birmingham, I heard something at the sauna which scared me. The women were talking about other foreign girls they knew like me and thought I couldn't understand what they were saying. Hearing English every day had helped me learn quickly though and I was shocked when I heard them say that some girls like me worked for years. I thought about it again and again until one morning I got into bed beside Ardy after work.

'It won't be long before I can leave you,' I said. 'Because soon my debt will be paid.'

He looked at me suspiciously. 'What do you mean?'

'Well, I've given you so much money.'

'But none of your debt is paid off.'

'I don't understand.'

'It's easy. The money you've given me has covered your rooms and food that's all. You haven't paid back any of your debt. You've just covered your costs and kept your children safe. Anyway, you shouldn't think about that so much. Soon we'll be able to buy a house and car, and bring your children here to the UK.'

I felt sick as he pulled me to him. Did he really believe that we would be together for years? Everything I'd done was to protect my children from him – not bring him closer to them.

'Come on, baby,' Ardy said as he started touching me and I lay like a dead body under his hands.

I couldn't stop thinking about what Ardy had said. I'd been so stupid again. He'd never let me go. I just wanted to scream at clients as they touched me, beat Ardy as he lay next to me, but I was as trapped as ever. I was either locked in the house or the sauna, Ardy's Albanian friends were everywhere, the sauna knew he was my pimp and told him exactly what I made, and my children needed to be protected.

The only good thing in my life was Jackie, a woman who worked with me. The other girls looked down on me because I had a pimp, but Jackie was different. We had started talking when I saw her looking at a photo one day.

'Who's that?' I asked.

'My son,' she told me, and held out the picture. The baby was so sweet with blond hair, blue eyes and fat cheeks.

'He's beautiful!' I exclaimed. 'What a pretty baby.'

She smiled. 'Do you have children?'

I didn't know what to say. I never spoke about them to anyone at work. But I could see as I looked at Jackie that she was just one mother asking another about her children.

'Yes,' I replied. Slowly I told her a few things about my children and then about myself, and soon we became friends. Jackie was a single mother who'd started working in the sauna because she couldn't survive on government money, like a lot of women I met who wanted to give their children something better and sold themselves to do it. I talked to her about Sasha and Luda, and a little about Pasha, but I couldn't tell her everything – she would never understand.

'One day we'll all be together again,' I told her, but I stopped myself talking about the children too much because otherwise I knew I would drive myself crazy just as I had in Italy.

I was expert now at shutting off my emotions. I didn't cry or scream in the bathroom anymore – I hadn't done that for a while. Instead, whenever I felt sad I'd just drink two double vodkas at the sauna to make me feel better. I didn't allow myself to think about my children and most of the time it worked, but there were still days when I'd see women with children as Ardy and Defrim took me to work and I'd have to turn my head away as I pushed down tears.

Talking to Jackie brought the faces of my children back into my mind. The pain was almost unbearable when I realised that it was now a year since I had seen them. I longed for them desperately and I kept remembering the promise I'd made to phone home again. The last time I'd called was nearly four months ago from Roberto's house. But how could I ever keep my promise?

'Do you know how I'd make a telephone call?' I asked Jackie one day. 'I don't have a mobile.'

Ardy had taken back the phone I'd had in Italy soon after we'd left.

'Use the pay phone in the lobby,' Jackie said. 'You'll need a phone card, though. I can buy you one if you like. Just give me the money.'

The only money I had was the five pounds Ardy gave me every day for food. Could I use that without him finding out? I trembled to think about it but knew it was the only way I'd be able to have any contact with home, so I had to take the risk.

One night, with the phone card Jackie had bought me, I dialled Ira's number with shaking fingers.

'It's me, Oxana,' I said as she picked the phone up.

Ira gasped. 'Oxana! Where have you been?'

'I'm so sorry. It's difficult. I'm in England now.'

'What? But why are you there?'

'Working.'

'Where?'

'In a bar.'

'Oh,' said Ira.

I knew she didn't believe me but I couldn't tell her the truth. I could never tell anyone how stupid I'd been. No one at home could know.

'How are the children?' I asked quickly.

'They're fine, they're all well. They still miss you. Some people from Pasha's school came looking for you not long ago. They wanted to know why you hadn't been to see him and to tell you that he'll be moving school soon.'

'What did you say?'

'That you were working abroad.'

'Did they say where he was going?'

'No.'

'So we don't know where he is?'

'No.'

I couldn't speak for a moment. Then I managed to say, 'How are Sasha and Luda?'

'Well, they need money to be looked after, Oxana,' Ira replied, her voice hardening with anger. 'It's been months now without any.'

'I know,' I whispered.

'What are you thinking? I've borrowed money to pay Tamara but I can't pay anymore. Why don't you send money? Why don't you call?'

'I can't explain it all. I've had problems. Please be patient just a little longer Ira. I'll get some money to you. I'm waiting for wages.'

'Well, I've borrowed two hundred dollars so far and I can't do it again.'

I felt so ashamed. It was a lot of money for someone who earned just $70 a month. 'Thank you so much Ira for all you've done. I promise to get money to you.'

'What will I tell Tamara?'

'Tell her the money will be coming soon. I have to go now, Ira. I'll call again when I can. Please believe me, I'm doing all I can. I think of you all every day. Give the children my love and a big kiss from me. I have to go. Goodbye.'

I put the phone down. Now I had made a promise and I did not know how I could ever keep it.

We had been in Birmingham for a month or two, and England was beginning to seem less strange to me. I was learning English quickly – it was all I had to do when the nights were quiet. I was still not popular with the other girls or with the clients, but I had Jackie to talk to when neither of us were working, and books and magazines that lay around to read.

My days were very shut off and quiet. I hardly ever went out, as I was locked in the house most of the time. Once or twice Defrim took me to the supermarket to help with the shopping but I was always closely watched to make sure I would not escape. I sensed that Ardy and Defrim were less in control in England than they might have been elsewhere: the city was so big and so full of people, it would be easy to disappear here. So they kept a close watch on Anna and me.

In the house during the day I cleaned and cooked. Then one of the men would take me to work for most of the night. From the early hours until just before midday, I slept. Then my slavery began again.

It would have been unbearable but for one thing: the promise I had made to Ira had given me hope. I had something to work for now. Somehow I would get her money so that my children could be looked after.

I listened to check everything was quiet before pulling out the dressing table from the wall. Ardy was downstairs but he'd come back up to the bedroom soon so I had to move quickly. Bending down, I searched with my fingers for the gap I'd cut between two sheets of wallpaper. When I found it, I slid a £5 note inside. The money would be hidden there until I wanted it again.

Excitement bubbled up as I moved the dressing table back into place. I'd started saving my tips a couple of weeks ago and already had about £60. Before then I'd always given the extra five or ten pounds that customers sometimes gave me at the end of an appointment to Ardy. But now I'd started hiding some of the secret money and putting it in my bra or shoe until I got home. Ardy was so relaxed with me, so certain that I'd never give him any trouble, that he didn't even watch me get undressed anymore. After all these months, he thought that I'd accepted what I was and that I was now tamed. My spirit had been broken.

But since my conversation with Ira, a part of me had awoken. There was hope, there was a chance – I just had to seize it and do whatever I could to make it happen. I was a mother and must do everything within my power to help my children. I did not know where Pasha was, but one day I would find him. Meanwhile, I would help Sasha and Luda. Slowly, slowly I would carry on saving until I had enough to send back home. I wouldn't phone again until I could fulfil my promise. I would deny myself the chance until I could provide.

I felt scared but excited as I hid the money. I needed more customers to get more tips and to do that I tried my hardest to please them – looking them in the eyes, smiling when they spoke to me and flattering them as they touched me. I didn't think about the fat man or any of the others as they pushed into me. I just thought of the money hidden behind the wallpaper.

Everything was quiet as I stood up and looked at the dressing table. Smiling to myself, I walked towards the shower.

'Take everything off,' Ardy said quietly.

I'd just got back from work and he had followed me upstairs.

'What do you mean?'

'I said take everything off.'

'But why?'

'I just want to see you.'

Ardy was angry. I didn't know what to do. There was £15 hidden in my bra. Did he know about the money behind the wallpaper?

'I'd like to tell you something,' I said in a rush. 'I got tips today.'

'Really?'

'Yes.'

'Just today?'

'Yes.'

'Hmm,' he said as he looked at me. 'Well, do you know what also happened today? I found some money.'

'Really? Where?'

'Behind the wallpaper. There were marks on the carpet in front of the dressing table and I realised it had been moved so I had a look.'

'That's strange,' I said. 'Where did it come from?'

Without a word, Ardy punched me and pain exploded in my face as I flew backwards.

'What are you doing?' I screamed.

'You're asking why? You fucking bitch.' He grabbed my hair before pulling me to the dressing table and opening a drawer. The notes I'd saved were lying in it.

'This is why,' he shouted. 'This is your money isn't it? Do you think I haven't noticed how happy you've been? That Defrim and Anna haven't seen it too? Do you think we're fucking stupid?'

He punched me again and anger bit inside me. I had to think quickly.

'What are you doing?' I screamed. 'It was for your birthday. It was for you.'

'What?'

Ardy suddenly let me go and I felt blood trickle down my face as I looked at him beseechingly. 'Yes, your birthday or don't you have one? I know it's in a few months but I wanted to get you something nice. A surprise.'

Confusion washed across his face. 'So what did you want to get me?'

'I saw something.'

'Where? You never go out.'

'At the supermarket one day. Defrim took me.'

'What?'

'A surprise.'

'Really? What?'

I stared at him. I could hardly remember what I'd seen. I knew there were clothes there.

'A jacket,' I said in a rush. 'And a watch.'

'I didn't see watches.'

'Well, there were.' I didn't know for sure. Surely he wasn't stupid enough to believe me? I held my breath as Ardy looked at me.

'Okay,' he said uncertainly. 'But you're going to show me the shop.'

'Okay. I'm telling the truth. I wouldn't lie to you.'

'Well, you were hiding money from me.'

'I was but for a good reason and now you've found it I won't be able to surprise you,' I said as I started to cry. 'Why didn't you ask before punching me?'

'I was angry.'

'You won't get a present now,' I said quietly as I walked towards the bathroom to wipe my nose.

Bending down to the sink, I splashed water on my face to wash away the tears. How could I have ever believed I'd be able to keep a secret? Ardy would watch me even more closely now and I knew I wouldn't be able to try anything again. Just like Serdar, he was too clever for me. I just had to survive – feel nothing and wait for the day when it would end. One day it had to.

Chapter Twenty-Nine

We left Birmingham soon after that night.
'Everybody tells me there's better money to be made in London,' Ardy said as we packed. 'There are hundreds of saunas there, and not enough police to make trouble. They say it's easy.'

I hid my sadness. I would be losing my friend Jackie and with her, the ability to phone home. How would I be able to get a phone card without her? I wished I'd called the children while I had the chance – now it was taken from me. I was glad though to leave Anna and Defrim behind – the sight of them together was unpleasant for me. I knew there was nothing I could do to save her.

We took the bus through the night from Birmingham to London where we were met by another of Ardy's contacts. He took us to a studio flat where we'd be staying. My heart sank when we walked in. It was tiny with a cooker in one corner and a shower and toilet in a cupboard in the other. I'd never get away. I'd be with Ardy every moment I wasn't working. At least in Birmingham I'd been alone sometimes.

'Don't worry,' Ardy told me. 'It's only for a couple of weeks. We'll soon make enough to put down a deposit on a house.'

I almost laughed. Apparently I'd only earned enough to pay for my food and rooms – the miserable cheap food and the disgusting shared rooms I'd endured – and yet, soon 'we' would have enough to buy a house.

Later his friend took us to a massage parlour in Tottenham where I asked for work. Ardy couldn't go in with me because the parlour had three rules – no pimps, no alcohol and every girl had to wear a knee-length uniform which looked like a nurse's. Ardy was very happy when I told him I would start the next day.

A Russian girl called Nastya showed me round when I went back to start work. There were five rooms to see clients in and each had a massage table but no bed.

'It keeps the parlour looking legal like that,' she told me. 'If anyone official asks then we just give massages and nothing more. Customers get half an hour. Ten minutes for massage, five minutes for oral and the rest for sex. If he doesn't want massage then try to think of something else otherwise you'll be having sex for half an hour and it's horrible. You get all sorts here – Turkish, English, black, white, brown.

'Half an hour costs forty-five pounds and the customer pays you. You give thirty of that to reception, twenty for the second customer and after that you pay just ten pounds per client. You'll also have to do shifts in different places. Men like seeing new girls and the British woman who owns this also has three others around London where you'll work sometimes.'

'Where are the other girls from?' I asked.

'Everywhere – Moldova, the Czech Republic, Slovakia, Romania, Slovenia, Albania, Bosnia, Serbia and a few English,' Nastya said as we turned to leave.

We went back to reception where girls were waiting on leather sofas and a man sat at a table.

He obviously wasn't a customer. He looked like a pimp and introduced himself as Ali.

'Do you speak any other languages?' he asked me.

'Yes, Turkish.'

'We'll call you Aysel,' he said excitedly. 'Turkish men like a woman from home.'

Ali got up and started dialling on his mobile as I sat with the women. I didn't speak much and neither did they as we waited for men to come in, look us over and pick one of us.

About 11pm my first customer arrived – he was a small, fat Kurd who smelled of kebabs and sweat. I felt sick as I took him to the room and explained the prices.

'I'll give you thirty-five pounds,' he said when I'd finished.

'No,' I said. 'This isn't a market. The price is forty-five.'

'But that's no good. Thirty-five's fair. It's all I've got.'

I looked at him. I wasn't going to fuck anyone for nothing. 'Then I'm going to talk to Ali,' I said as I walked out of the room and slammed the door. 'He wants to get the price down and I'm not going to do it,' I said as I walked into reception.

Ali looked at me. I could see he knew exactly what the man was like and had wanted to find out what I'd do. 'Okay,' he said. 'Just tell him it's forty-five pounds.'

I did but the man couldn't agree to anything. I massaged him and he wanted more, I asked him to sit up and he turned around to try and hug me. He smelled of urine and there was hair all over his back, chest and stomach.

'Get your hands off me,' I said as he tried to grab me.

'But don't you want a kiss?' he asked.

'No, I'm not your wife.'

'Oh, come on. You do really.' He kept touching me as I stood beside him. 'I just want a kiss,' he whined. 'Can't you just give me a kiss?'

'No,' I almost shouted. 'I can't and I won't.' I pushed him away. He was like a dog trying to lick a bone as he kept reaching for me. 'Just take your fucking money back,' I told him. 'I've had enough.'

But he refused and we were still arguing half an hour later when Ali knocked on the door to say our time was up.

'She's a bitch,' the man said as I followed him into reception. 'She wouldn't do a thing. Where did you get her from? So fat and old.'

I wanted to scream as I looked at Ali.

'He wanted extra massage,' I said in a low voice. 'Then he tried to kiss me and I wouldn't do it.'

'All right, all right,' Ali replied. 'I'll sort it out. Don't worry – you've got a busy night. There are other customers waiting for you.'

Five men were sitting on the sofas. I looked down at my hands. They were covered in oil and hair.

'Get moving,' Ali hissed.

The next customer had come from a casino where he'd won some money. He wore a suit, was in his twenties and was very handsome.

'Don't touch me, don't kiss me, just one position and no changing,' I told him as we walked into the room.

He had to understand. I wasn't a woman to touch and caress. I was just a hole to be paid for. A thing. That's all he would get.

I didn't have time for a shower, coffee, glass of water, food, cigarette or even the toilet that first night and didn't finish until 7am as customer after customer came to see the new girl. Ali knew many people who liked Turkish girls and I saw thirteen men, one after the other for seven hours. At first I looked after them properly – I was like a robot as I did their massage, bent down to them, lay back for them and got up off the bed to start my job again. But slowly anger built up inside me and I was almost rough with the men by the time morning came. I pinched their skin and didn't smile or look at them as their bodies moved above me.

Ardy was so impatient by the time I walked out onto the street that he asked to see the money then and there. Usually he waited until we were hidden inside.

'Good, good,' he said excitedly as he took it. 'They were right, London pays much better.'

I said nothing. I had pain like the pain of childbirth in my stomach and thought I would fall down. I wondered if I would ever wash the stink of that night away and all I could think about was sleep. But after I'd had a shower and got into bed, I felt Ardy's hand reach out to touch me.

'Are you crazy?' I asked him.

'Just a blow job,' he said.

'No.'

'Oh, come on.'

'Please, please don't touch me.'

Ardy turned over and left me alone that night but I had to do as he wanted when I woke up the next morning. Afterwards I turned over and closed my eyes again. I could still feel pain deep inside me and knew the night wasn't far away. For now I'd hide in sleep and let blackness wash over me.

* * *

The days that followed were the same. I felt like dying by the time Ardy picked me up. I just wanted to lie down, close my eyes and dissolve the anger racing in my veins. A strange thing had happened to me since the night we'd arrived in London. Perhaps it was because Ardy had discovered my stash of money and destroyed my hopes again, but more and more the deadness inside me was being replaced by anger. I could not get rid of the feeling. Rage boiled inside me constantly and it was all I could do to control it. At work I'd sit on top of customers and imagine putting a pillow over their faces or plunging a knife into their hearts. They made me sick. Some were rich men who would have looked down on a woman like me in public; others didn't care that they were dirty as they took off underpants stained brown and they didn't even bother washing me off their skin before going home to their wives.

Putting a condom on them, I'd close my eyes and switch off my mind so I wouldn't have to see, taste or smell them. But I hated them more and more. It was as if the feeling inside me just kept growing and sometimes I felt it would burst out of me as they called me a bitch or stared at my body as I got dressed.

Soon I started having a quick cold shower after every customer or slapping my cheeks to calm myself down. But I saw a different person when I looked in the mirror. She had hard eyes, bleached blonde hair, black roots and too much make-up. You could see she had a dark heart and I was scared that one day it would show itself to the world. I didn't want to be like her. I wanted to love people, believe in them, laugh and have fun. But then I'd look down at my body – the bruises on my arms, finger marks on my neck and handprints on my buttocks where I'd been slapped – and know I never would. Each one was another piece of dirt scarring my soul. Someone had told me the red bruises customers left were called lovebites and I hated the word. This had nothing to do with love.

I kept quiet most of the time while I was waiting for customers. I didn't trust other girls and the only people I spoke to were three sisters who ran reception. They were nice but it made me sad because one was having a baby and she'd sit and knit for her child. I remembered how I'd sewn for my children in that dark, dirty room with no food, how they'd screamed when they were hungry, how they were sick and cold and it made me sad to think of the life we'd lived. All I'd ever wanted was to make it better and now I wasn't even with them.

But there were also good things about the sauna. I liked the fact that no one would speak to any of the pimps so Ardy never knew how much I made. Of course I didn't try to take any of it but it was nice that, even for just a few moments, I knew something he didn't as I walked down the stairs at the end of a shift. Sometimes I'd worked thirty-six hours in a row with no sleep but I could still enjoy those few seconds before I saw him.

The parlour also allowed sexual health workers to come in and see us which I was glad about. One day I even made Ardy take me to a clinic in central London to be tested for HIV and I was so relieved when they told me I was all right.

Sometimes the other girls tried chatting with me but I didn't really want to speak to them. It made me angry that they always asked about my boyfriend, never pimp. Couldn't they see? Some English women might work for themselves but girls from Eastern Europe didn't. The only one I'd met who did was a woman who'd been a doctor in Russia. But all the rest of us were controlled – maybe not every one had been sold like me but a man was still making money selling a woman's body.

The women didn't get angry with those men, though – instead they'd turn on each other, fighting and quarrelling among themselves. In particular they didn't like a young Czech girl. She looked very young and was busy all the time so the girls kept whispering that she broke the rules by letting men kiss her, give her oral sex and not use a condom. Ali made sure fights didn't break out and kept everyone in control. All the girls were scared of him – he'd scream if you were late out of a room, didn't clean it properly or wash up a glass you'd used. He was a pimp in all but name so I made sure I got on with him. I saw up to seven men a day and that kept Ali happy.

Ardy was happy as well. He'd bought himself a car, a false driving licence, a fake passport and expensive clothes thanks to me.

He'd been watching me ever since finding the hidden tips in Birmingham and his eyes never left me now as I undressed. I knew he also checked my bag and underwear while I showered and sometimes I'd hear him lift up the top of the toilet or find my socks separated when I'd left them folded in a pair.

'You'd never do bad things to me again?' he asked a few times. 'I'm right aren't I?'

'Of course, Ardy. You know I wouldn't hurt you.'

'Good. Because I trust you, Oxana.'

But I knew he didn't.

By the time July came he was so pleased with me that he took me to the pub with three Albanian men to celebrate his birthday. I said nothing as they got drunk, I was just glad that for one night no one was touching me.

Chapter Thirty

The smoke rolled thickly from the man's mouth and his eyes were red as he looked at me.

'I want a blow job and then I want to fuck you,' he said in a lazy voice.

I looked at him. He was Asian, middle-aged and smoking a cigarette packed with cannabis.

'Okay,' I said and sat down on a chair in front of him.

'Take off your uniform. I want to see you.'

Sighing, I stood up and started unbuttoning my dress. I hated men looking at my body and had learned to hide myself by wearing a long camisole and stockings. That way I only had to remove my uniform and underwear when I saw customers and they got what they paid for but nothing else.

I could see the dark shadow of cruelty in this man's eyes and it made me nervous. But my mind went blank once again as I sat down to start work. Everything was silent except for the occasional hissing crack of the joint as the man took a puff but suddenly there was a rustle and I saw a hand in front of my face. Black dirt huddled underneath his fingernails as he held a lighter in front of me.

'Can I put it in your pussy?' he said, his voice suddenly light with excitement.

Fear rippled inside me. Did he want to hurt me? I wondered if I should leave the room and get Ali but knew I couldn't. He would get very angry if I cut short an appointment and lost money just because I was scared. The only time he'd help was if something actually happened.

'Put it away,' I said softly.

'Oh come on,' the man said as he started to laugh. 'If you'll fuck for money then why won't you do this?'

'Because I won't,' I replied. 'And if you want someone else to then you'd better leave.'

The man's eyes glittered at me as he stared down but he was silent and I bent my head to him once again. I could feel him looking at me. I just had to carry on, make him forget what it was he wanted to do.

'Do you want to lie down?' I said a few minutes later.

He was ready now and hopefully the sex would be quick.

'No – I want you to lie down and I'll go on top of you,' the man said as he stubbed out his joint in the ashtray.

I looked at him. Most of the time customers liked me to be on top and I did as well because that way I could touch them as little as possible. What did this man want?

Without a word, I lay down on the massage table and waited for him to take off his trousers.

'Have you had children?' he asked as he stared at my breasts in the low-cut camisole. 'I think you have – your tits and stomach show it.'

'I have no children,' I replied as he lay on top of me.

It's what I always said. I didn't want anyone to know anything about me.

'Oh come on, you have. Why lie? Do they know you fuck for money? They must be so proud of their mother.'

I closed my eyes as the man moved on top of me but I could feel the smile in his as he looked down at me below him. He was in charge now.

'Open your eyes,' he snapped.

I didn't want to. I wanted to shut him out and let this all be over with.

'I said open your eyes.'

He was everywhere, pawing at me, trying to touch me all over. I put my hands on his chest to keep him as far away from me as possible. His body smelled bitterly of sweat. But he was moving quickly on top of me now – maybe if I did as he said he would finish quicker and I could get away from him.

I opened my eyes and stared at him.

'Touch me,' he panted as he moved above me, his voice snapping with frustration. 'I want you to touch me, tell me how good I am.'

I didn't move. He had paid me for one thing – nothing more.

'Now kiss me,' he snapped.

I didn't speak – just turned my head to one side to let him know he would never have that part of me. He moved heavily against me as he grabbed at my breasts.

'Kiss me,' he moaned.

Still I kept my head turned from him.

'You fucking bitch,' he screamed. 'What do you think you are? Do what I say.'

His face came towards me and his weight pushed the breath out of my chest as he lowered himself towards me. I strained to move my face as far from him as possible.

'Kiss me,' he shouted.

I wouldn't. I couldn't. I mustn't give him that.

Suddenly I felt his teeth sinking into my cheek and his hand pulling at my hair.

'Do you like that?' he panted. 'Is that what you want? Is that what this is all about?'

I held my breath as he moved inside me. I just wanted this over with. I wanted him away from me. I wanted him and all the ones like him to leave me alone.

He shuddered as he lay on top of me and his body jerked against me. His hand tightened around my hair once more and his teeth bit softly into the corner of my lip.

'Yes that's what you like isn't it?' he said with a laugh. 'But remember – you're just a whore. I'm the one who's here to enjoy themselves – not you.'

One afternoon I arrived at work to find someone new working in reception. Her name was Naz and she was from Turkey.

Somehow I knew I could trust her from the moment we met. She was friendly, open and generous, and even though I was so closed off, I quickly warmed to her. I liked the fact that she didn't ask me too many questions about my life or tell me too much about hers. All I knew was that she was in her late thirties, single and had been in England about seven years.

I found myself looking forward to getting into work a little early so that we could have a coffee and a cigarette together. I enjoyed being with her, just relaxing and chatting like I'd done all those years before with Marina. Naz was a good person – she'd let me hide if a customer came in who I didn't like or cover me if I was late to work and Ali started asking questions. Where I always felt a little uncomfortable with the working girls, I didn't with her.

Naz didn't ask anything about Ardy until a few weeks after we met.

'I see him waiting for you every night,' she said. 'Is he your boyfriend?'

'No,' I replied, and said nothing more.

'Do you work for him?' she asked quietly.

'Yes.'

'Where's he from?'

'Albania.'

She understood. There was a pause before she looked up at me. 'So how did it happen?'

'It's a long story. I had a friend who sold me, I couldn't escape.'

Sadness flooded into Naz's eyes and I hated seeing her pity.

'But you have three children at home,' she said. 'What are you going to do?'

'I don't know.'

Naz didn't say anymore and I was glad she didn't. I hated talking about what had happened to me, felt too ashamed and stupid that I had been tricked as I had. I must be the most stupid woman in the world to have believed what I had. But as the days passed I kept thinking about something that had been on my mind for a long time. I'd tried talking to the other girls about it but they just fell silent if I asked any questions.

'Is it true that if you're illegal in England the police will put you in prison?' I asked Naz one afternoon as we sat together.

'Did your pimp tell you this?'

'Yes.'

She took a deep breath. 'It's not the first time I've heard the story but it's not true, Oxana,' she said. 'You wouldn't get put in prison here in England. If you're caught then you could get put into a centre for illegals and you'd have to apply to stay in this country from there. Sometimes they send people back and sometimes they let them stay. It just depends. Other people are let go when they're caught and have to sign on at a place called the Home Office once a week while the decision is made. There are many people in England who shouldn't be here and they get sent home but if you have a good reason then this is a kind country.'

Disbelief flooded through me. What did Naz mean? How could it be that you weren't put in prison for breaking the law? What about all the police who had chased us on our journey into Italy? The shots fired and the lights that shone as they looked for us? Surely England would be the same.

'I don't understand,' I told Naz. 'Ardy told me I'd face years in jail if anyone found me. He said I'd never get home to my children.'

She was silent for a moment before leaning forward to take my hand. 'It's simple,' she said slowly. 'Ardy is lying to you. He made it all up.'

In the days that followed I couldn't stop thinking about what Naz had said. How could I ever have believed Ardy? Once again I felt the animal rise up in me as I lay staring at him while he slept and shame filled me one minute with anger following it the next. I was so weak. How easy it had been for everyone to fool me.

One evening before work, Naz and I sat together smoking.

'I've been thinking about what you said,' I told her. 'If it's true, then I've been so stupid. Perhaps I deserve all this if I'm so stupid. How could I have let Ardy trick me so easily?'

'Don't be so hard on yourself, Oxana,' Naz said. 'I've met other girls like you. You're not alone. It's hard to know the truth when you don't know a country.' She took a drag of her cigarette and looked at me seriously. 'So what are you going to do? Work for him forever?'

I frowned. 'What do you mean?'

'Just what I say. Are you going to be a prisoner like this forever?'

'So what can I do?' I asked angrily. Naz didn't understand what it was like. She had no idea – it wasn't as simple as it sounded.

'Escape, go to the police, do anything but this.'

I looked around to make sure no one was listening. I felt scared even talking about this. 'Don't be stupid, Naz. I can't just run away. He'd find me in a day, he has friends everywhere and I don't know anyone or have any money. Most importantly, he knows where my children are. He'd hurt them if I ever left. I just have to wait until my debt is paid.'

Naz leaned forward towards me and took my hand in hers. 'Don't you see, Oxana?' she said softly. 'It never never will be. Ardy will keep you with him forever.'

'But how?'

'Because he knows you're too scared to run.'

I stared at her. I didn't want to talk about this or even think about it. What she was saying was impossible.

'Think about it,' she asked. 'What could Ardy do if you left him?'

'Call someone, ask his friends to help him,' I replied. 'I've been there, Naz. I've seen it – the guns, the drugs. These are dangerous people and they have pictures of my children, their names, everything.'

'But you've left all those people behind and now you're here with just him.'

'And?'

'Well, do you think you're worth all that to Ardy? Do you know how much it would cost him to find your children? He's new in this business and I'm sure he's just as afraid of the gangsters who sold you to him as you are. But he knew that you were so scared by the time he met you that you'd believe anything he said and he's brainwashed you ever since to keep you with him.'

I looked at Naz. I wanted to believe what she said but I felt so afraid and angry. Why was she making it all sound so simple? I hadn't thought about escaping for so long, I'd accepted that I would be with Ardy until he let me go.

'Listen to me, Oxana,' Naz said. 'You can do whatever you want – escape, go to the police, get away from here. But you'll need to be clever, you'll need to make a plan. I could help you to hide some of your money. If you have ten customers, I'll just write down eight and put the rest away. No one will ever know.'

'But he'll find out.'

'How? Who will tell him? The girls here? They won't tell anyone, they're like you but even more scared to escape.'

I gazed at her silently.

'We'll save the money slowly,' Naz continued. 'I'll miss out a customer from time to time until there's enough for you to get away. I have a friend who works in a sauna far from here and you could use the money to go to her. Please, Oxana, listen to me. I want to help you.'

'But what about my children? He'll kill them.'

'All I know is this,' Naz said. 'Ardy is a boy and has just you, your money and your fear. I'm sure he wouldn't hurt the children. I really believe that. Please trust me.'

'But how? I can't put their lives at risk without being sure they'll be safe.'

'You'll never know, Oxana, and because of this Ardy will always keep you. He knows the most precious thing in the world is your children and that's what makes you stay. But he's afraid of something too – trouble, the police finding him, losing the money you make him. It would be a big risk for him to go to Ukraine and hurt your children. He knows the trouble he could be in. It would be much easier for him just to buy another girl.'

I stared at the table, trying to understand what she was saying. Could it be true that Ardy would simply let me go and forget about me?

'He could get another girl in England,' Naz went on. 'I've heard of women being sold four times in London. Trust me, each pimp has a bigger pimp and then another and there are many girls here. For Ardy it would be far easier here than going back to Albania.'

My head was spinning. Blood rushed into my ears. I couldn't believe what Naz was saying. She made it all sound so simple, so easy. She didn't know what these people were capable of.

'Listen to me, Oxana,' she said quietly. 'Ardy wouldn't do anything to your children for two good reasons: it's too much of a risk and far, far cheaper for him to buy another girl here. So. What shall we do?'

'I don't know. I need to think ... I need to think it over.'

Chapter Thirty-One

I thought again and again of what Naz had told me as I walked in and out of rooms with men, as they handed me their money, as Ardy counted it again at the end of the night. Her voice kept playing in my head.

I felt scared even thinking about what she was saying. I couldn't take the risk. What if Ardy did something? I'd already been so selfish, I couldn't let anything happen to Sasha, Pasha or Luda because of me. Over and over it kept swirling round my head. There were ten different stories of my future dancing in front of my eyes and I had to pick one.

Two days later, I went to Naz and asked her to hide some of my wages. 'But I'm not going to escape,' I said. 'I'm going to send it home to my children. I can't take the risk just because I want to be free.'

'All right. It's your decision. I'll do whatever I can to help you, you know that,' Naz said quietly, but her face was sad.

We didn't hide money every day because we were scared Ali would notice, but we managed to save £20 one day and £40 the next week until we had about £200. Now I could tell Tamara that I had money to send her and phone Sasha and Luda again. I had to be brave. It had

been months since I'd spoken to them and part of me felt
too ashamed to face them. But I couldn't just disappear,
make the same mistake again. I needed to build a picture
in my children's heads of the day I would see them again.
Naz was showing me that. I might not want to escape but
I had to learn to conquer a little bit of fear.

I was shaking as I picked up the phone. Sasha had had
his tenth birthday about three months before and I
wanted to find out how Luda was enjoying school. I spoke
to Tamara quickly, telling her I'd be sending money. Then
Luda came on the line.

'Hi, Mamma,' she said in her bright little voice.

'Hello, darling.' A huge smile came over my face at the
sound of her.

'I've just come in from playing.'

'What have you been doing?'

'Just skipping. So are you going to come and see us
soon?' She sounded hopeful.

'Yes, my darling. But I need to work a little longer.'

'Oh.' Luda didn't believe me. Her voice sounded
hollow and my heart beat. My daughter knew I was lying
to her. I was never going to come. I'd made a promise,
broken it and everyone was telling her I'd let her down.

'My friend has just arrived,' she said suddenly. 'Here's
Sasha.'

Luda put down the phone and I heard her running
away as she screamed her brother's name.

'Mamma?' Sasha said as he came on the line.

'It's me,' I said, pushing down tears which made my
throat feel tight. 'How are you?'

'I'm good. Where have you been? I thought you'd be
here for New Year but you weren't and now it's August.
It's so long.'

'I know, darling. But I can't come yet. I just need to make some more money, I need to buy us a house and then we'll all live together. You, me, Pasha and Luda.'

'But I miss you so much. I don't like it with Tamara.'

Tears ran down my face as I swallowed to keep my voice steady. He had to understand that I hadn't chosen to leave him.

'I miss you too, my darling, and I want you to know there are good reasons why I left you which I'll tell you one day. But for now I want you to know that Mamma loves you and will come back for you.'

'Are you sick?'

'No, I'm fine.'

'So when will you come?'

'Soon, darling, and no matter what happens, or what anyone says, remember that I love you, I love Pasha and I love Luda.'

'Okay.'

'Goodbye now, darling, I have to go. Be a good boy for Tamara, okay? And look after your sister. I love you. I'll come for you soon.'

'Okay. Bye bye, Mamma.'

His voice sounded so small as I put the phone down and knew that on the other side of the world my son was crying for me just as I was crying for him. How long would it be before my children hated me so much that, even if I got home to them, they wouldn't want to see me? Luda hardly knew me, Sasha was upset and I still did not know where Pasha was. I had to do something.

The next day I went into work early to see Naz.

'I want you to give me the phone number you told me about.'

'What number?'

'For your friend. You once told me you could help me to escape, that you had a friend who could help me. Will you give me her number?'

Naz spoke. Her voice was almost a whisper. 'So you've decided to escape?'

'Yes.'

'When?'

'Soon.'

It was a rainy morning in late September 2002. I had been away from home for fifteen months. Ardy was sleeping beside me and I lay still as I looked at him. For weeks now I'd been so good with him – cooking, smiling, talking and having sex whenever he wanted. But all the time I knew there was a small bag hidden behind the wardrobe. In it was some underwear, a top and gold ring that Ardy had given me as a present. I wanted to take it with me as a reminder of what I should never forget and how one day I would pay him back for what he'd done to me. In the past few weeks I'd sent more money home and now had £150 for myself – enough to get far away.

Ardy had been so pleased a few days before when I'd bought him a present. Sometimes he gave me money to spend on cosmetics or underwear when he took me to the shops and I'd used it to buy him a purse for all the money I'd made. It would soon be empty.

'Maybe I've finally fallen in love with you,' I said as I handed him the gift.

'Oh, come on,' he replied with a laugh.

Ardy had no idea what I was planning to do and my heart twisted in my chest as I looked at him. I was afraid but just kept reminding myself of how I'd felt after speaking to Luda and Sasha and months of anger had hardened into courage. I didn't know what I was going to do – I would still be in a foreign country with no money, no documents and unable to go home. I just knew I had to be free.

A few days earlier I'd phoned Naz's friend – a Russian woman called Lara who worked in a sauna in Essex.

'I need somewhere to hide,' I'd told her. 'I can't tell you everything but there is an Albanian who will look for me and I don't have anyone here. Naz told me you could help.'

Lara said I could stay with her for a few days until I decided what I was going to do and I told her I'd ring when I'd got away.

I got out of bed and walked towards the fridge. I would make some breakfast. I sighed as I bent down to open the door but suddenly my heart started beating as I looked inside. My chance to escape had come. We didn't have any food. Ardy would have to go shopping and leave me alone.

I'd already dressed and written him a list by the time he got up – eggs, milk, sugar, salami, rice, carrots and onions.

'Can you get me some chocolate?' I asked.

'Yes, okay.'

He turned away and put on a jacket.

'I'll be back soon,' he said as he unlocked the door.

'See you later,' I told him.

I held my breath as the door closed and the lock clicked. I had to be quick. The supermarket was just down the road. Running to the window, I watched Ardy from behind the curtain.

'Come on,' I whispered as he walked slowly up the street before turning out of view towards the supermarket.

Running to the wardrobe, I pulled out my bag and went back to the window. There was a catch on it so it didn't open very wide. I would just have to break it. We were only on the ground floor so it wasn't far to jump. I wrapped my hand in Ardy's T-shirt before hitting the glass with all my strength. It cracked into a million pieces but didn't shatter.

Come on. Hurry up.

Time seemed to slow down as I hit the window again and again. I pushed at the glass but it wouldn't shatter.

Hurry. He'll be coming back soon.

I pulled back my hand, made a fist and hit the window with all my strength.

Please, God. Let me get away.

Suddenly the glass started to fall. I could make a hole in it. Putting my head out of the window, I looked down the street. I couldn't see Ardy. I turned back to pick up my bag and took one last look around. Finally I was leaving my prison.

Breathing hard, I jumped down into the little garden in front of the house. The fresh air filled my lungs as I hit the ground. I was free.

Chapter Thirty-Two

I ran.

I couldn't look back. I didn't want to know if Ardy had seen me or not. I'd just wait until his hand grabbed my arm, his scream echoed in my ear, but until then I'd run. I saw a minicab office and went to a car waiting outside it. I showed the driver an address that I'd written on a piece of paper. He nodded and I climbed in. As the car started moving, I couldn't stop turning around to look out the back window – had Ardy seen me? Was he following me?

The traffic lights in front of us flashed red and the car slowed down. Please don't stop. Please let me get away.

Turning my head, my eyes scanned the road behind us which led to the supermarket. Was Ardy's face among those walking along the street? He must be on his way back by now. Had he reached our room and found I wasn't there, was he searching for me?

I felt something stir on my neck and flicked my head forward again. It felt like someone's breath on my skin. But there was no one beside me on the seat. I was alone.

'Calm down,' I told myself as I stared ahead once again, my eyes searching for what might have caressed my neck.

I looked at the window – it was open a little. A draught must have found its way onto my skin.

'You're safe now,' I told myself. 'You've got away. You've done it.'

But as I looked up I saw the driver's eyes staring at me from the mirror. Was he a client? One of Ardy's friends?

My hand reached out to take hold of the door handle. If he looked at me anymore then I'd run again. I'd throw myself out of the car if I had to. I couldn't go back now.

The sound of my heart hammered in my ears as I stared at those eyes. Either I was finally safe or a prisoner again – which was it? Should I run or stay still?

The eyes slid forward as the lights turned to green.

'Finally,' the driver sighed as we started driving.

I said nothing as I looked at the street passing me by – every second a step further away from my prison.

'I don't want to be nosey, love, but are you all right?' a voice suddenly asked.

I looked up to see the driver looking at me once again. But now his eyes were kind instead of hard, questioning instead of knowing. I took a deep breath and exhaled slowly.

'Yes,' I said. 'I'm fine.'

I didn't feel happy as the minutes turned into miles – just numb. I knew I had no choice now but to ask Lara for a job in the sauna where she worked as a receptionist. I had no money or friends and couldn't ask a stranger to save me. I had to survive. At least it would be hard for Ardy to find me if I was just another nameless whore but I felt sick at the thought of going back to prostitution now I was free. Surely God would punish me.

I couldn't ask anyone for help though. Naz had told me the English police could send me back to Ukraine if they wanted and I couldn't risk that. Ardy, Olga or Serdar could find me and kill me. Besides, Sergey was also out of prison and I was sure that sooner or later he'd come back to get me and the children. I would just have to earn enough money to buy the house I had always dreamed of in Moldova.

When the taxi stopped outside Lara's house, I rang the doorbell and a tall, blonde woman with a kind face opened the door. She didn't ask too much but I told her a little of what had happened and why I needed to hide. That afternoon she took me to the sauna to meet her boss. He was a kind Turkish man who agreed to let me work for him and stay in one of the sauna's rooms while I saved some money.

'Would you be able to give me a loan?' I asked. 'It's very urgent.'

I needed to send money home. They had to know I was going to be a good mother who kept her promises from now on.

'Will you vouch for her?' the boss asked Lara. 'Pay it back if she disappears?'

Lara looked at me. 'Yes,' she said.

I knew I was lucky. Once again I'd found a true friend and couldn't let her down.

The new place was far nicer than anywhere I'd worked before. Upstairs there was a sauna, two Jacuzzi rooms and a small kitchen, while downstairs there were three rooms with a shower and toilet in each. There was also a sitting room where we waited for customers with leather chairs and a table with a big bowl of fruit on it. No alcohol was allowed on the premises, everything was clean, and two security men helped us with things like cleaning, towels and restocking the fridge. They also threw out customers who behaved badly by doing something like biting or shouting at a girl, or having their half an hour and then lying that they hadn't had sex.

In some ways I was safer now than I ever had been before. There was CCTV on the door to the sauna and Lara could also turn away customers at reception if she didn't like them. The men also had to pay £10 just to get inside so, while most came for sex, there were those who wanted just a sauna and massage after finishing work late. But none of it mattered to me as I started working because I couldn't stop think about Ardy. I was sure he would find me and take revenge. The first thing I did with the £500 the boss gave me was to buy a mobile phone and call home. I gave Ira and Tamara the number but told them they mustn't give out any information about me.

'If anybody comes to your house, if anybody calls, then you don't know me. I've had some problems so please don't say anything about me or the children. If Sergey comes then you don't know where I am – just say I'm sending you money but you don't know my number.'

Night after night I anxiously watched the CCTV screens to check the face of every man coming into the sauna and would hide if anyone had their head down because I couldn't be sure if it was Ardy or not. A couple of Albanian girls also worked with me and I was careful not to talk too much to them or anyone else really. I just wanted to be like a shadow no one noticed.

I was so scared that I didn't even leave the sauna for the first two weeks – staying inside all day and only eating the food the security men bought for us. When I finally did go out I either ran to the money transfer shop to send cash home or to the pub across the road where I'd get a coffee and read the English newspaper to try and improve my language. But I couldn't stop looking up into the faces of the men around me, convinced someone would be there ready to jump out and suck me back into my old world.

I also found sleeping more and more difficult. After the sauna had closed at around 5am, we'd cleaned the rooms and the other girls had left, I'd lie in bed unable to switch off. I hated being alone and would jump at every noise as my head filled with thoughts and I begged God for forgiveness. Once I had been forced to sell myself but now I was choosing to do it.

'Dear Lord,' I'd pray. 'I'll leave this job soon. I know this is wrong.'

I felt so confused – I needed money but hated what I had to do to get it, I wanted to be with my children but was too scared to go home to them. I was happy of course that I could now talk to Sasha and Luda more, and send money every two weeks. I usually made about £100 a week and kept just a little for myself. At least I knew they were eating well now and had warm clothes to put on, and I also sent Ira something to help with Vica's schooling. But I couldn't stop thinking about them, how long I'd been away and my worries about Pasha. I still didn't know where he was – he was all alone without even a brother or sister to keep him company and I couldn't contact him. How would I ever make up to him what he'd been forced to suffer without us? Would I ever be able to explain to him that I'd never wanted to leave him?

Questions turned over in my mind as I wondered what I was going to do and, when I eventually got to sleep, black images would fill my dreams. They weren't faces or people I recognised but, just as I had as a child, I knew it was the devil who'd come to kill me, and I'd dream I was being strangled and wake up choking. My mother had always told me that praying three times would make nightmares go away but sometimes I was so scared I couldn't even get the words into my head. Instead I'd drink coffee, smoke cigarettes, switch on the television or read books for hours until the sun came up when at last I knew I'd be safe.

As the weeks passed I began to realise that instead of being really free, I'd just swapped one prison for another. I might have smashed a locked window to run from Ardy but the iron bars of fear he'd created in my mind would take far longer to escape.

I felt tears rise up in me as I sat in the living room at the sauna. It was about 2am and I'd only had one customer. Less money meant less food on the table for my children.

'You've got to smile a bit more, relax a little,' Lara told me as she walked in and saw me sitting alone. 'If you carry on like this it will take you a year to make any money.'

'I know. I'm trying.'

'But you're not. You look as if you want to kill someone. No wonder no one wants you – you're frightening customers away.'

I looked at Lara's back as she walked out of the room. She was right. I was scaring customers and couldn't seem to stop myself. I just felt so angry all the time and, where once I'd forced myself to wear a mask, it now almost strangled me. All I could feel was anger and at times I couldn't breathe as I fought to keep down the feeling.

Lara kept telling me that I had to stop being rude to customers. We'd become close in the weeks since I'd run to Essex and sometimes now I went over to her flat to cook for her. It made me happy to have someone to look after a little and Lara had quickly become my friend, my mother, my daughter, my sister, everything in one. She was also the person who explained things and showed me little bits of this new country – we'd even gone to a night-club.

I followed her out to reception.

'I'm trying, I really am,' I insisted as she sat back down. 'But they just don't like me here.'

'Well, they might if you smiled a little. I know it's hard but you've got to try, Oxana.'

Anger pinched at my throat. 'I'm going to get a drink,' I said and turned away.

Alcohol was the only way I could face my job now. With vodka inside me I was different – relaxed, happy, not caring anymore. I'd put on music and dance, laugh and be crazy. I didn't understand why I couldn't make myself be a good girl without it. The customers weren't like those in Tottenham. They were regulars, better behaved, not rough and rude. Here no one screamed that I was a bitch or tried to make me do things I didn't want to do. But still I couldn't stop my rage if they said the wrong thing.

'So do you like your job?' a man might ask as he got dressed after sex. 'It's a good job, isn't it? Just fucking and getting money.'

'What do you mean?' I'd shout. 'Do you think it's easy to fuck you, smile at you and pretend I like you?'

'Oh come on,' he'd laugh. 'You just need to take your clothes off and lie back. There's nothing to it.'

Bastards. They had no idea how it felt as the smell of yet another man filled my nose – an Indian with the scent of curry on him, a Turk with kebab fat stuck to his clothes, an Englishman stinking of beer. I just couldn't hide my feelings any more and recently I'd gone for five days without a single customer. Lara had given me money for food but I didn't know how I would ever bury the anger as it poured out of me.

Tonight it was my job to make tea and coffee for customers and I looked up as the door opened. Two men walked in and I felt annoyed even looking at them. I had on very high heels and if they wanted a drink then the kitchen was all the way upstairs.

One went straight to have a sauna and didn't take a girl. He must work in a restaurant or kebab shop and just want to relax. But his friend – who was tall, slim and wearing a bandanna on his head – didn't even do that. Why did these men come in to stare at us like animals in a zoo?

Lara asked him if he wanted a drink as she showed him in.

'Coffee. White.'

I slammed my book shut. 'How many sugars?' I sighed.

'If it's a bother then don't worry,' the man said.

Lara stared at me.

'No,' I said in a flat voice. 'It's okay.'

'Two, please.'

I looked at the man. He was obviously Turkish. 'It will be here in a minute,' I told him in his language and left.

A few minutes later I returned with the coffee and picked up my book again.

'So how do you know Turkish?'

'Does it matter?'

'No but I'm trying to make conversation.'

'I worked there.'

'So where are you from?'

'Russia.'

'What is your name?'

'Marilyn.' Since leaving Ardy, I'd cut my hair, dyed it blonde and wore red lipstick.

'Do you do good massage?' the man asked softly.

'I don't know. Some people must like it.'

'Well, can you give me one?'

'It's thirty pounds for twenty minutes.'

'Okay.'

We walked into a room and the man sat down in a chair.

'So how many customers have you had today?' he asked.

'No one yet,' I lied.

'And how much do you give reception of what you get?'

'Twenty pounds,' I lied.

'So you'll get just ten pounds for seeing me?'

'Yes.'

'And how much is sex?'

'Forty-five pounds.'

'And how much do you give them?'

'Thirty-five.'

In fact we only gave reception £35 from the £45 our first customer gave us and £15 for each one after that. But the man didn't need to know that – hopefully he'd feel sorry for me. He held out £45. He wanted sex. I walked out to give Lara what I owed before returning to the room.

'Here,' the man said as I closed the door. 'This is for you.'

He held out another £40.

Good.

'Thank you.' I walked towards him and unbuttoned his shorts.

'Can I have a shower first?' he asked.

'Of course,' I replied and he got under the water as I undressed, wrapped a towel around me and sat on the bed. I stared into space. How long would this take? I was enjoying my book.

'Come here.'

I looked over to where he was washing. 'What?'

'Come here,' he repeated. 'I want to wash your back.'

'No,' I said wearily. 'I don't shower with customers. I'll get water in my hair and my make-up will run.'

'I'll make sure it doesn't. I want you to come in with me.'

Sighing, I got up off the bed. If I wanted to get this over then I should do as he said. Anything which excited them meant they finished quicker.

The man looked at me as I stepped into the shower but said nothing. I turned my back to him. So this was what he wanted – to clean me of my sins before using me. I stared ahead as he rubbed my back with a sponge. Soap bubbles trickled all over my body and the water was warm. At least he was gentle, not pawing at me like some of the men did. We said nothing.

Suddenly his hands started to massage my shoulders and I almost flinched. His touch was soft, gentle, unlike any I'd ever known. From the day at the beach through Sergey and his friends to Serdar and all the rough men who'd paid for me, no one had ever touched me so tenderly, as if I was delicate. His hands ran down my back and around my waist. I felt his lips on my shoulder. I said nothing.

I felt alive.

It wasn't butterflies in my stomach, it was more than that – like waves pulling me up and crashing over me. My skin was sensitive, my body alert. Without a word, the man turned off the water and we got out of the shower. I lay down on the bed.

'It can't be like this,' a voice kept whispering. 'He's a customer. That's all he is.'

But there was something inside me which couldn't stop. All my life I'd dreamed of the kind of tenderness I'd seen in Bollywood films and, for some reason I didn't understand, this man was giving it to me. He was touching me like a real woman – not a faceless whore. Maybe he was imagining I was someone else, maybe he wasn't even thinking about it, but I didn't want it to end however wrong it was.

We were silent as he put on a condom and went inside me. His lips touched mine. I ran my fingers across his skin – it was covered in goose bumps – and my body started shaking as he moved on top of me. I couldn't think of anything anymore, my life was forgotten as everything tensed up inside me for a few moments and I screamed softly. I didn't understand what had happened. I'd never felt like that before. I felt free, warm.

'Is everything okay?' Lara asked as she knocked gently at the door.

'Fine,' I said hurriedly.

The moment was finished and I got up off the bed to start dressing. I didn't look back. Shame filled me. What had I done? How could I have been so stupid? How could my body have betrayed me as it had? How could I have allowed it to take pleasure from what every part of me hated so much? Maybe I really was what all those men had told me – a dirty whore who wanted it.

The man got up off the bed and walked back to the shower.

'We're going to an all-night restaurant,' he told me. 'Do you want to come?'

'No.'

'Why not?'

'Because I'm working. There'll be others after you.'

I didn't understand what he was trying to do. He knew what I was, where I worked. Did he want to make a joke out of me?

'Here,' the man said as he walked towards me after getting dressed. He pressed a piece of paper into my hand as he turned to leave. There was a phone number written on it.

The door closed and I sat down on the bed. I felt almost scared. I didn't understand what I'd just done. All I knew was that it must never happen again.

Chapter Thirty-Three

Even though I didn't use the phone number, I couldn't stop myself from ringing it sometimes. I just wanted to hear the man's voice. My heart would beat as the number started ringing before stopping for a second as a click and a pause told me his recorded message was about to start. I loved hearing him speak but couldn't say anything back. Instead I waited every day for him to return for me. But I felt so confused. How could I have feelings for a man who'd paid for me?

'Don't trust him,' Lara told me. 'He's a customer. What are you going to do? Fuck him for free?'

I knew she was right when the weeks passed and the man didn't come back. Then Lara told me he'd been in when I was off and taken another girl. I'd been so stupid – I was just a prostitute and he just wanted sex. How could anyone want me in the same way that they'd want a normal woman?

It was in early December, about a week after I moved into a bedroom in Lara's flat, that the man finally returned. I felt almost angry when he walked into the living room.

'He's just a customer,' I said to myself as he smiled at me. 'He's forgotten you.'

'Will you come with me?' he asked.

I didn't look at him as I got up.

'I should tell you my name,' the man said as we walked into a room.

'Whatever you want,' I told him as I stripped off.

'It's Murat. And you?'

'Oxana.'

'Not Marilyn?'

'No.'

He started undressing. 'I've been away.'

'Really?'

'To my brother's wedding in Turkey. That's why I haven't seen you.'

'Oh.'

'I came to look for you a while ago but you weren't here.'

'No. Shall we start?'

I wouldn't let myself feel, I had to push my emotions into the tiniest hole inside me, lock them up and forget them.

We had sex. It was quick, clinical, just like all the others. But as Murat got up off the bed he looked at me softly again. 'Would you like to come to a restaurant sometime?' he asked.

I stared at him. Why was he doing this? Well, I wasn't going to be a fool again. 'No.'

'Why not?'

'Because you're a customer.' I turned, walked out of the room and sat back down in the living room to read my book. I didn't look up when Murat left, I didn't want him to see my heart in my eyes.

Later I went to the kitchen to pour myself a vodka. I felt confused and strange. The alcohol would numb me inside until I got control of myself again. But one drink followed another until I felt brave and crazy. I picked up my phone and dialled his number.

'It's Oxana. I want to see you,' I said as he answered.

I would just use him and leave. I could do whatever I wanted now I had vodka inside me.

'Okay.'

Murat told me where he lived and I got a minicab to a petrol station near his flat before calling him again to come and pick me up. Waiting for him, I felt my coat brush against my bare skin. I was wearing just underwear and stockings. I wanted him to touch me as he had before, make me feel like a person again, make me forget.

He came to pick me up and immediately I looked into his eyes, I knew he was going to heal me, even if just for a short while. We went back to his flat and made love as we had that first time: with a sensuality I'd never known except with him. Only he could make my skin – dead for so long – come alive and thrill to the touch of a man. At last I understood what sex could be. I'd always seen it as something to be endured, something that women suffered and men took. I never thought I could enjoy it.

'You're beautiful,' Murat told me later as we lay in bed. 'I want to see you again.'

'Of course you can,' I said. At the moment I felt as though I'd discovered buried treasure. 'I want to see you too.'

I left before morning and by then my mood had turned to depression. The wild courage that the alcohol had given me had vanished. I cursed myself. I'd been weak. Why had I come here? How could I be so stupid as to open up my heart even just a crack to the thought that a man could ever love me properly? This man would hurt me, just as all the others had.

Lara smiled when she saw me walk back in the sauna. 'How was it?'

'Okay.' I shrugged.

'So will you go back for more?'

I felt my heart harden inside me. I could feel the old anger, bubbling away just below the surface, ready to spill out at any minute. Nothing had really changed. 'No. He's just like the others, I'm sure of it.'

I didn't want to think about Murat but I couldn't get him out of my mind. I kept thinking about his voice which made me feel as if the anger inside had disappeared and his touch which was so soft it made me want to cry. Somehow I felt I could trust him. Maybe he could see something different in me. Maybe I wasn't as worthless as I thought.

'Don't fall for it,' the other girls kept telling me. 'He's just a client and you're stupid to give it away when you could charge.'

But something in me had come alive again. It had been hard to control my fear and shame in the past, but I had managed. Now I realised the heart was far more powerful when it came to love and tenderness, and there was nothing I could do to stop how I felt.

'Maybe this is your chance for happiness,' a voice kept whispering. 'Perhaps Murat will help you decide what you're going to do, how to be with your children again.'

Dreaming of him was a bright spot in the darkness that I still lived in. I may have escaped from Ardy – I was finally beginning to believe that Naz was right, and that he wouldn't come after me – but I still felt so lonely and unsure. I had always believed that when I was free from

Ardy, I'd be reunited with the children. If I were free then I'd be able to do whatever I wanted. But I was as far as ever from Sasha, Pasha and Luda, and I was beginning to realise the truth: I was still trapped. I had no money, no documents and no friends but Lara. Even if I could get back home with no money or passport, I was terrified of what waited there. I was sure that Sergey would come for me and then there was the risk that any of the people whose paths I'd crossed could track me down: Olga, Serdar or Ardy. But most likely of all, people would guess what had happened and what I'd been forced to do. Women like that were hated, and I would bring shame on my children. I would never find work or earn enough to feed my family. No, I could never go home now. There was no future for me in Ukraine.

Perhaps I could hide in England forever and bring the children to join me. I could buy a false passport like Ardy had, adopt a new name and disappear. I'd heard about people who brought their children illegally to England and if I could earn the money, I would find out how to do it.

At least I could now talk to my little ones. I phoned them once a week, to chat to Sasha and Luda about the things they'd been doing and what was happening at school. Even though it was only over the phone, I could feel our relationship growing again. They knew I was their mamma and that I loved them. Every time we spoke, I told them how much I loved and missed them and that we'd be reunited as soon as possible. The little kisses they sent me down the phone were the sweetest things in my life.

* * *

'Hello, Oxana.'

I looked up. It was Murat, his brown eyes soft and kind.

'Hello,' I said, trying to sound cool. Keep your distance, I told myself. 'Are you here for the usual?'

'No, I've come to ask if you are coming out with me.'

I stared down at the carpet and reminded myself why I wasn't going to let myself be hurt. 'I don't know …' I muttered.

'Look, when are you free? Tomorrow?'

'I suppose I could be,' I said slowly, feeling my resolution weaken.

'Good. You and I will go out for dinner. I'll call you tomorrow about where to meet. Okay?' He smiled at me. There was no way I could refuse. So I nodded.

I was so excited before our meeting that I couldn't think about anything else. Murat took me to a place he knew and we ate dinner together, talking about ourselves shyly at first and then with more confidence. I could hardly believe it: here I was, sitting and talking and laughing with a man who didn't want to use me or hurt me – at least not as far I knew. Later, we went home to Murat's flat and made love again.

'You won't go cold on me again, will you?' Murat asked.

I shook my head. It was no good – I was too far in to go back now.

Soon Murat and I were seeing each other regularly and he became my escape from the sadness about my children and shame at the work I was still doing. Like me, he worked until the early hours of the morning in a kebab shop and we'd meet up as dawn approached. I loved the time we spent together. He cooked for me, ran me baths or poured me a glass of wine as we sat in bed looking at the city lights until the sun came up. My time with him was like a bubble of happiness that lasted until the moment I had to go back to the sauna and everything I hated.

'So how long will you do this job?' Murat sometimes asked.

I knew he didn't like it.

'I'll do it until I've got money for my children,' I said. I'd told him about how I'd come to be here and the pain I felt at being separated from Sasha, Pasha and Luda.

Murat frowned. 'Couldn't you find another job?'

'I don't think so. I've got no papers. I keep thinking about it but I'm scared of being caught by the police. Maybe I could work with you making kebabs?'

'No,' Murat said as he laughed. 'It's not a job for women. I can't help you but you should find something else. The job you're doing is no good.'

Chapter Thirty-Four

It was Christmas Eve. I had a day off and went to the supermarket to buy some vodka and fruit juice. I wanted to be drunk. This was always the hardest time of the year for me because all around me the happiness of families and children was being celebrated. I couldn't stop thinking of home and how my children would be getting excited about New Year. Yet again I wasn't with them and I didn't want to be alone. I wanted to drink, dance and forget.

Murat was working, so I decided to go to the sauna and see who was there.

'Hey, it's Christmas. Who wants a drink?' I asked as I walked into the living room where we lounged about when we weren't with customers.

Over the years I'd come to rely on large quantities of vodka to numb the pain of my life. Even now, although I was no longer Ardy's slave, I needed to forget the reality of my situation and the distance between me and the people I loved most in the world. I knew it was bad for me but I simply didn't care – without it, I would not have been able to cope. I was sure that when my life improved, I'd be able to let go of vodka. Until then, it was my comforter and friend.

Lara and five of the regular girls were sitting about and delighted to see me.

'Yes, why not? It's Christmas,' said Lara, so I started pouring vodka and quickly gulped some down as we wished each other a happy Christmas. Soon my head began to feel light and I relaxed. Now I could forget my sadness.

A new girl who I didn't know walked in. I could see she was English but she didn't say a word as she helped herself to a drink. I felt anger stir in my stomach.

'Is that yours?' I asked her.

'No.' She looked at me boldly and took a gulp of my vodka.

I smiled coldly. 'Well then, you need to ask me. It's my stuff and please don't take it without asking.'

The woman didn't say anything and I turned to carry on talking to the girls. Soon she poured herself another drink.

'Listen,' I said, my voice low and angry. 'I don't know who you are and you don't know me so don't touch my stuff. Even if you don't respect anyone else here then I'm asking you to respect me.'

'Oh, fuck off,' the woman said as she looked at me with cold eyes.

I stared back at her, rage filling me.

'Oxana,' Lara hissed. 'Calm down.'

She had seen what I could be like sometimes when I had drunk far too much – aggressive and argumentative. I took a deep breath and walked out of the room. The girl could just piss off. I was hungry. I wanted something to eat.

Everything swam in front of me as I walked upstairs to the kitchen where I started cutting up salami and cheese to put on a board for everyone. We were going to have fun tonight, we were going to forget where we were and this time of year when families celebrated together. But I couldn't stop thinking of the girl. Did she really think she could treat the rest of us like dirt just because she was English? It was one thing when men did it but another when it came to a girl. Anger pumped through my veins as she walked into the kitchen.

I spun round to face her, feeling my rage come to the surface. I shouted, 'If you think that because you're British and have the law on your side that you can do whatever you want because I'm illegal then you can fuck off!'

'Fuck off yourself!' the girl yelled back.

How dare she? I was sick of being treated like some faceless piece of shit. This girl had to know she couldn't push me around. I took a step towards her with the bread knife in my hand and screamed, 'Don't tell me to fuck off!'

She glanced down at the knife in my hand, her eyes wide, and I realised that she thought I intended to use it on her. Before I could do anything, she backed quickly out of the kitchen, tripped on the tiny landing and slipped backwards on the top of the staircase.

I flew forward to help her but it was too late: she fell heavily to the bottom, screaming as she went.

There was hardly time to realise what had happened before the girls came rushing out of the living room to help her. As I stared down, I saw them help the girl up as she started crying. Lara made sure she was all right and then stared up the stairs at me.

'What have you done?' she shouted, furious. 'You've just tried to kill her.'

It was so ridiculous, I laughed. 'What are you talking about? I'm making a sandwiches, not killing anyone. It was an accident.'

'Don't pretend, Oxana. We heard you shouting at each other and then the thump as she fell downstairs. Tell me what you did.'

'Nothing. I was cutting up cheese and salami. She came in, we shouted, and she tripped and fell. I didn't touch her.'

I went back into the kitchen, trying to calm down. It was a ridiculous accident, I knew that. How could Lara think otherwise? Sometimes I was aggressive and loud but I'd never try to hurt anyone. A few minutes later, Lara appeared in the small kitchen.

'Is she okay?' I asked.

'Yes, she'll be fine. But she's called the police. They're coming now. She said you tried to kill her.'

I lifted my cup and took another mouthful of vodka. My chest burned as I swallowed it. 'They can come if they want to. I didn't do anything.'

The alcohol made me brave and when two police officers arrived to arrest me, I brazened it out, acting bold and fearless, even laughing a little. But by the time I'd been in the police station for an hour, and the effects of the vodka began to wear off, I felt differently.

I was in trouble. They were going to ask me for documents and I didn't have any. Why had I been so stupid? They'd find out I was illegal and put me in prison. Fear filled me.

I was taken into a room where two officers sat. One had a pen in his hand while the other started asking me questions.

'So why did you assault this woman?' he asked.

'I didn't.'

'You had a knife.'

'I was making a sandwich. We had an argument and she tripped and fell. I didn't touch her.'

The man looked at me disbelievingly. 'So what's your name?' he asked.

'Alexandra Kolesnikova,' I lied.

'Date of birth?'

I made up a date. '26 April 1971.'

'What are you doing here in the UK? Do you have permission to be here?'

'No.'

'And where is your passport?'

I covered my face with my hands and started to cry. Now I was afraid.

'Do you have identity documents?'

I said nothing. There was a long pause. I tried to stop crying and looked at the two men.

'All right. This is now an immigration matter,' one said slowly. 'Somebody else will have to come and see you.'

They left the room and it was another three hours before someone else arrived. This time it was a young woman and a man who told me they were immigration officers. There was also a woman interpreter with them who started translating their questions. Who was I? When had I come to England? Why was I here? I didn't know what to do. Tell them my story and hope they'd have pity on me? Or lie and hope they'd believe me?

I didn't have a choice. I had to tell them the truth and trust that they would let me go. I started crying again as my head pounded and my mouth felt dry. 'I was brought to this country by a man who forced me to work as a prostitute,' I whispered. 'I was kidnapped nearly two years ago and sold by gangsters. This man bought me and arranged for us to be brought here. First I had to work in Birmingham but after a few months he brought me to London because he said there would be more money here. I was forced to prostitute myself and give him all the money, and I was never allowed on my own. I managed to escape from him but I've had to work in saunas and massage parlours ever since.'

They listened silently and recorded everything on tape.

'Please let me go,' I begged.

They didn't reply but only took my fingerprints and then left the room. I sat on my own, terrified, for fifteen minutes. Had I done the right thing telling them the truth? Was I about to be marched to prison?

Fifteen minutes later the woman returned and gave me a letter with the words 'Home Office' and a telephone number on it.

'We won't be keeping you,' she told me. 'But you are in this country illegally and must apply to the Home Office to stay. You'll need to take this letter, explain what happened to you and they can help you.'

I didn't understand. She was letting me go? How could she after I'd broken the law?

'Will I be sent back to my country?' I asked.

'I'm not sure,' the woman said. 'But you could be.'

In that moment I knew I would never go to the Home Office. I couldn't risk the terrible life that awaited me back in Ukraine. These people didn't know who I was or where I was from. I'd disappear.

The girls couldn't believe I had been let go when I got back to the sauna.

'How did you do it?' they asked in disbelief.

'I don't know,' I told them. 'I just don't know.'

* * *

I knew I'd had a lucky escape but it didn't make me any happier. The anger that had been boiling inside me for months seemed to be growing fiercer and bigger until it possessed me. It lived inside me like a demon and was getting so strong that I could hardly control it. When I worked, it bubbled up hour by hour until I was almost blinded by rage. I hated what I had to do but I couldn't see a way out. I had to send money home to the children while I found another path that would allow me to start a new life and get my babies back.

The only time I was content and able to forget my grief and fury was when I was with Murat, but I knew he hated my job as much as I did.

Early in the new year, I rang the sauna to say I couldn't work because my period had started.

'Just a moment,' said the receptionist and went off the line. Lara wasn't working that day and I didn't know this girl well. A moment later she came back on the line. 'I've talked to the boss and he wants you to come in and show him.'

'Why?'

'He wants to be sure you're not lying.'

Rage filled me. It was like working for Ardy again. Why should I be humiliated like this? 'Tell him to fuck off!' I screamed. 'I'm not doing this anymore.'

I felt liberated as I slammed down the phone but not for long. Where would I get money for food and rent? How could I send any home? I called the sauna back, explained that I'd been a little rash but had now calmed down. Could I go back to work in a few days when my period was finished?

'You should have thought before you told me to fuck off,' the boss said coldly. 'You're not welcome here any longer.'

Once again, Lara came to my aid. This time she gave me an introduction to a Turkish woman called Gul who ran a brothel at a flat and who needed a receptionist. I went to meet Gul and we got on well. The flat seemed clean and well run.

'Do you want to work in the bedrooms?' she asked cheerfully as she showed me round. 'You'd earn a lot more there.'

I thought about it for a long moment. Of course I needed money, but here at last was the opportunity to take a different path. I desperately needed to stop selling myself. Unless I did that, the awful anger inside would eventually destroy me, I knew that. I could do it no longer. This was my chance to end, at last, what had started against my will so long ago.

'No,' I said.

'Are you sure?'

I looked her straight in the eye and said firmly, 'I'm sure.'

Finally I would be able to look at myself in the mirror.

Two weeks later Gul called and said the flat had been closed. There'd been a murder nearby and police were everywhere. I felt sick as she spoke. There was £200 due for my rent in two days and I had just £30.

'What am I going to do?' I cried to Murat. 'I'll have to go back to a sauna. I don't have any choice. There's nothing else I can do. I can't ask for a legal job and I have to stay hidden otherwise the police will find me.'

He was silent for a moment. 'You could stay with me,' he said.

I could hardly believe what he was saying. Did he really want me to live with him?

'I have a spare bedroom and you're in trouble,' he said.

I did not speak for a moment. Murat had offered to help me. Maybe this was a second chance at life, maybe after all these years of dreaming my happy ending had finally come.

'Thank you,' I said, and hugged him.

Chapter Thirty-Five

I loved Murat almost too much. I believed he was an angel sent from God to help me and couldn't stop feeling everything for him which I'd built a wall around for so long. Apart from my children, I'd never known anything like it. Murat protected me, knew so many things about England and gave me advice on all of them. He also read a lot of religious books like the Koran and talked to me about things I'd never heard of before. Soon I'd told him about how much I'd prayed to God to forgive me for all the wrong I'd done.

'I think I must have been punished. Perhaps I was not a good enough mother. Perhaps I failed Pasha. I must be a bad mother because now I don't even know where he is.'

'But you did what you thought was right,' Murat kept telling me. 'God has tested you and you've shown you're strong. He will always be with you and you must never forget that or say it's your fault. Think of all the people in the world who have no water or food. They are living their lives and you should try to as well.'

Murat was like no one I'd known before and helped me see the world differently. Everyone else had always blamed me but he didn't. He looked after me and, even though he wasn't a millionaire, paid all the bills. In return

I did everything I could to care for him like cooking, washing and ironing. For me it was the marriage I'd never had. Murat did not hit me – he was kind and would hug me sometimes as we lay on the sofa or suggest what I should wear which showed me that he cared about me. He was a good and gentle lover but nevertheless he found it hard to show me affection. I started to understand why when we were sitting in a café one day and his friends walked in. Murat's face changed and he looked shifty.

'Could you sit somewhere else please?' he asked urgently. I understood and moved away quickly and quietly. I waited until his friends had left and then we walked home together.

'Why didn't you want us to be seen together?' I asked.

'There's nothing to worry about,' he said with a shrug. 'We're just talking men's talk. You don't need to hear it. It's about jobs, work, things like that, boring stuff.'

'But are you embarrassed by me? Are you ashamed?'

'No. Of course not. But in my world, men don't include women when they're talking together, that's all.'

I knew he was lying but I accepted it. He never had to ask me to move again – I always made sure his friends didn't see us together in public. They wouldn't see a woman, just a prostitute.

Deep down, despite the happiness Murat brought me, I was sad that he didn't love me as I loved him but I understood. I was ashamed of myself so how could I expect Murat not to be? I told myself he'd learn to trust me. I'd stopped selling my body, I was on the road back to being able to respect myself and soon Murat would too. In my country it is said that time is everything and I just had to be patient for the day when he'd tell me he loved me and ask me to marry him.

It was a great relief not to be working and selling myself any longer. The anger in me began to boil less fiercely. But the problem I had feared arose.

Ever since leaving Ardy, I'd sent money home every couple of weeks. It meant so much that I was able to support the children and I had vowed I would never let them down again. But now that I had left the sauna, I had no income and it seemed impossible to find another job. I was too scared to ask English people because I didn't have any documents and they might report me to the police, so I instead looked in the Turkish community. But when I rang up about adverts for cleaners, men would ask what I looked like and whether I had a boyfriend so I knew what they were really looking for. Other people also wanted references and I had none to give them.

After a few weeks of looking I found work in a café but was sacked three days later when some customers recognised me from the sauna. So I was happy to get a phone call from Gul asking if I'd like to go back to working on reception at her flat which had now reopened. Although I didn't want to go back to that world, I needed money and so I agreed.

Soon after I returned, Gul brought in a new girl one day. British girls didn't work for her because she demanded half of what they made and this one, very young and scared, was obviously from abroad. I knew instantly that she was like me.

'She's going to sleep here so you can keep an eye on her,' Gul said. I stayed at the flat on the nights I worked.

'She owes money to a friend of mine and needs to earn quickly so give her every customer you can.'

I made sure I was friendly to the girl and, as the days passed, she told me her story. She thought she was coming legally to England from Russia with all the right documents and a contract for a job. But when the men who'd organised her trip had met her at the airport, they'd locked her up, raped her and told her she owed them £12,000 for the work they'd done getting her into the country.

'I'll have to do this for six months and then they'll let me go,' she said tearfully.

But of course I knew it wasn't true.

'You've got to run,' I told her. 'You'll never make that kind of money here. They'll keep you forever.'

Just as Naz had once helped me, I now encouraged the girl. I'd been like her – so full of fear that I was paralysed – and it only needed one person to help me see a way out. It took about a week to convince her to escape and in that time I secretly saved about £100 for her until she was ready to run.

'I'll leave the front door unlocked when we go to bed and you can leave early in the morning when I'm asleep,' I said.

'But don't you want to know where I'm going?' she asked.

'No,' I replied. 'If I know then someone may make me tell them.'

The next day Gul told me the girl had gone. I pretended to be shocked and furious.

'Little bitch,' I said. 'She said she wanted to buy a sea sponge so I let her out to the shops.'

'But how could you have been so stupid?' Gul screamed.

'Well, she'd been out before and always come back so I didn't think. I'm sorry.'

Gul was so angry she took me to a pub where the girl's pimps were waiting. 'You can explain this to them,' she hissed.

The men were real gangsters and I felt afraid as I looked at them. They questioned me for hours, asking me what the girl had said and where I thought she might have gone, what we had talked about together, but I summoned all my courage and told them nothing. My years as a prostitute had at least taught me how to hide my emotions and to pretend things I did not feel.

'Look, I'm as shocked as you are, and furious with the little cow,' I said. 'The last thing I need is to risk my job or get into trouble with you guys. I just want a quiet life, okay? I don't know where the bitch has gone, I wasn't interested in her. She was just a beginner with nothing to talk about. She never said a word to me about where she came from or where she was going. I'm surprised she had the guts, to be honest.' I smoked casually, concealing my nervousness while men stared at me suspiciously. To my great relief, they believed me and I had to spend a few hours with them and Gul, laughing and smoking and drinking.

I walked home feeling triumphant because I'd cheated these disgusting creatures out of the money they'd hoped to make from that poor girl. But I also knew I'd been lucky. I had to get out of this world. I hated it too much to survive inside it.

I had a new life now, with Murat.

It was all very well to leave the seedy sex industry behind me, but I still couldn't find work. As the summer turned to autumn, I felt more and more worried. Murat had given me £200 to send home but I couldn't keep asking him. What would Sasha and Luda think when Mamma didn't look after them yet again as she'd promised? I just didn't know what to do.

With no money or job, I spent hours alone in the flat. The time alone did something strange to me. All the feelings I'd kept frozen ever since I'd been kidnapped, even after escaping Ardy, began to well up inside me and escape. Once it had started, it became a flood. I couldn't stop thinking about all the terrible things that had happened to me and the bad things I'd done. My life was trash, I realised. For the first time, I felt scared about seeing my children again – would they hate me for what I'd done? How would I ever find Pasha? How would I face him if I did? The thought of all three had kept me alive for so long but now I didn't know if I could see them. I was dirty, shamed, marked forever and, however much I asked God for direction, I couldn't find one.

The depression pulled me down into a dark place. Murat tried to be supportive and help me but eventually even he began to lose patience with me.

'Just go back home if you're so sad,' he'd tell me. 'Go to your children.'

'But I can't. I have nothing there. We'd starve again and there are people who would want to hurt me.'

'Then stop crying.'

'But what will I do?'

'Look, we'll find a way to work things out. Let's find a lawyer who can tell us how you can become legal and live here.'

It was the suggestion that helped me find a purpose in my life. I knew I had to do something – I couldn't live in the shadows forever and, besides, how would I feed my children if I couldn't work? Murat and I found a lawyer through the Turkish newspaper and I made an appointment to see her.

The interview was not a success. The lawyer did not seem to understand what had happened to me and fired many brisk, sharp questions at me. When I stumbled with my answers or couldn't remember exactly what she wanted to know, she was obviously angry. In the end, I lied that I'd only been in England six months because I thought if people knew it had been longer then I'd be sent away. The lawyer told me she'd put my case into the system and I just had to wait.

'It's not easy becoming a legal citizen here, you know,' she said. 'It will take a long time and cost you a lot of money. You'll have to come and see me often.'

I was dispirited by her attitude and by the many meetings I had to attend and documents I had to fill out. Then weeks went by without news and my depression was replaced by fear. I had finally trusted someone in authority and I was sure that I would be betrayed. They would send me right back to where I had started – penniless, starving, without a future.

As the time passed with no news on my status and no work I got more and more depressed, and sometimes I'd stare down from the flat windows at the floors disappearing below me wondering if I could throw myself off. I felt so helpless. God was testing me again but I still couldn't find the answers. I couldn't find work or look after my children and there was something every day which reminded me of the past – a pair of knickers I'd worn at the sauna, a lipstick that I'd used, small things which made my head fill with pictures. Sometimes my mind would even try and take me back there when I was with Murat but I wouldn't let it.

What made it worse was that, even though I was no longer working, Murat could not forget so easily either.

'I'm not your boyfriend,' he said to me one night when we were talking.

'But we're living together,' I said, surprised.

'Well, we're just having fun. You're my friend.'

'But friends don't sleep together, do they?'

'You knew how things were before you came here so don't try and change them now. Don't rush me.'

I thought for a moment and then said in a small voice, 'Do you think you'll ever love me?'

'I don't know.' He stared up at the ceiling. 'I can't say.'

My dream of marriage would never happen, I knew that now. Murat had rescued me and I was grateful to him but long ago, on the night I met him, he had offered me just a morsel of affection, and deep down, I knew it was not enough to sustain me. I felt as lost as I always had done.

Chapter Thirty-Six

I walked into the hallway and saw two envelopes lying near the door. As I bent to pick them up, I saw one was from Ukraine. I recognised Tamara's writing. I opened it at once.

'Oxana

This is urgent. Send me as much money as you can at once. Call me as soon as you can. Big problems.

Tamara'

I couldn't phone because I had no money and fear filled me all day as I waited for Murat to get back from work. He gave me £10 and the next morning I bought a card and picked up my mobile after he'd left for the day.

'Oxana, I've been waiting for you,' Tamara said in a rush as she heard my voice.

'I'm sorry. I only got the letter yesterday.'

'But why didn't you call then?'

'I've got some problems with money.'

'Yes, of course,' she snapped. 'It's been months without any.'

'What's happened?'

'Sasha and Luda have run away.'

'What?'

'They've gone, no one knows where, the police have been looking for them for ten days.'

The ground fell from under my feet as my legs started shaking. 'But what do you mean?'

How could Sasha and Luda be lost? I'd only spoken to them two weeks ago and everything seemed fine. I could hardly hear what Tamara was saying.

'Does Ira know where they are?' I asked. I felt so confused. They couldn't be missing. They were just children of eleven and eight. Ira had sent me photographs and they still looked like babies, with their big eyes and fair hair.

'Of course not,' Tamara snapped. 'But there's something else. They stole five hundred dollars that I was looking after for a friend and he's supposed to be coming to get it in a few days. If he finds out it has gone then he's sure to tell the police so I need to pay him back.'

I couldn't say anything about any missing money. Where were Sasha and Luda? Ukraine was a dangerous place. Ten days? It was so long for children to be alone on the streets. 'I don't understand,' I whispered.

'It's simple. We woke up. No money. No children. Oxana, are you listening to me? I need five hundred dollars.'

Why did she keep talking about money? What about my children? 'I'll find it for you,' I said without thinking. 'But were can Sasha and Luda be? Did you give the police their descriptions?'

'Yes. They're looking for them.'

I was silent. I felt so far away and helpless. My children were all alone and there was nothing I could do to help them. I was their mother, I should be protecting them.

'You'll have to send the money you owe me as well,' Tamara continued. 'It's been more than two months since you paid me so you'll need to send about nine hundred dollars.'

'Of course,' I told her. 'I'll call you tomorrow.'

But I couldn't think about money as I put the phone down. Had Ardy done what he'd always promised? Or maybe Serdar or Olga? Where were Sasha and Luda? Who had taken them? Were they dead?

It was as if my body shut down that day. I sat for hours and hours as the sky first turned grey and then black wondering if this was my final punishment. Had my children disappeared because I wanted to be free? Had they been pulled into my awful world? Had I lost them forever? I should never have run. I should have just accepted things. I should have been their mother.

'Oxana?' a voice said.

I looked up to see a face in the dark.

'I've been ringing you,' Murat said.

'I didn't hear.'

'So what has happened?'

'Children. Lost. Gone away. Nine hundred dollars.'

He stared at me. 'What do you mean?'

I opened my mouth but couldn't speak. I stared at the floor.

'Come with me,' Murat said and I felt his hand take mine. 'You need to calm down.'

He led me into the bathroom and turned on the water. 'Now get undressed and get into the bath.'

Without thinking, I did as he said and took my clothes off. The warm water closed around me and I felt my muscles relax. Now I could tell Murat my story.

'Please help me,' I begged him as I finished. 'If I don't send Tamara the money then the children will go to prison when they're found. I know what those places are like, what they did to my husband. My children can't go there. Can you lend me the money? I'll pay back every penny.'

'But if you get it will the children definitely come back?'

'I don't know but I can't run the risk that they may be reported for theft.'

Murat looked at me. 'But I don't have that kind of money, Oxana. I've only got a hundred pounds in the bank and I can't give it to you because I need to pay rent.'

'Can you give me just some of it? Something to send Tamara?'

'I haven't got it.'

'Please,' I whispered.

'I'm sorry,' he replied.

'Can't you borrow it? Ask a friend? Your boss?'

'No.'

I moaned softly and turned my face away.

The next day Murat gave me another £10 so that I could call Tamara again.

'They've been found,' she said excitedly. 'Last night. They were at the airport asking people to buy them tickets to London. They didn't have any money with them. It had all gone. My friend says that if you don't pay then he'll go to the police.'

'But how are they?'

'Fine. They're at the police station and I've been there but they won't let me have them back because I'm not their legal guardian.'

'What do you mean?' The delight and relief I'd been feeling turned to horror.

'Just what I say – the police won't give the children back to me. They're going to be transferred to an orphanage.

'I'm sorry but there's nothing we can do. I haven't got any documents proving that I look after them and the police won't even give them to Ira even though she's their aunt.'

I felt sick, faint. My children in an orphanage?

'You need to pay me as quick as possible you know,' I heard Tamara say. 'The man needs money so I've borrowed some but the police won't like hearing about this.'

Panic filled me. I had to get that money. My children would be in even more trouble if the police found out about it. Maybe if I paid Tamara back she would find a way to stop them going to the orphanage. 'All right, I'll do it. But I'll need a few days. I'll call as soon as I can.'

Later that night, I begged Murat to help me. 'I'll do anything. I'll work. I'll pay you back. I promise I will.'

'But I don't have it.' He looked at me sadly and I knew that he was telling the truth.

For four days I cried, drank and shouted, all the time hoping that Murat would change his mind and give me just a little of what he had. But all he said was that he couldn't help me.

On the fifth day, I went to the mirror and looked at myself. My eyes were puffy and red, my skin was grey and my hair lank. I reached out and touched the face reflected back at me. It had only been a few short months that I'd been able to look at myself.

'You have no choice,' I said to my image. Coldness filled me and made me shudder. 'You have to go back to the sauna. It's the only way to make the money you need to save them.' Tears filled my eyes. 'I'm sorry. I'm so sorry.'

'So that's your decision is it?' Murat shouted when I told him. 'To go back to fucking?'

'But there's no choice,' I sobbed. 'You can't help me and Lara doesn't have that kind of money. I have no one else. My children need me. I must do this.'

Murat looked at me angrily. 'You know that if you go then my door is closed to you,' he said in a low voice. 'I will never take you back.'

I stared at him and my heart broke even as I stayed strong. 'I know. But my children come first. It doesn't matter how much I love you. I have to do this for them. They need me.'

Hours later I left and went back to stay with Lara. I knew what I had to do.

Chapter Thirty-Seven

The man's face swam in front of me. I couldn't make my eyes stay still as I looked up at him. My head was spinning. I lifted the glass to my lips and swallowed.

'Are you free?' he asked.

I wasn't in the room. I was somewhere far, far away. I started to get up and staggered a little. I felt a hand on my arm.

'Are you free?' the man said again.

'Yes,' I replied. 'Come with me, darling. We'll have a good time.'

I walked out of the living room and towards a massage room. Suddenly acid sickness burned the back of my throat. I swallowed as I opened the door.

'Think of the children,' a voice said inside me.

It was my second day back at the sauna. The boss had forgotten the argument we'd had so long ago and was happy to give me work once again. I'd just got ready for the evening: I was wearing a white nurse's uniform, black high heels, a blonde ponytail hair extension and thick make-up to hide my real face. It was about 9pm and I was sitting in the living room with the girls – there were six of us tonight.

'Looks like we're going to be busy,' someone said and we looked up at the CCTV screens to see a group of men arriving.

A minute later Lara opened the door. 'Police,' she whispered.

A ripple of fear ran through us. Some of the girls didn't have documents just like me. But I didn't feel too scared – after all, a lawyer was looking after my case even if I hadn't heard anything in a long time.

A group of men walked in, some in uniform and some in office suits. I wanted to laugh. I knew one of them. He was a regular customer. I was always too scared to see official men when they came in. Once I'd taken one to a room where he'd asked for a full service and I'd told him I didn't know what he was talking about – we were just a sauna and massage place. But I knew some of the other girls would do it.

'We need to talk to you,' one of the men said. 'This is a routine immigration check and there are officers here both from the police and immigration service. We'll be speaking to you individually but first we need your names.'

We each told him and then were taken on our own to one of the massage rooms. A policeman and a policewoman were waiting for me and started asking questions.

'What is your name? Date of birth? How did you get here? Do you have a passport or residency documents?'

I told them what they wanted to know, giving my real name this time, and gave them my lawyer's details. They said nothing as they left but I didn't feel too scared. I kept telling myself that I had a lawyer, I would be safe.

Then the police went away and we forgot about them.

* * *

I can hardly remember the details of the next few days. Today, coldness fills me when I try to think back but I can't picture much. All I know for sure is that I sold myself and made enough to start paying Tamara back. I don't remember the customers I had, what I did or who they were, the smell or touch of them. I was too blank, too drunk, and thought only of Sasha and Luda, getting the money, sending it home and keeping them safe. I had already lost Pasha and I would not lose them too. Tamara had told me on the phone that Sasha and Luda had been moved to the orphanage but no one knew where it was. They had vanished.

I thought constantly of them as I tried to forget where I was. It was the worst week of my life, the closest I ever came to killing myself. Going back to that world almost destroyed me and I prayed day after day to my father.

'Please take me, Papa,' I'd ask him. 'Let me be with you.'

I thought about hurting myself all the time – standing in the kitchen, I'd put the bread knife to my wrist and see the grey metal against the white skin or walking along the street, I'd stare at a bus and wonder if I could throw myself under it. But I was too scared to do anything and that upset me even more. I was so weak I couldn't even do that.

The sauna was quiet because everyone had heard about the visit from the police and I kept asking God to send me customers. I just wanted to finish this and felt so angry with Him. I knew what I was doing was wrong but couldn't He just help me? I also cried hour after hour and Lara would hug me.

'It won't be long,' she'd tell me. 'You just need to work hard and you'll have the money.'

I knew she was right but I felt so dirty again. I must be a terrible person to be punished so badly – so weak and stupid to be back in this place. I couldn't let myself think about Murat. I knew he didn't understand and part of me felt angry that he hadn't helped me.

'He's just a man,' I kept telling myself but in my heart I felt very sad and alone.

For a short while, I'd really believed that with Murat, I could finally leave the past behind, that he was the prince who'd come to rescue me. Now I knew I never would be.

I called him just once when I was drunk.

'Why are you phoning? he asked. 'I'm busy.'

'I just want to hear your voice.'

'I can't talk. I'll call you back later.'

He never did.

Six days after their first visit, the police returned, this time just two of them in uniform. They told me and two Thai girls that we had to go with them.

I was surprised but too numb to be frightened. I had almost stopped caring what happened to me. If I'd lost the children, then it didn't matter if I spent the rest of my life in prison. We were taken to a police station. Inside, an officer standing behind a counter told me to take off the belt holding up my jeans. When I handed it to him, he put it into a plastic bag. Then he opened my handbag and wrote down what was in it.

'Is that it?' he asked as he opened my purse and saw a £5 note in there.

One of the Thai girls had been carrying about £1000 in cash with her. I pointed to the most recent receipt for a money transfer that I'd made back to Ukraine. I had managed to send a little to Tamara to start paying off the debt.

'I see.' He smiled and I did too but only because it was ironic – he obviously thought women like me had a lot of money. In reality, I had nothing.

The officer took my jewellery and put it in another plastic bag before giving me a form listing what they'd taken. Then I was led to a cell and the door was locked.

I looked around. The room was bare with just a plastic mattress on a platform, a pillow and dark blue duvet in it. I couldn't see through the glass in the window because it wasn't clear and there was a toilet in the corner. So it had finally happened: I was locked up in a prison like a criminal. I sat on the bed and started crying. Now I began to be afraid. Why was I here? I needed to be back at the sauna earning money for Sasha and Luda, to repay what they'd stolen.

I stuffed the pillow over my face as I slid to the floor but even my silent screams couldn't dissolve my fear. This had to be the end. It was the third time I'd been caught by the police and now my luck must have run out. This time they wouldn't let me go. I'd be sent back to Ukraine to watch my children starve again and to my death. I banged my head on the wall as my mind raced. I wanted it to be still, for my fear to leave me. I had to be brave.

'Are you all right?' a voice asked and I looked up to see a policeman standing above me.

'Yes.'

'Why are you sitting on the floor?'

'I like it.'

'Well, if you're sure.' He bent down towards me. 'Would you like something to drink?'

'A coffee? Strong, no sugar.'

'Okay then.'

A couple of minutes later the man came back with my drink.

'You shouldn't worry,' he said as he handed it to me. 'It's late and you should get some sleep.'

'But what's happening to me? I don't understand.'

'We're waiting for a lawyer and interpreter to arrive. You don't have a passport or travel documents so the likelihood is that you're here illegally.'

The man seemed very kind as he spoke to me. I'd always been scared of policemen in Ukraine because they beat you up or made you sign documents saying that you'd done things you hadn't. But this man seemed different. After a while he went away.

I don't know how long I was in the cell – for me one minute was like hours and soon I began to panic. I banged on the door.

'Please can I have a cigarette?'

This time another officer came to see me. 'A cigarette? I'll have to ask.' He was gone a few minutes before returning, unlocking the cell and taking me outside. He handed me a packet of cigarettes and a lighter.

I lit one gratefully and puffed out the smoke. I felt so cold. I couldn't stop myself shaking and, when I'd finished smoking two cigarettes, the officer moved towards me to start going back.

'Let's get back inside,' he said.

'Please let me stay out here a little longer,' I asked. 'I don't want to go in that room again.'

The man stopped. 'Just five minutes then,' he said.

The cell door opened and I looked up to see a woman at the door. Fear filled me again.

'We're ready to interview you now,' she said. 'Come with me.'

I was taken to a small room where two men were waiting.

'This is your interpreter and this is your lawyer,' the woman told me. 'And I am a member of the immigration and vice team.'

I said nothing as the lawyer started speaking and the interpreter translated for me. He finished by saying, 'If you have something to say but you're too scared to tell us, you don't have to say anything. It's your right to remain silent.'

I sat up straight. 'Remain silent? I don't want to be silent. I want to tell you my story.' I had the overwhelming feeling that I had to speak the whole truth at last. This woman had to know what had happened to me, to know that she couldn't send me home. I couldn't lie any longer.

I began with the day that Sergey went to prison and the desperation I had felt. I explained the need to feed my little children and why I had made the difficult decision to leave them when I went to Turkey. Then I told them how I had been duped, kidnapped and sold into a world of slavery and imprisonment. I told them about Olga, Serdar and Ardy; that I had not seen my children in nearly three years and that I yearned for them so desperately I could die from it. I spoke for two long hours.

The immigration officer listened carefully and when I'd finished, she asked me many questions. It was impossible to tell what she thought of my story but I tried not to think about that. I knew that I just had to be as truthful as I could to make her see that I wasn't a bad person.

I told her about the lawyer I had gone to all those weeks ago.

'But we can't find any record of you, Miss Kalemi,' she told me. 'There has been no application for you for residency or asylum in the UK. When did the lawyer take on your case?'

'Six months ago.'

'Six months?' She looked surprised. 'Why has it taken so long?'

'I don't know. She said she'd be in touch and I haven't heard from her.'

'We can't phone her now. We'll have to do it in the morning.'

'But what will happen to me?'

The woman looked at me seriously. I could see sadness in her eyes. 'Women like you are usually deported. You're illegal here and may very well be sent home.'

I started crying. 'But you can't make me go back. Don't you see? I'll die.'

'It's not my decision, I'm afraid,' the woman said softly.

No one spoke and I wanted to scream into the silence. Hadn't these people listened to what I'd told them? Did they really think they could send me back?

The woman looked at me. 'There is just one thing. Wait for a moment.'

She stood up and walked out of the door. She was gone for about fifteen minutes before returning.

'I have some news for you,' she said. 'A special charity was set up in the UK earlier this year. It's called the POPPY Project and it works with women who've been sex trafficked. They have houses for women like you to stay in and help you to plead your case with the Home Office. There aren't many places but I've rung a friend who knows them and she'll find out if there is one available. We'll know in the morning.'

'Does that mean I could stay in England?' I asked.

'I don't know,' she replied. 'Nothing is certain. Let's just hope they can help.'

I was taken back to my cell and, as I watched the light turn towards morning behind the window, I prayed for the day not to come. Maybe it would be the one on which I would be sent to prison just as Naz had told me I would be, maybe it would be the day when I was finally made to leave England. I knew I would never survive if I was. I couldn't do it again. Would I ever get out of this place and rescue Sasha and Luda and find Pasha? Be their mother again?

Breakfast arrived a few hours later – a plate of sausage and beans. I didn't want to eat but I was grateful for the cup of hot tea that came with it. I took a gulp. It scalded my throat but I didn't care. I was exhausted with lack of sleep and weeping.

'Miss Kalemi?' a voice asked.

I looked up to see two women standing in front of me. They had come into the cell behind the man who'd delivered my breakfast. One had dark hair and looked middle-aged while the other was slim, with blonde hair and looked very young.

'Hello,' said the younger one. She smiled at me.

I could hardly lift my head to look at her. I felt so weak.

'Oxana?' she said.

I looked up at her properly. Her eyes were kind. She had a sad look on her face.

'My name is Sally,' she said softly. 'I'm from the POPPY Project. I'm here to help you.'

Chapter Thirty-Eight

I was standing in front of a tall terraced house. Sally was beside me and the dark-haired woman, the interpreter, was also with us.

'Here we are,' Sally said as she smiled at me. 'This is the house where you'll be staying. There are three rooms but only one is occupied at the moment.'

'How long will I be here?' I asked as she unlocked the door.

'Four weeks to start with but it depends on your case. We'll have to see.'

'Will I be sent back to Ukraine?'

'It's complicated so we'll have to talk more about it but let's show you your room now.'

I was so tired. Earlier I'd seen myself in a mirror – my face was swollen and red, and my eyes were small with black circles underneath them.

Sally carried on talking but I didn't listen. All I could think about was what would happen to me when the month ended. I didn't really understand what kind of organisation POPPY was. In Ukraine charities just handed out money or food, not houses.

'Oxana?' Sally said.

I looked at her.

'We've got to go all the way up. Your room is in the attic.'

We climbed the stairs and I almost gasped when Sally opened the door to my bedroom – it was beautiful. The walls were painted a purple pink, there was a single bed with new sheets in packets lying on it, a sink with a cabinet underneath and two windows sloping in the roof. I'd never had a room of my own before.

Sally handed me a bag with soap, a towel, a toothbrush and shampoo inside before giving me a mobile phone.

'We're going to give you a number which you can call anytime if you need us. If you have any problems then just ring me. Let's just show you around the rest of the house and then you can have a rest.'

Sally took me to the kitchen and living room before handing me £90.

'This should last you a week,' she told me. 'Shall we go and get you some food?'

We walked to a supermarket and I bought some things before going back to the house where Sally left me. She said she would come back to see me the next day. It was only about 2pm but my legs felt so heavy as I walked upstairs. Pulling the sheets out of the packets, I made the bed before lying down and falling asleep immediately.

Hours later I woke up in the middle of the night, wondering where I was. I looked up. I could see stars shining through one of the windows. Then I remembered that I was far away from the sauna, the police station, the flat I'd shared with Murat, and all the dingy, horrible places I'd lived in. What had Sally called this place? It was a 'safe house', she'd said. Somewhere no one would find me if I didn't want them to. For now, I was protected, at last.

I sighed, turned over and fell back into a deep sleep.

Even though I was in a safe house, I was still scared. I hardly understood where I was or what was going to happen to me. I was still in the hands of others, out of control of my own life. I could only trust that I was going to get help.

Sally came back the next day and the one after that. Gradually, she was able to explain to me what the POPPY Project was, and how it could help me.

'We are specifically here to help women who've been trafficked into this country and forced into prostitution. We provide you with accommodation and support, and can help you if you wish to apply to stay here.'

'I do want to stay,' I said quickly.

'Then our first job is to help you apply for asylum,' she said. 'I'm not sure what your lawyer has done but there is no record of you at the Home Office. We know people who can represent you. It's a long process but we'll make sure you get the best advice possible.'

'Will I be able to stay in this country?'

'We can't say for sure. No one can. But we hope so.'

'What must I do in return?'

'Nothing. But you could consider helping us by cooperating with the authorities here. We want to stop this awful trade in sex-trafficked women and if you can tell us what happened to you and how, it might stop this happening to someone else. You don't have to do anything now – just think about it.'

The idea of telling the authorities the truth was terrifying – when they found out what bad things I'd done, I'd surely be sent away. But Sally didn't put any pressure on me.

'Just think about it. Perhaps you'll be ready one day.'

In my first few weeks in the safe house, I learned about POPPY and they learned about me. It was hard to trust anyone after all that had happened but gradually I began to believe in Sally. She did many things for me: she took me to see a doctor, and a dentist who sorted out my bad teeth – I'd always been too scared to go in Ukraine because free appointments meant no anaesthetic and I couldn't afford to pay. She also explained that POPPY had trained people called counsellors whom I could talk to about what had happened to me if I wanted. I would also be able to apply to go to school while I waited for my asylum case to be processed – I could take language courses and learn English properly.

'I would love to do that!' I exclaimed when Sally told me, excited by the opportunity to learn English. 'I want to apply, definitely.'

'Good,' Sally said, laughing. 'I wish all students were as keen as you.'

As the days passed and I realised that the POPPY Project really was there to help me, I began to adjust to my new life. I spent long hours alone, thinking or reading books from a Russian library, or walking about the city and buying food at the market. I had never really seen London, even though I had been there a long time now, and I didn't know it at all. I was a long way from Tottenham and so occasionally I went out to explore London. But I found the outside world frightening – it was so big and busy, and I never knew if Ardy's face would suddenly loom at me from the crowds of people – so, apart from going to visit Lara occasionally, I hid away a lot.

In those long and lonely hours, I thought back over everything that had happened to me. How could I have let it happen? I must be weak, pointless, stupid. I had ruined my own life, and my children's. Every morning when I woke up, I felt scared and ashamed. I had been easy to trick, simple to control, scared to fight and a bad mother who did not even know where one of her children was. Why were these people even helping me?

Rage and grief shook me, coming upon me suddenly at all hours of the day or night. Out walking, I would suddenly lose the strength in my legs and have to sit down as I began to shake and weep. In the dead of night, I would jerk awake from a nightmare, sweating and trembling. Sometimes I wanted to scream and tear myself to pieces. At other times, I wanted to lie down and go somewhere silent and dark, and be alone forever.

One day I went to Sally.

'I'm ready to talk,' I said. 'I will help the authorities if I can. If they can stop these bastards, maybe punish them, then I'll tell them what they want to know.'

'That's very brave, Oxana,' Sally said softly. 'You're doing the right thing. I know how hard it is.'

The next day, a detective from the Vice Squad came to POPPY and I told him the entire story of what had happened to me. I told him how women like me were treated, where they were hidden and how they lived. I told him about men like Ardy and how they traded women and lived off their work, how they bought fake passports and driving licences, how they liked to spend the money they took from their slaves and where they went to enjoy themselves.

But I was too scared to tell him where I'd left Ardy and where he might find him. I was terrified that any contact would make him think of me, and then of my children, and awaken his thirst for vengeance.

Thoughts of the children obsessed me. I had grown used to being able to speak to them and now that they were shut away in the orphanage, the pleasure of that small contact was gone. It was torture.

I used some of the £60 Sally gave me each week to phone Ira. I begged her to do what she could to get the children back.

'I'm doing my best,' she told me. 'I went to the orphanage to apply to become their guardian but it's impossible.'

'Where are they?'

Ira told me the name of the orphanage and I wanted to scream. I knew about the place – it was full of children who stole or took drugs.

'They won't let me see the children,' Ira went on. 'I asked if they could come to me but they said no, because I've only got the two bedrooms, no hot water or toilet inside, and I already look after Vica. You know what it's like, Oxana. They say that they need lots of documents and I simply don't have them, so they won't release Sasha and Luda to me.'

I knew the reality of the situation: the authorities moved slowly in the Ukraine and the only thing that oiled the wheels was money. But I had only enough to live on and nothing to send back to help Ira.

In the worst hours, I considered going back to prostitution. No one from POPPY would know, I could just stand on a street corner at night like I had in Italy and then Tamara would have her money and Ira would have something to pay the officials. But however much I thought about it, I couldn't make myself do it. Sally had told me that if I was granted asylum in the UK then my children would be able to join me and I was sure that if I was caught working again then I'd be made to leave. I had to do everything I could to stop myself being sent home.

The children were already in an orphanage. Even if Tamara's friend brought in the police, they were unlikely to do more than that. I would do my best eventually to repay what the children had taken but for now all I could do was pray that Sasha and Luda were still together.

Chapter Thirty-Nine

The noise hit me as I walked into the restaurant. I'd been alone for so many weeks now that I wasn't used to it. It was 23 December and I had been invited to POPPY's Christmas party. A couple of days before I'd moved from the safe house to another in the north of the city and in a few weeks I would start my English course.

It was the worst time of the year for me. I'd grown to hate Christmas as it only reminded me of how far away I was from my children. Thoughts of them filled my mind. I knew Ira was doing all she could but it felt so wrong that I was safe now and my children weren't. I still had no idea where Pasha was, although Sally had told me there were people who could help put families back in touch with each other. I hoped that together we would find my son. Until then, the knowledge that he was lost would torment me.

Anger bubbled up as I looked around the restaurant at the tables of smiling people. It was never far below the surface these days. One minute I felt okay and the next I was filled with rage. Sometimes it was directed at someone – Murat who'd let me down, Ardy who'd sold me, Sergey who'd beaten me – but at other times it just filled me for the smallest reason. Today I was angry because I didn't have anything nice to wear. In a long knitted skirt and polo-neck jumper, I felt terrible. I didn't want to speak to anyone. I was too embarrassed about how bad I looked.

'Oxana?' It was Sally. She was sitting at a long table full of women. 'We've saved a space for you and we also have something to give you.' She pointed to a big bag. 'There are presents inside so pick one.'

I walked over, reached into the bag and took a parcel. It was wrapped in silver and blue shiny paper with the words 'Happy Christmas' written on it. Sitting down at the table, I opened it and saw a body cream, soap and perfume. Someone was wishing me a happy Christmas. I couldn't remember the last time I'd been given a present. Tears burned in my eyes.

Lifting my head, I looked down the table at the other women. I hadn't really noticed who was at the table but now I could see there were more than thirty women sitting around me. Black faces, white faces, Asian faces – women from all over the world. My breath caught in my throat. They must all have a story like mine to tell.

I felt so shocked. Of course I'd met a couple of women along the way who'd been sold but I had no idea it was like this – there were so many of us. It wasn't just me. I wasn't the only one stupid enough to believe the lies I'd been told. I felt tears rise up as I looked down at the table and saw all those faces. Some were laughing, others were serious but they were all there. Just like me, they had survived. But how many more like us had not been so lucky? How many tonight would be selling themselves to men who refused to see the fear in their eyes?

At last I knew it wasn't just good luck that POPPY had found me. God had chosen a road and now He was showing it to me. All I had to do was follow. For too long people had been locking me up, pushing me down and keeping me prisoner. Now I had the real chance of a new life and I must take it. Like all the other women sitting around me, I wasn't the only one this had happened to. It was finally time to stop being afraid.

My heart was beating as the phone rang.

'Yes?' a voice said.

'Hello,' I replied. 'This is Oxana Kalemi. I would like to talk to my son Sasha Kalemi and my daughter Luda Kalemi.'

'Okay. Can you wait please?'

I heard the phone being put down and footsteps walking away down an echoing corridor. On the other end of the line, I could hear children's voices, shouts and laughter. A few days earlier, Ira had finally got me the number of the orphanage where Sasha and Luda were living. Soon I heard footsteps coming back towards the phone.

'Hello?' a fearful voice said.

Sasha.

'It's me,' I replied.

'Mamma!' he screamed.

'Yes, darling. I couldn't ring you before but I'm so happy that I can now. How are you?'

'Okay.' His voice sounded small.

'Really?'

'Yes.'

We were silent for a moment.

'Why did you run away?' I asked gently. 'You can't take your sister away like that and steal from people. I don't understand. Why did you do it?'

'We missed you, Mamma,' Sasha said in a rush. 'We wanted to come and see you, and I thought that if we had enough money then we'd be able to get onto a plane and fly to England.'

My throat tightened with tears. 'Oh, Sasha,' I whispered. 'I miss you too but you can't take money that isn't yours.'

'I know, Mamma. I'm sorry.'

'Well, it's done now and I don't want to shout at you but you must promise me that you'll never do such a thing again.'

'I won't.'

'So what food are they giving you? Do you have clothes?'

'Yes. Ira and Tamara came and brought us some, and the food is good – we get beef stew with potatoes, tea with sugar.'

'Do you like it there?'

'Yes, Mamma. It's fine. Please don't worry.'

'That's good, darling.' I heard a voice in the background.

'Luda wants to speak to you. Will you phone again?'

'Of course. Every two weeks from now on, I promise.'

'Bye, Mamma.'

'Bye, Sasha.'

I could hear sobs as Luda picked up the phone.

'I hate it, Mamma,' she wailed. 'I don't want to be here.'

My heart twisted as I heard her tiny voice. 'Oh, darling,' I said softly. 'Why don't you like it?'

'Because I don't know anyone. When are you coming for us, Mamma?'

'As soon as I can. I'm studying English and I'm working very hard at school. Every day I come home and carry on looking at my books so I can learn as much as possible.

You see, if I'm a good English person then I will get documents to stay here, and if that happens then you will be able to come and live with me.'

'Really?' she screamed. 'In England?'

'Yes.'

'But will people really let you do that?'

I took a deep breath. 'Yes, they will. I'll make sure they do and then I'm going to find Pasha so that we can be together. The four of us will be a family again.'

'I can't wait, Mamma,' Luda whispered.

'Neither can I, my darling. Neither can I.'

Epilogue

There are four small pictures on my wall which I once found in a bin. Someone had thrown them away but to me they were beautiful. They are tiny oil paintings and, while each is different, they all contain the same things – a house under a blue sky, a green field and flowers with a stream. One day I will live in a place like that with my children.

It has been five years since I made my promise to Sasha and Luda, and at times it has felt like a hundred. Time has a way of slowing down when you are waiting for something you want more than anything else in the world.

I tried to make it pass by doing well when I went back to school with the help of the POPPY Project. Studying hard, I completed exams in six months that most people take a year to do. I was just as much of the classroom good girl as I always had been! I wanted desperately to be able to work, pay my way and make something of myself, so that I could make my children proud of me. As well as English, I studied computing and business, and was able to get a job in the catering industry. At last I was independent, earning my own money for myself.

Those achievements couldn't dull the pain though and the years were not easy for me – even though much in my life improved, there was still sadness, loneliness, and the demons of anger and despair sometimes possessed me, despite my efforts to stay strong. I suffered from what had happened to me, and from the separation from my children. I tried to hide from my pain in alcohol and brief relationships with men who weren't able to love me and comfort me in the way I needed. I mourned the loss of Murat, and I developed chronic insomnia, only able to sleep a few hours a night. Instead I'd lie on the sofa staring at the television, putting off the moment when I'd have to get into bed and let the devil come to find me in the darkness.

At night I couldn't stop thinking of my past – the nightmarish journey packed inside a crate aboard a lorry, a world of slavery and degradation where my fate was out of my hands. By day, I walked along streets and wondered if any of the women I saw were now in that kind of existence. I hoped not. I scanned faces to see if I could recognise the familiar dead look in the eyes that I'd known so well in my own.

The worst time came in June 2004 when I received terrible news: the Ukrainian courts had taken my parental rights away because I was an absent mother. I knew nothing about it, had no chance to defend myself, and suddenly my children were no longer my own. I lay in bed for three days after getting the news, sure that I no longer had a reason to live. How could I ever get them back? I knew only too well how things worked in my country. There was endless paperwork and things moved at a snail's pace unless you had the right connections or bundles of money to provide an incentive for people in authority.

But I knew that I had to fight. I had come so far and couldn't let myself be defeated now. Besides, I had a promise to keep. I got out of bed, found a lawyer and started the long process of winning my children back. At times the authorities stood in my way, people refused to help me and it would take forever just to get one piece of paper signed. I wondered if I would ever be a mother again. But I fought on and told myself, as months turned into years, that I could not give up.

In 2005, two wonderful things happened. On one of the happiest days I'd known for years, I was granted asylum in the UK. Finally I was truly safe and as soon as my children were returned to me, they would be able to join me in England for a brighter, better future.

My most joyful moment, though, was finding Pasha again. He was at a deaf school for older children in Simferopol. I was so scared to make contact with him again but knew that my heart had never let me forget my son and I hoped his had done the same. It was the first time in many years that we had communicated and I soon got a letter back.

'Hello, dear Mamma,' he wrote. 'I'm studying in four classes, my teacher's name is Larissa and my nurses are Nadia and Ludmilla. I'm studying speaking, reading and writing. I love my school but I really wish to go home with you. I love you, I kiss you, your dear son Pasha.'

His handwriting was clear and strong, and his teacher had added something below it.

'Hello, Oxana,' she wrote. 'When your letter arrived, Pasha was very, very happy. He looked at the photos you sent and showed everyone that he looked similar to you. Now he's asking all the time when he'll go home. We've explained to him that he needs to wait a little bit. He's changed so much for the better – he's studying well, and his reading and writing are better. He made very sure there were no mistakes in this letter to you.

'Pasha is a very communicative and interested child. He's good at drawing, makes things out of paper and is respectful in class. He also has a lot of friends, and everyone remembers his birthday and celebrates with him every year. We drink tea with cake and make cards for him.

'Oxana, I wish you the best and hope you can do everything you need to have your son with you. But, for now, Pasha will be waiting every hour for your letters.'

I wept when I read it, kissed his letter, smiled and then cried again. My son, who was lost, had been found.

* * *

I know that I would be nowhere today if it wasn't for the POPPY Project and I will always thank them. They rescued me when I thought I had finally lost everything, gave routine to a life that had fallen apart and kindness to a woman who had known so little for so long. With their help, I was able to start afresh and in December 2006 left their housing to live in my own flat in the same block as Lara. I've tried to give back a little of what I've had. Besides paid work, I've done voluntary work in an animal charity shop and at the Women's National Commission, an independent advisory body. Now I am at college studying hairdressing and hope one day to have my own business.

Today I live in the north of England – a place of green trees, fresh air and friendly faces. It is a home for me at last.

Sometimes I think back over the terrible things that happened to me and they seem far away. But then the terror comes back to me in dreams or at moments when I'm low and depressed. Then I taste again the fear, the violence and the sense of being a worthless nothing. I feel so sad that I've seen the worst of human nature: greed, callousness, cruelty and selfishness. I wish that I hadn't witnessed and experienced the awful power men can wield over women, the way they can use them and throw them aside and treat their bodies as instruments for their own pleasure, or imprison them as slaves to make them money.

What happened to the men who used me and passed me on? Where are they now and who are they tormenting? I think of Ardy – that stupid, greedy boy – and hope that no one else is suffering under him as I did. I hope that one day he begins to understand what he has done, and the damage and pain he inflicted.

Then I remember kindness – the tenderness of Roberto, the encouragement from Naz, the loyalty and constancy of Lara, the help and support I received from the POPPY Project – and I try to hold onto that and trust in goodness.

The dreadful trade in sex workers must be stopped, and we must do all we can to prevent this modern-day slavery. The POPPY Project is one way to reach women, rescue them and learn from their stories how we can stamp out trafficking. Please, if you are able to help, don't forget my story and the thousands like it.

But of all the scars inside me, the way I failed my son Pasha is the one that will never heal. I tell myself that I was young, trying to survive and he had many needs which I didn't understand. Today though, my guilt and sadness is as strong as ever. I just hope that one day he will forgive me. I don't know if I will ever be able to learn to forgive myself.

At times as I wait for my children it seems as if my hope is being stretched to breaking point. We talk regularly on the phone, we write and I am as involved in their lives as I can be, but it is not the same as having them with me.

I think of them every day and long to return to them but know I can never go back to Ukraine. I fear for my life if my traffickers find me there, and I've also been advised not to return to Ukraine because it might threaten the refugee status I have here in the UK. I know I must keep it if I am going to provide a good future for my children, but it is hard to be apart from them year after year.

I have a lawyer in Ukraine working for me and all I can do is keep believing that one day I will see my children again. Every part of my being yearns for the day when I will hold them in my arms again.

I am desperate to be the mother that I wasn't for so long. I have made so many mistakes that I think I will live with regret forever. But I hope that when my children join me, we can build a life together and they will come to understand that while I wasn't always there, I never stopped loving them. Because in all the darkness I experienced, the evil which nearly submerged me, they were like a thread of gold which kept shining. My love for them guided me forward. It rescued me when all else was lost.

Further Information

- Prostitution and the trafficking of women is the third highest 'black market' income-earner globally after arms and drugs

- The Home Office estimates that up to 4,000 trafficked women are being forced into prostitution in the UK at any one time. Experts say the real figure is far higher

- The POPPY Project is the only specialist service in the UK for women trafficked into prostitution. It has 35 bed spaces

- For more information on the POPPY Project or to make a donation go to www.eaves4women.co.uk

- Many trafficked women rescued from prostitution are currently classed as illegal immigrants and sent to detention centres

- The Council of Europe Convention on Action against Trafficking in Human Beings states that trafficked women should instead be given time in safe housing during which they can be assessed by experts on violence against women

- In March 2007 the UK government signed the convention but, at the time of going to press, had yet to ratify it – meaning its recommendations have not yet been fully implemented

- For more information on trafficking go to www.amnesty.org.uk/svaw

what's next?

Tell us the name of an author you love

Oxana Kalemi	Go ▶

and we'll find your next great book

book army

Mummy, Come Home

A brutal kidnapping.
A terrified prisoner.
A mother desperate to
reach her children.

OXANA KALEMI

HarperElement
An Imprint of HarperCollins*Publishers*
77–85 Fulham Palace Road,
Hammersmith, London W6 8JB
www.harpercollins.co.uk

and *HarperElement* are trademarks
of HarperCollins*Publishers* Ltd

First published by HarperElement 2008
This production 2013

© Oxana Kalemi and Megan Lloyd Davies 2008

Oxana Kalemi asserts the moral right to
be identified as the author of this work

A catalogue record of this book is
available from the British Library

ISBN 978-0-00-725196-4

Printed and bound in Great Britain by
Clays Ltd, St Ives plc

MIX
Paper from
responsible sources
FSC™ C007454

FSC™ is a non-profit international organisation established to promote the
responsible management of the world's forests. Products carrying the FSC
label are independently certified to assure consumers that they come from
forests that are managed to meet the social, economic and ecological needs
of present and future generations, and other controlled sources.

Find out more about HarperCollins and the environment at
www.harpercollins.co.uk/green